choose dupage
It's all here.

Compliments of
Roger G. Hopkins

Choose **DuPage**
630.955.2090
www.choosedupage.com

CHICAGO'S WESTERN HORIZON
DuPage Regional Development **Alliance**

The Little Black Book of Economic Development

The Little Black Book of Economic Development

"The Clandestine Art and Practical Science of Building Local Economies"

Don Allen Holbrook

Copyright © 2007 by Don Allen Holbrook.

Library of Congress Control Number: 2007906219
ISBN: Hardcover   978-1-4257-8414-0
              Softcover   978-1-4257-8413-3

All rights reserved. No part of this book may be reproduced or transmitted in any form or by any means, electronic or mechanical, including photocopying, recording, or by any information storage and retrieval system, without permission in writing from the copyright owner.

This book was printed in the United States of America.

To order additional copies of this book, contact:
Xlibris Corporation
1-888-795-4274
www.Xlibris.com
Orders@Xlibris.com
40890

Contents

Author's Acknowledgements 7
Foreword 9
"Introduction by Cathy Katona: Researcher's Journey of Discovery
during the Book Project" 13

Chapter One: "The Global Economy is the 21st Century
                  Economic War for Survival" 25
Chapter Two: "Global Combat for Survival and the
                  Emerging Trends of Winners and Losers" 28
Chapter Three: "Community Cycles Usher in Times of Opportunity
                  or the Curtain Call for Sustainable Renewal and
                  Survival is not Guaranteed" 39
Chapter Four: "You are Your own Destiny and Best Chance of
                  Survival in Today's Workplace" 42
Chapter Five: Fearless Leadership "The way of the Dragon Slayer
                  the Knight Errant in Today's Context" 45
Chapter Six: "Place Based Evolution and the Power of
                  Progress to Change City Destinies" 55
Chapter Seven: "The World-Class Journey" 66
Chapter Eight: "How Economic Developers Can Create their
                  Own Art of the Deal" 77
Chapter Nine: "Gaining Perspective on What to do and Why and
                  How Others have Faced Similar Issues." 97
Chapter Ten: "The Great Debate to Incentivize Deals or Not . . ." 99
Chapter Eleven: "Education Matters in Economic
                  Development Matrix" 108
Chapter Twelve: "Political & Fiscal Policy Reform Considerations" 117
Chapter Thirteen: "Retooling Business Retention &
                  Expansion Strategies: A Lost Art that Deserves
                  Rediscovered Focus and Purpose" 128

Chapter Fourteen:	"Understanding and Managing the Technology Paradigm Shift: Catching the Wave of Transformational Technology Critical to Economic Development Information"	136
Chapter Fifteen:	"Technology-Led Entrepreneurial Business Retention Efforts: Planning for Succession and the Economic Development Team"	141
Chapter Sixteen:	"Hybrid Capitalization for Economic Development Purposes: Cash is King in the Global Economy; it Builds Flexible Capabilities and Mitigates Growth Barriers. Those who have the Gold will make the Rules . . . Do you have the Midas Touch in Economic Development	146
Chapter Seventeen:	"Rural Economic Development Renaissance: Leveling the Playing Field for Equilibrium in Rural Economic Development"	162
Chapter Eighteen:	"World-Class Communities do World-Class Economic Development: Getting the Job done is Their Playbook for Success."	170
Chapter Nineteen:	"Been There Done That and Bought the T-Shirt: Lessons learned!"	185
The Final Chapter:	"The Pillars of the Next Frontier, for Economic Development, for the Future"	191
Author's Notes		195
Index of Key words		201

Author's Acknowledgements

Anyone who writes a book knows it is not only a work of passion and expression, but it is also deeply personal. Most books cannot be accomplished as a solo effort, and my first book is no exception. There has been a cadre of professional economic development friends, colleagues, and mentors involved in the advisement of the major issues discussed in this book. As with many relationships, both personal and professional, my thoughts do not always represent those who have advised me. To know me is to know I am a typical Alpha Male; head strong and candid but honest and benign in my intent to disclose to my readers a glimpse of my own life as a professional economic developer. I have been called a forward thinker and a pioneer. I have also been called provocative, among many other colorful expressions I shouldn't disclose. This book is not politically correct, and it does not shade these major issues with soft edge's, rather it openly discusses the trials, tribulations, trends, and tumultuous economic battles yet to come, without fear of reprisal from the media, community leaders stuck in denial, or politicians offended by their own inability to lead communities. Our states and our nation face tough times ahead, especially in the global economy.

This book has been dubbed the book from within a book, and it evolved as part of my monumental effort to write *"Who Moved My Smoke Stack?"* and because there was so much specific to the trade and craft of economic developers, I had to give it its own venue. Those who are professional economic developers know this profession is a hybrid of many skills and traits. Our approach is part academic, for our need to develop a deep intellectual knowledge in our niche areas of specialization; part diplomatic and statesman because of our dealings with politicians; part athletic in the way we guide a rag tag underdog team to victory; and part special forces commando, for our tactical and strategic approaches when it comes to addressing economic threats and opportunities. We are expected to be the last line of defense against our communities' dragons that assail our residents and destroy their stability, and then we are expected to ride out as their knight champion and vanquish such threats, at our own peril. Then we set off to pirate, plunder, and raid in order to gather our own community's trophies. Yes, we are indeed a special and hard to grasp cadre of very capable individuals.

I want to thank all my 50 plus professional economic development colleagues for their fresh opinions of our industry. They believe, as do I, that giving back and sharing experiences might make our nation more competitive, and our time here more meaningful.

I want to especially thank my good friend and colleague Jeff Finkle. His tireless belief in my maverick ways and my professional passion for our shared love of our trade and our nation makes him a true American economic patriot.

I want to thank Cathy Katona for her hard work and earnest time spent. She is not only my friend, but she is also the director of research for this book and my upcoming book, *"Who Moved My Smoke Stack?"* Cathy is passionate when it comes to economic development, and she is one smart lady. She not only managed these 50 professionals, but she also placed their wisdoms on electronic paper. She is my trusted colleague in the development of this book from within the book.

To my parents, Floyd & Elizabeth Osman, my hope is this book makes you proud of the years of love and pain you have had to endure while watching me struggle to reach the top of the proverbial mountain. I love you both. I know my path was not how you would have wanted it to be attained. There have been many tumultuous moments and I have added stress to your life during those worrisome years.

To my In-laws, Gary & Gloria Lutz, thanks for keeping me grounded in the reality that I am just a man, and an opinionated one at that. I enjoy our spirited debates. Thanks for being my best critics, giving me honest advice, and helping me to keep my feet on the ground.

Finally to Aunt Sandra Hilary (Nanna to my sons Ian & Aidan), you're the toughest, smartest and most passionate politician I ever met. Thanks for endorsing me in landing my first economic development position.

Last, and most importantly, I want to thank my wife, Laurie Ann Holbrook. Laurie's continuous belief in me and her inspirational encouragement began the first day we met, and it will continue through eternity. No man is luckier than I. I met and married my soul mate, and she loves me without condition. She lights my path, and she creates balance and equilibrium in my life. She gave me our sons, our gifts from God, and we hope our actions and words will inspire them to someday raise the bar and help others in some special manner related to their own communities, profession and our nation.

Foreword

Jeff Finkle, President/CEO International Economic Development Council

In over 20 years of working in the economic development field, nothing has challenged our communities and the profession, as a whole, as much as the effects of globalization. As communities struggle to remain competitive, economic developers are under pressure to step light years ahead, becoming fluent in international affairs and technology, in order to translate policies to fit their local business landscape.

The 21st century has bestowed a multitude of queries, as well as opportunities, in the economic field, and the solutions to managing them are not ready-made. Today's businesses have a myriad of options for where they can operate and maintain a vibrant business community means, and economic developers will need to demonstrate a commitment to society's values, as well as an understanding of the economic bottom-line, through their actions. This is a tremendous task, and it requires leadership, vision, and courage to achieve these goals.

The key source of real competitive advantage for economic development is leadership, and leaders will need to be more strategic, more creative, and more innovative in their approach to getting their tasks done. Economic development leaders need to follow a well thought out methodology and resolve to educating themselves in order to develop and implement the types of policies that will not only work for them, but their communities, too.

To successfully steer ahead into this new century, it will be required that economic developers adapt quickly and use significant standards of self-monitoring. Don Holbrook truly understands the challenges economic developers face while carrying out their missions on a daily bases and what needs to be done to remain relevant in today's volatile environment.

Holbrook is straight forward in his views of economic development practices, and "The Black Book of Economic Development—*The Clandestine Art and Practical Science of Building Local Economies*" is a must-read for everyone in the industry who is seeking to make a positive impact on both his or her communities and the profession. I wish all my best to Don Holbrook, and I salute him for this meaningful piece of work.

"Each person has the spirit of the
dragon slayer deep within them . . .
they thirst to overcome
the obstacles to knowledge
of their greater purpose in life.
This sets many of us
on modern day quests
for building our legacy.
This is our noble calling
to serve others through prosperity
with a purpose to the greater good
of humanity."

Don A. Holbrook, CEcD

"Veritas vos Liberabit"

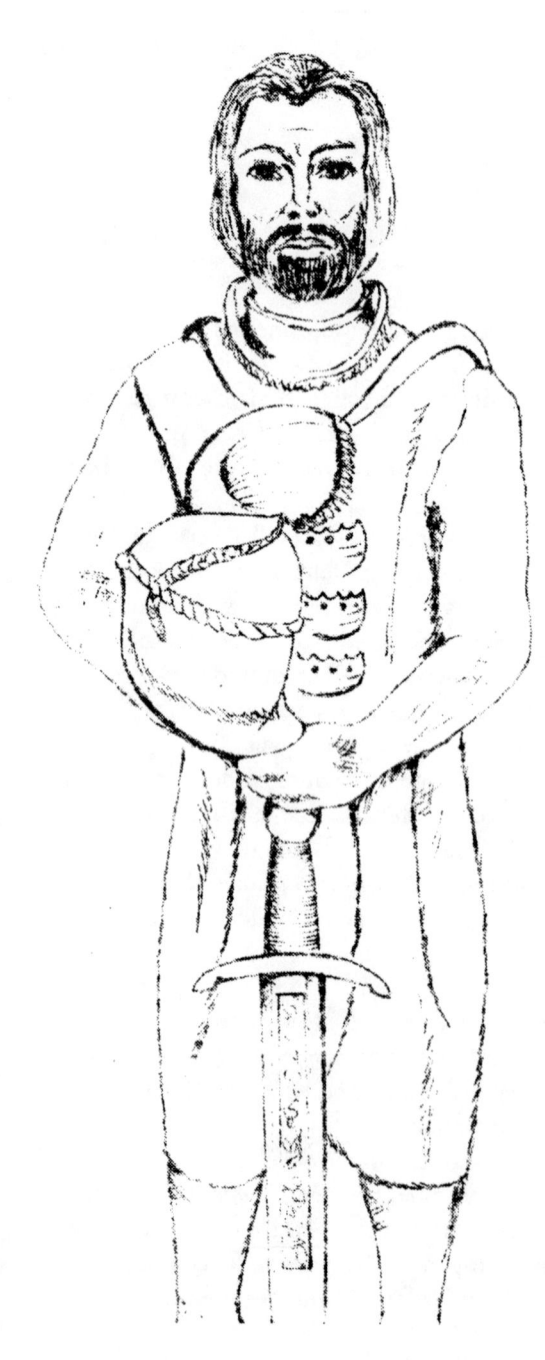

Illustration by George Harlan

NO FEAR

By Laurie Ann Holbrook

"I wear the mask of no fear because that's what I am suppose to be-

Fearless!! Being born in my generation it was understood from the beginning you are to always be a man and be brave, keep your chin up, don't cry, take it like a man because that really didn't hurt. If you are a man you are invincible.

As a young man I was taught to do the right thing and live with integrity. I practice this each and every day but in a world of corruption, deceit and unaccountability I am finding it hard to be fearless. Do the right thing but pay a price that is equal if not greater than those who did you wrong. I have been lied to, cheated, robbed and defamed and yet I am still to provide and survive unscathed.

I am a husband, a provider, a father and a son. To my wife I am to be the oracle and have every answer to every question even when I don't know it or she is not going to like it. I am the primary economic provider.

As a provider I brave the workplace where I have made a career in politics until recently because if you are in politics you would know corruption still exists today and the minute you don't play ball you are looking for another place of employment. That doesn't erase the fact you still have a mortgage, car payments, utilities and your wife's shopping expenses.

As a father I am suppose to be fearless with my children when they ride their bikes for the first time and drive for the first time If they want to go on top the Arc D'Triumph or Eiffel Tower (and I have a fear of heights), I still have to go. Or when they need a simple operation and you fear the outcome. How about the day your boy is up to bat, bases loaded and the count is 3-2, talk about trying to have no fear.

As a son, I am an only child and I am to have no fear with my parents approaching 80 and surpassing those milestones. Soon the day will come when I will get that dreaded phone call and all that follows. No Fear, I don't think so!"

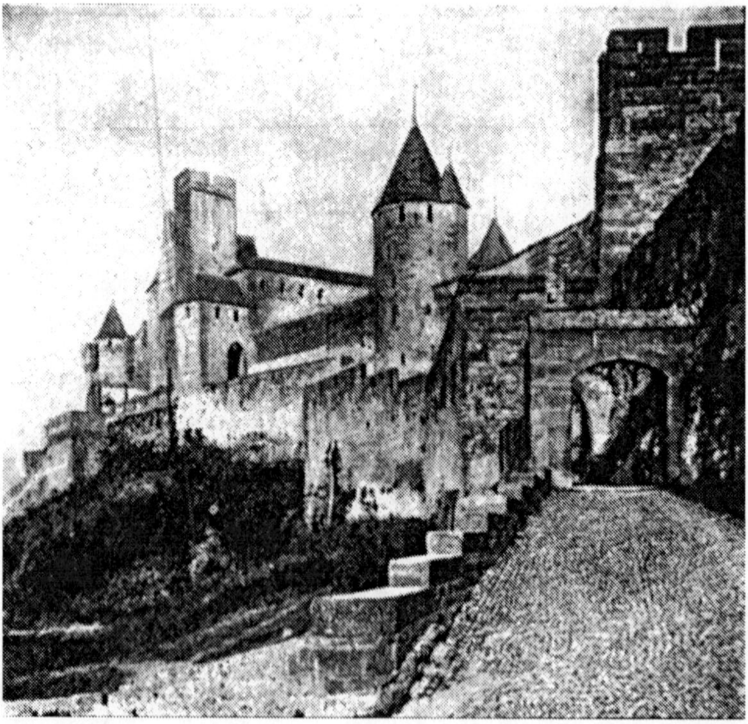

"Introduction by Cathy Katona: Researcher's Journey of Discovery during the Book Project"

We must open our eyes and see what is happening, locally and globally. This is the main message our experts have for our local leaders and those involved in local economic development. Given the state of our many economic development organizations, and the way our local cities are run, we are due some real troubles, not 20 years from now, but as near as 5 years from now, when it comes to keeping competitive on the global basis.

I interviewed over 50 economic developers from around the country, each identified as the top thought leaders in the field of economic development, both consultants and practitioners. The news they had was dismal. Although one never spoke to another prior to these interviews, each message was surprisingly succinct: as a nation, even ranked as one of the top developed countries in the world, we are not prepared for globalization. In fact, if we don't change the way our leadership leads, we are going to inherit a bleak future.

Several factors were identified, but competing in the global market has nothing to do with the strength of the global market, it is the emphasizes on the weaknesses that we see at the local level, whether this weakness deals with the local leadership in economic development, the understanding of where to put local investments, or the understanding of what each community has to offer. Holbrook describes these weaknesses as being stuck in a denial of reality, and the unrealistic proverb of waiting or expecting the market to provide acceptable answers. At the core, a real lack of willingness to get things resolved on a community's own initiative is part of this weakness. Communities are immobilized by their fear of change and lack of vision, and there is no thinking outside the box or ahead of the curve.

Communities in general have a lot of issues to work on, internally, before they can consider competing globally. A community's first issue to address is the most fundamental issue, the building block to any community's success, and this is its leadership at the local level. Not even a remedial economic development program is going to work at the local level without solid vision, financial fortitude, and support from a community's local leaders. Don Holbrook calls for a fearless leadership, one ready to step out and take calculated risks while bearing the brunt of uninformed critics; the "Heel to Hero Syndrome."

Local leaders need not only understand how to make their communities competitive, but more importantly, what economic development actually encompasses. This term is tossed around quite frequently, and when traveling to different-sized communities, economic development is defined differently. It has become politically correct lingo, lost in translation by the leaderships of our communities. With this lack of a common defined economic development program between leaders, there is no point in taking any steps, until this is resolved. Resolving this often needs to come from an outside expert because a local economic developer is not often in a position to help local leaders better understand the requirements for a successful economic development program, and he fears offending his local leader's intellect. In fact, Dennis Donovan actually gives an astounding D+ to most economic development efforts and the people who lead our economic development boards and serve as our economic development leadership. Though we are considered the nation of the best and brightest, it doesn't show in our selection of local, state, and national leadership. Wayne Schell (CALED) believes the number one step to becoming competitive is to insist the teaching of an Economic Development 101 to our local community leaders and each elected and appointed official. Doing this will constitute defining economic development in terms that local leadership will understand, teaching them what to watch out for, how to talk to economic development staff, the understanding of the economic development measurements, and how to ask the right questions. More importantly, there is the hope these leaders will grasp the paradigm shift necessary to help their communities become or remain competitive in the economy.

It usually takes an outside voice to come in and give local leadership the dirty news they don't want to hear. Local leaders, including policy makers, need to be educated on local issues and become unified in order to enhance their ability to compete locally, let alone globally. According to Jay Garner, "You need leaders who are focused on the big picture and vision, with the understanding that they have to put their self-interest secondary to the community as a whole, or nothing moves forward." As the old adage goes, egos need to be checked at the door. A city will be at an extreme disadvantage if local leadership cannot get their act together. A sign of a true leader is one who is able to unite with others, share his visions for the community, and is willing to learn from outside experts when it comes to economic development.

Another common mistake communities make is not understanding their competitive advantages. Competitive advantages are those aspects of a community that positively set it apart from other communities, giving it a competitive edge over other communities competing for a specific industry. At one point, comparative advantages were national; for example, cheaper labor in the South resulted in the move of many industries in the 1970's, from the North to the South. However, today's comparative advantages must be thought of in a global context. Geography is no longer the deciding factor; human capital now creates these advantages, coupled with progressive business climate investments.

A solution can be used to force a community to identify its competitive advantages and its weaknesses; a strengths, weakness, opportunities, and threats, analysis (SWOT). Through this analysis, a community can identify its community assets, which can then be grown and cultivated to attract new businesses and residents. It is from the SWOT analysis that most communities' economic development plans are formed. This analysis tells where to target investments, how to make a community more attractive, and what to stress during a community's attraction efforts. Yet, according to Don Iannone, "Too many SWOT analysis are canned activities, focusing on generic questions every community thinks a site location specialist wants answers to," and Holbrook also states too many communities claim to be unique in their features; therefore, the entire lot is more or less discredited from such claims.

Unfortunately, the trend in economic development is for localities to overestimate and overvalue their product, their community, in order to receive attention from possible investors. During the time of identifying competitive advantages, it is crucial to be realistic in the representation of any local strengths that come from the SWOT analysis. There are hundreds of small communities in our nation which have identified themselves as being "THE" center for biotech, yet most do not have a single local strength justifying this statement.

Most experts emphasized their frustration with communities that do not properly represent what they have locally or create unrealistic economic development goals for themselves. Communities need to formulate realistic economic development goals, focusing primarily on local critical masses of existing industries or strengths. Holbrook claims that communities give business retention and expansion a great deal of lip service, causing an overzealous focus on business attraction for the next "big deal." Business retention and expansion can be the springboard to better transformative and innovative entrepreneurial opportunities because existing companies already believe in their locale. Communities need to work at meeting their customer's needs not what their customers don't need. A community cannot be all things to all people, so there needs to be focus on realistic potential.

Once a community has its comparative advantages identified, it then becomes apparent that most communities do not effectively communicate these comparative advantage. From the 1950's to the 1980's, the most common way to communicate a community's comparative advantage was through advertisements and media placements ads. This was also a time when economic development revolved around the availability of real estate for development. However, this rather generic marketing approach has lost most of its meaning in today's economy.

When marketing a community's comparative advantage, the point is to envision and articulate the strengths of the hometown. Yet, according to my interviews, it is quite evident that a lot of communities still do not know how to communicate their message. According to top marketing guru and economic development media consultant, Andy Levine, only "5-10% of the communities out there are marketing themselves properly." In addition to faulty, incomplete, or out of date data, communities are simply not honing in on their specific community advantages, and they continue to stress meaningless factors such as the "qualify of life" or the number of incentives the community offers for the relocation or attraction of a company to their community. According to Holbrook, communities develop messages that lack meaning to the target audience. Rather than focusing on issues that can be gathered at the local level, such as operating costs, workforce costs, or transportation issues, communities continue to tout generic advantages that don't really set them apart.

The most common mistake a lot of communities make when trying to communicate their comparative advantages is to target their marketing efforts based on desires rather than competitive advantage. Too often the community doesn't properly match its desires to what it actually has as far as its competitive advantage. Hundreds of thousands of dollars are focused on paid or controlled media, and these media lack credibility, particularly in their advertising. Holbrook reminds us of his long struggle to create meaningful and measurable information (data standards) only to be largely ignored by the economic developers and technology vendors. Holbrook further points out that the effort was led by the very audience economic developers wish to impress; the site location professionals. This need for a paradigm shift in the technology foundation and its exchanges information failed. In fact, according to Andy Levine, "The three main marketing mistakes are ineffective targeting, lack of a meaningful message, and focus on a paid media rather than an earned media like editorial placements. There is a huge focus toward making the mass media work when it comes to selling communities. Although this may work for some commodities, like televisions or automobiles, it simply doesn't work when it comes to economic development." Holbrook mentions that this approach refers to the accuracy of a rifle's pin point focus versus the routine shotgun approach of shooting wildly from the hip.

Important community investment decisions are made through local leadership, the SWOT analysis, and marketing efforts, and if we set aside the millions of dollars spent yearly on paid economic development advertising, we still have to consider how local community investment decisions are being made.

If a community makes a decision on a poorly constructed SWOT analysis, poor data, or false data, this improperly reflects the local comparative advantage it leads to a huge amount of money poorly allocated to improving the product; however, experts point to four areas where communities should be putting their money, and they certainly don't point to paid advertising. First and foremost, money should be placed our workforce. Because the global economy now aims toward the knowledge industries, a more productive and qualified worker is crucial. Second, money should be placed in our local physical infrastructure, the fiber superhighway, utilities, regular highway or transportation investments, and shovel ready sites (fully permitted and improved, with utilities at the curb) and their future development. Finally, money should be placed toward creating places attractive to people.

The most frightening aspect in the United States is our lack of workforce development, not in its current job employment, but in its preparation for future jobs. Communities need a workforce that is talented. Focusing on the attraction of talented individuals will, in turn, attract the types of companies' communities' desire. These types of companies no longer make their location decision on real estate but rather where the intelligence and knowledge is found; in fact, Holbrook believes the new power of place is the creation of communities where people want to live, work, and play, and where others want to visit. All these dynamics must be present in order to sustain a diverse and robust economy. A major business attraction feature is its communities' productive workforce. Yet there are a plethora of training programs that do not help in the development of a better workforce. Economic developers must be more engaged at the high school level. Because students are not learning skills needed in the future, we are frighteningly behind in our competitive transition, so we are quickly falling woefully behind our major international competitors. Our continual objective to fill workforce needs for traditional workforce positions may be strong, yet it is these traditional professions that are declining in importance. Holbrook found that our biggest failure is in transitioning our workforce to become valuable to new businesses' skill requirements, and this is our Achilles heel when it comes to the global economy. Workforce development is a long-term issue. We need to look seven to eight years down the road; instead, we fill jobs now, rather than thinking about what jobs we will need to fill in the future. We must give students the skills needed for future positions. The lack of a robust best practice program that can financially support the actual cost of this transition is a critical flaw in our renewed opportunity to remain the greatest economic superpower, especially in the 21st century. Because we are a society based on immediate satisfaction and immediate results, we don't think strategically toward the future. Our leaders constantly look at what they can do in their next quarter, not what they can do in a year. As a result, largely strategic thinking and required preparation for the future are being forgotten. In fact, many economic developers still use a 1950's methodology while working with today's companies.

No economic development discussion is complete without the mention of incentives. Incentives are tools offered at the local and state level, and they encourage new community investments, like a company's relocation from another community due to expansion or the attraction. Incentives, or corporate welfare, allow a corporation to receive a tax break on its property tax, so both company and community benefit. Yet, however important incentives are to the economic development, there is no doubt the average economic developer puts far too much emphasis on these tools. Even our site locator experts identify a gross overuse of incentives. Bob Ady agrees," I have never worked with someone who said 'Let's go with the place that gives us the most incentives.'" and Gene DePrez further emphasizes that "incentives only make marginal differences." yet communities nationwide oversell incentives simply to "close the deal."

Furthermore, there has been little creative use of existing incentives. However, as with any tool, there is the proper time and place to use these tools. Experts recognize that "smart communities" are changing their use of incentives, intelligently using incentives and understanding their financial implications. Although it is Bob Ady's job to take advantage of incentives offered his clients, he is constantly amazed by the number of communities that offer incentives in this manner. The creative part of an incentive is driven by the needs of the company, yet many communities continue to offer generic incentives without listening to the company's needs.

In order to determine the most palatable use of incentives depends on the local community culture. How much the local community is willing to invest to attract said company and if its benefits don't outweigh the detriments then incentives need to be addressed. Incentives are usually offered on a project by project basis to lower risks of market entry. Most experts agree that communities need to take a better look at their incentive packages in order to develop a clear and precise incentive policy based on real numbers. Holbrook also points out that incentives do play a major role of leveling the playing field for new business investment in tight races between communities. Communities that create innovative incentives that matter to businesses, like key barriers to their investment and reduced, up front risks will be winners more times than losers. We live in a highly competitive environment, and according to Holbrook, it is all about the W's not the L's, just like in sports.

At this point, I have only discussed basic economic development, but I have not spoken of our communities and how they can compete with the larger global economy. If our American communities are to continue to be competitive in the near and not so near future, all the above weaknesses must be resolved. Our current economy, whether it is called "global economy," "new economy," or "today's economy," is an economy that no longer relies on real estate or a business' processes to be in one place. Today's businesses have more choices as to where it places its services, its research and/or development of products, or its distribution of products. This is where our focus should lie; in fact, Holbrook believes that with today's volatile political, social, and economic climates, there will be a resurgence of investments made by companies that want to get closer to their various markets because they no longer need to place too much dependence on any one market for their business fortunes.

Local leaders and economic development professionals need to understand the world around them, a better understanding of the environment we function in. In fact, according to Laith Wardi, "the economic developers need to ask whether they really provide the tools that are germane to year 2007 and beyond. Are they really helping their local companies become globally competitive?"

In today's global market, the difference between the haves and the have-nots has been the ability to assimilate technology into their own products or services. This applies not only businesses but also our workforce. To be relevant in the global economy, economic developers have to ratchet up the use of technology in both the projects and services they provide the private sector and in their dialogue with the local business owner. Most economic developers are unable to share a technological dialogue because those running the economic development organizations aren't familiar with technology issues. Holbrook further points out that the vast majority of today's economic development leadership is techno-phobic, literally stuck in the last economy when it comes to their approach to business procedures and innovative uses of technology. These dinosaurs will soon be replaced by a newer tech-savvy generation, and this will cause a significant growth, internally, in the field of economic development.

Meanwhile, companies in China and India have the competitive advantage because they can make things at a cheaper rate, and the only way we can level the playing field is by bringing technology to the forefront in order to make our local companies more competitive. As Eric Canada says, "If [economic developers] understood the global competitive environment, they would be walking in the door to determine how economic development can help the company be more competitive in the global stage while operating from that community." Furthermore, Holbrook points out that the economic development industry needs to get in touch with developing new innovative processes for conducting business decisions and creating deal structures in the complex environment of today's global capital markets.

Yet how many economic developers truly understand what is happening across the ocean. Most economic developers don't see that what is going on locally is symptomatic of what is happening elsewhere. Technology is imperative to this type of discovery. North American economic developers are unaware of their foreign competitors, and this lack of knowledge has allowed their competitors to build an unmatched momentum, slowing the ability to respond to these competitor's vulnerabilities. Holbrook warns that this slow surfacing of enlightenment has thrown a full additional decade into our recovery process because we were too self confident for too long, and this was undeserved and inappropriate.

Internally, economic developers need to be cognizant of the computer equipment they use, the type of information they receive, and the day to day checking of industrial information. They need to look at global factors and the impact these have on global industries. No longer can they look next door or across the country to see what their competition is doing, they have to open their eyes and look more globally to find out what certain industry sectors are doing and what other communities are doing to support those sectors. Today's competition is global; therefore, our economic developers, no matter how small their community, need to look internationally in order to learn what is going on locally as far as the implications for local economic health.

All businesses, no matter how small their community, will be affected by global changes in that industry. As a result, local businesses must be competitive in this global environment. Economic developers constantly need to reach out to local businesses and work with them in order to make them more competitive. Economic developers must be aware so they can adapt to this changing business landscape. They must communicate with their local businesses, and there are a myriad of questions they should ask. As Karin Richmond suggests, "Listen to the people who are directly involved in both management and production decisions." Direct dialogue with company executives will save the community and the economic development practitioner a lot of time and money. Before designing a program, it is important to hear what types of job skills the community needs to prepare for in order to keep that business open. The question they should ask is not what skills are needed now, but what job skills are needed in three or four years. This will give economical developers time to work with the local technical colleges and the preparation for the needs that will keep the company competitive. Programs cannot be based on current data, but on speculation of future data. Based on this information, economic developers can instruct technical colleges to establish new students' skill sets based on what will be needed by the local business community; in fact, Holbrook calls our student population our future crop of profitable assets that can be harvested for renewed community growth and, just as in farming, we must care for and cultivate this crop to maximize its yield in the future.

The economic development practitioner and those in leadership positions need also understand market time issues. Each day a business can't operate it becomes impaired. The quicker economic developers can help a business into market, the more help they are to that business. The communities that help a company shorten its time to market will be at a competitive edge, and in order to do this there must be a better understanding for what this company needs to get to market. "Helping a business keep to its time line means we need to get cities to understand economic development better, helping these cities to improve their customer service side of doing business on a city level" (Wayne Schell).

Consequently, those working with local businesses also need to help local businesses to keep up to date both technologically and competitively. According to Laith Wardi, "understanding the industrial markets and the technology that will be needed both now and in the future will help our businesses. The erosion of the manufacturing base happens because companies don't make early investments to be competitive, so when the competition heats up and the market gets tight, they aren't able to compete globally. The ability to produce cheaply through the assimilation of technology and finding the right workers to use this technology creates human capital, a better understanding of these industries, and an understanding of their suppliers and whether these suppliers are adept to the technology.

However, determining what businesses to work with may be difficult; after all, practitioners cannot work with businesses that are impervious to change. In fact, "An example of the dilemma I [Eric Canada] am talking about was illustrated in Chicago through the survey the Alliance for Illinois Manufacturers did of about 10,000 companies. They found that 1/2 these companies were totally disengaged; using old production methods, old products, and disinterested in change. Only 1,250 were advanced manufacturers, using best practices toward bringing in the best technology. 4,300 were struggling, and 1,800 of this group were 'progressive.' Disengaged and struggling businesses amounted to 75% of the businesses in the Chicago area and 5,000 closed their doors because they couldn't compete. There is a need to focus on the struggling and progressive businesses because businesses that are disengaged won't engage unless they see the value in doing so. Their challenges are not necessarily the competition they're within the businesses themselves. 99% of an economical developer's profession is asking what is wrong with his or her community, yet he or she should be looking at a company's managements' thoughts about what is wrong with its business."

With all this said, what in fact is a world-class city? Interestingly enough, when it came to defining a world-class city, very few interviewed talked about the city itself, but instead referred to the people who live in the city. Diversity is the key. Diversity is people who come from different parts of the world, have different living styles, and display different talents, and a diversity of people make different levels of income. This also refers to a well-educated, highly skilled workforce. A highly skilled workforce does not mean that each person has to be a computer genius. Highly skilled people work for individual companies, skilled in the specific needs of that company. There needs to be a quality workforce, and a unique cluster of talent is important for communities to tout. Part of economic development attraction is the attraction of people with the talent to improve the local business climate of a community, and this important strategy will attract these types of people.

The other components to a world-class city are the presence of higher learning institutions, a city's positive attitude and its generation of pride and enthusiasm for its local population, and the actual infrastructure found in its city, like housing options, transportation infrastructure, accessibility, including its access to international flights, telecommunications infrastructure, and its infrastructure to promote the attraction of new companies. Once leadership issues, the better understanding of competitive advantage, and a network between local companies and the community are resolved, the city needs to benchmark against other areas that have that same strength. Understanding these comparisons will build an advantage with product improvement and marketing. "Case studies must be made on other studies, including taking political and private leadership to other communities that are facing or have faced similar issues. See how these other cities deal with certain issues. Use facts and data to prove a message. Create a case and show proof points from other communities where these ideas have worked" (Gene DePrez). Holbrook reinforces this type of knowledge, especially the knowledge of experience others have had in similar situations (best practices) as an essential element of a progressive world class leadership mindset.

In terms of dealing with individual companies, focus on "primary employers" who are importing wealth to the community. Bill Fruth points out, "Communities should do whatever is legally possible to reduce locally generated costs to its primary employers, enabling them to be as profitable as possible, so they can expand in the area," and there is a need to focus on the progressive companies that are trying to make the transition to the global economy and create an environment where those types of businesses can prosper.

In order to communicate strengths in a clear and concise way that truly sets a community apart from other communities, there is a need to really understand what can be offered locally and communicate this effectively. To do this, we must interview people who don't live in the same city. Holbrook believes leaders who seek and listen to third party expert's validations, especially external investors', is essential to getting a realistic perspective of the current community situation. A disconnected look at the community from an outsider's point of view is a needed skill. Although a local economical developer may be most familiar with what he or she has to offer, a valuable lesson can immerge about a community's image through outside sources. This can also help guide the determining what factors to stress when bringing attention to a community. Holbrook points out, however, that many community leaders not only seek outside expertise too late, but they openly chastise the concept, believing they alone can make such decisions, much like the electorate's benevolent rulers in a vacuum of real experience and knowledge, but this is merely economic folly, treasonous to their electorate.

Finally, no community should operate in a silo. For instance, our experts refused to speak of small communities, but they did mention regional approaches. A small community should partner with local neighbors to prove its points. Rather than referring to a small community's labor statistics, attention to the labor regional statistics is preferred. A small community should involve itself with a regional economic development marketing initiatives, and in order for a successful regional approach, there must be a "vision that is generated by leadership, so they can work together to implement that vision by enhancing or building the product" (Jay Garner).

Dealing with Don Holbrook and this project not only tested my own values but my understanding of the economic development industry, the global world we compete in, and those we serve. Holbrook brought significant realities to my awareness, and some of my favorite work idioms he professes are "No just means not today," and "there is no such thing as can't, just won't, in a community's resolve to reinvent its circumstances." I found Holbrook's view that world-class communities constantly seek catalyst projects to challenge conventional paradigms while taking calculated visionary risks refreshing to my research. While Holbrook is definitely an out of the box thinker and a maverick thought leader in the field of economic development, his compassion for those at-risk is refreshing, and his patriotic desire to see our nation, and others, thrive in the future is inspiring to me.

Chapter One

"The Global Economy is the 21st Century Economic War for Survival"

Globalization is more integrated, and this has made men and women wealthier than we have ever been. People, goods, ideas, and services are moving at a rapid pace, with no regard for political and/or national borders. The average global per capita income tripled between the1950s and the year 2000, and it is predicted to grow another 60% by 2025. However, though the richest 225 people in the world have more collective wealth than nearly half the global population combined, we no longer see the same signs of posterity as we did in the past. Years ago, the barons of industry had prosperity with a purpose, and they sought ways and means to leave legacies not merely inheritances to their own families and the greater good of society. Now we see a plethora of non-profit cause-related organizations spawn, yet our footprints seem shallow and faint in today's sands of time. Because we are fragile when it comes to a global society, our planet is beginning to rebel against our lack of thought for sustainable balance between men and women and Mother Earth. I am not going to talk about climate change or economic development because it is poignant to do so; however, our survival depends on our getting these next few decade's right.

The greater mobility of this global economy has not only created a mobile workforce, but it has also taken mobile and transportable jobs to new shores. This paradox in our global economy is heralded in an era of new opportunities, but it has brought the pain of economic insecurity and dislocation to our institutional employers in our communities, and it has torn the community fabric of corporate, citizen, and governance interdependence to shreds. In fact:

> *The economic forces of today's economy have created winners and losers at the community level. How can and should local economic development create the proper tools to fuel the knowledge and innovation opportunities? What is going on in San Jose?*
>
> *I believe that the growth of the global economy represents a growing pie and if you position yourself appropriately, emphasizing your strengths*

and identifying your weaknesses, you can be in a mutually beneficial relationship with other cities around the world. The size of the market is growing around the world; this represents an opportunity to grow for a lot of cities and regions across the world. (**Paul Krutko**, *Professional Economic Developer, San Jose, CA*)

Between 2005 and 2010, most communities will experience a major crisis that could adversely affect their economic growth opportunities, and this could have dire consequences on their workforce. Communities need to understand that conducting successful business has always been a risk proposition, left to the dominant forces of the times. Our leadership's decisions are whether they will act before they are forced to react to situations while our workforce hopes this invisible hand of leadership will act in their best interests and keep them informed. The workforce needs to know what to expect and how adversity will be handled. They don't want overly zealous optimisms; they want to be kept educated on the realities of the economic battlefront. They want to know the battle plan, and that our troops and logistics are moving and being deployed to confront the future and exploit our fair share of the opportunities for conquest in these new territories. Citizens must also be informed in order to allow them to make adjustments to their own situations and keep pace with the needs of both today's and tomorrow's employers. Once these citizens understand the impact of nonparticipation, they will better understand the need for individual and collective involvement.

Community renewal is no different than a corporate growth planning. Renewal identifies the critical infrastructure necessary to succeed, locates vulnerabilities in current landscape, and creates mitigation plans that can respond to these threats and weaknesses; therefore, turn them into new opportunities. For example:

In the US, we are in a situation where many communities built their piers during high-tide. Now that the tide has turned, it looks like we did something wrong. Not the case, but how we react will determine our future success. Unfortunately, most jump to the "hot trend" (entrepreneurship, venture development, technology transfer, etc.) like a drunk looking for solace in the bottom of a bottle. Leadership must focus on distinguishing our communities. Homogenizing them is a sure path to failure. (**Eric Canada**, *Greater Chicago Area, National Marketing Consultant*)

The flow of foreign investments is driving the global industrialization of nations. Most the world's population growth is in the nexus outside of the traditional industrialized nations and even beyond the boundaries of most emerging industrialized nations. The biggest problem we face on a global scale is the enormous strain that globalization and exploitation have on population growth, poverty, and increased environmental degradation. These factors create a vicious spiral that fuels short-term gains at the loss of long-term safety; in fact, according to a study done by the Anne Platt, water borne pathogens kill 25 million people per year. Environmental harm is exponential in the unindustrialized nations that lack proper infrastructure, and an educational advocacy to address the problems caused by industrialization is crucial.

The U.S. economy has a problem when it comes to its balance of payments for financial growth. A large amount of this deficit spending is paid for by foreign investors (creditors); in fact, we spend more than we earn from our processes, and this problem must be resolved. However, we cannot resolve this by tapping off our relationships and current sources of income; we must address our own financing and spending patterns, not only as a nation but as individuals. Furthermore:

> *In the global economy, many companies are dispersing their activities to become cost effective in order to create a world presence. Often we see that part of the business development process is either moved due to mergers and acquisition, or it is all together shut down. These decisions to move abroad are usually caused by looking at low wage nations rather than looking at a global strategy.* **(Tom Kucharski**, *Professional Economic Developer, Buffalo, NY)*

This also causes what is called the "Dual Vicious Circles" model, and if we continue to pile on debt and then must service this debt, we will eventually become an insolvent and debtor nation, beyond our own means of repayment, ruining our financial foundation and creating inflation and interest rate spikes that will implode the U.S. economy. Our only hope is to stop talking about balanced budgets and start making them a reality. A debt reduction plan that is sacred and untouched by politicians is needed in order to balance this budget. A balanced retirement system and cut entitlement programs, tying them to performance and ROI principles that create cash or reduce debts over the holistic life of our problems must be created. There are a zillion books on this topic, yet there has been little or no real movement toward a balanced budget. This should be our national focus, not the creation of barriers to immigration or global trading. A balanced budget can become the triad of our economic stool to stand on when it comes to a renewed national growth.

Chapter Two

"Global Combat for Survival and the Emerging Trends of Winners and Losers"

Our society's preparation for the near term and long-term future is essential to the successful navigation of the rapid changes in the global economy, our community attributes, and our own lifestyles. We have to understand the underlying principles of economy in order to understand the many diverse linkages to these many aspects of our lives. To do this, we must define economy and economic development.

An economy can be small and localized or widespread. States, nations, trading blocks, and the planet are economies. Economies are measured by the collective production, distribution, and commerce related to such from the measurable area of a designation. Economies are reliant upon the productivity of their workforce and the organizations, both private and public, that contribute to managing the enterprises that support the economy in general. Today's economies have quickened their pace with the worldwide speed of our information and communication networks. This array of connectivity has enabled the flow of ideas, capital, talents, products, and services.

Economic development is the management of both public and private investment collaborations to facilitate growth in an economy. Just as there are various sizes and shapes of economies, there are matching economic development responsibilities to monitor, match, and manage these sizes in the similar scope of roles and responsibilities economic development plays. At the root foundation of economic development is the underlying drive to create economic wealth for as many residents of the economy served as possible. This is done by creating positive job growth, increased earnings, and improved wealth for the underlying values of the economy. Economic development see to such things as buildings, homes, and businesses and their prosperity through the productivity of workforce and business climate. The balancing of these forces is similar to the Federal Reserve and its attempt to balance interest rates to keep inflation in check while stimulating investments at the same time. Economic developers must maintain the equilibrium between the necessary cost of doing business and the reward to local participants, both public and private, so that each maintains its fair share of profitability. This process fills the gaps that cause costs to rise and create offsetting assets, and it offsets any changes or problems in the local economy that creates economic hardships for either sector. This process, like the economy, is in a constant state of flux, especially when there is talk of globalization.

> *Learning from our practices both good and bad is essential. Today's implementation is the key variable, not policy. Focus must be made on the means to achieve end, not merely the end itself. Avoid copying policies from elsewhere without first understanding what makes them work. Good strategies and policies are important but meaningless without implementation; thus the focus on the reality of how to get things done changes the focus from sites and buildings to firms, people, and skills. Globalization has not created the death of the national state but rather created a need for a more precise set of roles within a more complex canvas.* (**Greg Clark**, Economic Development Consultant, United Kingdom)

There are pros and cons when it comes to globalization. The onslaught of a globalized economy is that it is neither biased nor empathetic to those not prepared to deal with it. In this era of electronic connectivity, it is far too easy to bypass slow takers in denial than to work with them and bring them into the fold. The global economy is about self-initiative and motivation. If communities, companies, individuals, and nations resist the impact and driving force of this global economy, they become prey to victimization, and once this cycle starts, it is difficult to reverse. Globalization means self-reliance at all levels of society. Globalization is driven by speed, innovation, borderless commerce, and trade opportunities. The teams that work in this environment are more loyal to their members than any company, community, or nation. These teams mobilize around opportunities, and cause related efforts are important to them. They feel that globalization is creating a freer citizenry for our planet, moving to create clean energy solutions and clean industries, and that knowledge is the supreme outcome of interconnectivity and participation in this new economy.

To fully participate in globalization, we must focus on many things, such as alternative solutions for today's common problems like energy, education, workforce development, healthcare, and affordable and sustainable housing. There must be awareness and involvement when it comes to addressing global terrorism and local crime. Solutions that involve the more at-risk people capable of participating in the economy are great starting points. Creating solutions to cyber crimes like identity theft, fraud, and theft of intellectual property are huge issues. Environmental issues such as conservation and alternative energy creation wage a counter strike-type economic war against terrorism.

Participation in globalization also demands the respect and support of laws that protect individual freedoms. This respect should also include the recent pressure on human rights and global warming, as these agendas are good for our existence and our planet. Economic developers must also claim a stake in the fight to create fiscal policies that are equitable to all levels of participants in the economy, from our least advantaged to our greatest. A fairer distribution of opportunities and a sharing of the burden, or a pro-rata share of social responsibilities, will create more realistic fiscal realities. This does not mean a free ticket for the at-risk population rather a cognitive focus on intervention that can allow each low-risk individual to crawl out of the cellar of ignorance, poverty, and crime. There must be a free flow of capital, products, services, ideas and communication so collaboration is paramount, not ethnic conflicts or religious differences, the two most significant mean for war and war crimes.

Global participation means the support and development of a healthcare system and an intervention methodology allowing all members of society a better chance at a healthy lifestyle. This includes the providing of both the most basic and advanced healthcare coverage. There must also be support for the development of food processing and distribution, so there is no longer subsidizing in industrialized countries, but a focus on self-reliance of infrastructure, allowing an attainment of dignity. In fact, humanitarian aid is the teaching of self-reliance. There must be focus on the need to reverse the environmental degradation of our planet without the compromise of commerce, keeping in mind there are possible hybrid solutions and partnerships that can harness the good aspects of this long, philosophical battle. Compromises, accountable actions, and real results are the key.

Finally, truly global citizens, nations, and communities best capable will start with a huge shift in focus on education and its educational attainment, and improving science, math, and its literacy skills are paramount. In addition, there must be an earlier teaching of the skills necessary in the business world and workforce. Learning entrepreneurial endeavors, finance, career outcomes and experiences, curriculum requirements for career choices, and skill assessments must be demonstrated toward such goals. Schools must encourage their students to make a difference in their community and the planet through the involvement of outside community service projects. Schools also need to promote diversity by linking their students to other students around the world. Cultural awareness, tolerance, and interaction are all essential to a better safe and secure population base.

Today, we are experiencing an economical balance for dominance; a World War III. Most of us do not realize 9/11 was the start of World War III. However, this war is very different than wars of the past. 9/11 will touch most of the planet's population, and in some manner, engage numerous tactics that will harm both commerce and citizens alike. Governments and societies will be pressured, against their will, to succumb to fanatic movements that will use any means necessary to drive their messages home (cyber attacks, terrorism bombs, environmental damages, bio-attacks, and hysteria fanned by media). As we now realize, this war cannot be combated by deploying troops. Though this does not mean force and military actions will not be required to combat this war, it also means other tactics will prove more invasive at shutting down this global offensive.

> *When it comes to what is actually the most important issue in today's US, foreign, and domestic policy—making ourselves energy efficient and independent, and environmentally green—they ridicule it as something only liberals, tree-huggers and sissies believe is possible or necessary.*
>
> *Sorry, but being green, focusing the nation on greater energy efficiency and conservation, is not some girlie-man issue. It is actually the most tough-minded, geostrategic, pro-growth and patriotic thing we can do. Living green is not for sissies. Sticking with oil and basically saying a country that can double the speed of microchips every 18 months is somehow incapable of innovating its way to energy independence—that is for sissies, defeatists, and people who are ready to see American values eroded at home and abroad.*
>
> *Living green is not just a "personal virtue," as Mr. Cheney says, it's a national security imperative.*
>
> *Today's biggest threat to America and its values is not communism, authoritarianism, or Islamism; it's petrolism. Petrolism is my term for the corrupting, antidemocratic governing practices—in oil states from Russia to Nigeria and Iran—that result from a long run of $60-a-barrel oil. Petrolism is the politics of using oil income to buy off one's citizens with subsidies and government jobs, using oil and gas exports to intimidate or buy off one's enemies, and using oil profits to build up one's internal security forces and army to keep oneself ensconced in power, without any transparency or checks and balances.*
>
> *When a nation's leaders can practice petrolism, they never have to tap their people's energy and creativity; they simply have to tap an oil well. And therefore politics in a petrolist state is not about building a society or an educational system that maximizes its people's ability to innovate, export and compete. It is simply about who controls the oil tap.* (**Thomas Friedman, Author**)

However, globalization has played a role in this war. Most of us were not prepared for the impact of 9/11, so it caught us on our hunches. Today, we are in a regroup status, responding in traditional manners (military intervention) when we need to respond in non-conventional manners (economic, social, and elite military interventions combined in a hybrid strategy). We need to starve the source of power, revenue, leadership, and followers from access to their supply lines. In this new globally fast era, the United States needs better diplomatic strategies and less military cops walking the beat. We need to be keenly aware as we rebuild our own internal society and economic capacities, negotiating others to do the same in creating a free trade movement that is equitable to all players. We need to lead the way in self-reliance, in issues such as poverty, education, workforce development, healthcare, debt, environmental protection, alternate energy, and in the innovation of new products and services that benefit mankind. In order to do this, we must be global statesmen, diplomatic and persuasive negotiators, rallying others to join us, and we should not allow ourselves to appear weak and less formidable. Our military interventions must be presented in a way that our enemies would never fathom an attack against us or our allies.

Our leadership can and should begin to understand that this shift in focus is more than a shift in military doctrine in the Middle East, it is a shift in our society, and it is high time we started pulling our heads out of the sand and making the tough decisions required in order to change our own nation and create less harm on others and less provocation of anger against us. We must put an end to peoples' ideas that we mean harm to their culture or society. A mutual respect that creates favorable conditions toward the abuse of rights must not be tolerated. Once we establish these new parameters, we will have to pull back and let it be known of our new manifesto, where America is going, and how we intend to get there.

Then we will need to recognize our workforce issues. By the year 2010, there will be a shortage of US workers, anywhere from 6 million to 10 million. These shortages will occur in the highest skilled-management and innovation science positions; hence the need of our educational system's focus on graduating more science and math prepared students. These jobs could very well stand unfilled, causing an even more severe consideration to push jobs to distant shores, where these may be better filled, places like India, China, and Eastern Europe. Globalization and technology will allow this shift of economic opportunity to happen, especially if they continue to be unchecked by our community, state, and national leaders. In order to address these shortages, the surge of immigration is necessary, but, more than just sheer quantities, we need to attract the world's brightest and creative to our shores and harness their ingenuity and contributions to innovation. For this reason alone, the current babble about immigration is rubbish. The only positive reality to building a wall around our nation to keep immigrants away would be the initial value of the wall's construction. This action to harm the proper and necessary immigration process is woefully inadequate. The real harm in the flow of immigrants across our borders, primarily in the south, is our not allowing them in openly because we don't think these immigrants pay their fair share, so we must change the system so they are able partake in these contributions. This will require an entirely new way of dealing with individual taxation. It is pertinent we know we need immigrants to assist in filling our workforce needs, and we will need them well into the next two decades.

So where must our economic development opportunities and focus areas be placed? Economic developers must work together to explore collaborative possibilities, allowing our various cultures, economies, political and business leadership, and societies to benefit from one another without cause of harm. The expansion trade to the International Economic Development Council (IEDC) and the surge in reaching out to others beyond North America is slowly opening necessary dialogues. These efforts no longer bare true competition for opportunities nor build safe havens for talented minds and professionals to gather, and this will affect our society as a whole.

However, economic developers, and our workforce and societies, face severe challenges when it comes to recruiting the best and brightest. In the next five years, there will be significant gaps in our workforce. Baby Boomers will be ready to retire, the greatest generation will be past its meaningful involvement, and the ranks of future professionals fall short when it comes to a needed leadership structure. Worse than this, the two major sources of institutional knowledge within the industry will have retired, leaving nothing behind as far as a legacy is concerned. There hasn't been any real cultivation for the institutional knowledge of these professionals who are passing in final honor guard review. The sources of their knowledge and best practices have remained sketchy and unrecorded, so our future generations will find it difficult to create their own innovations, leaving them a great deal of risky attempts at relearning what many of today's professionals might have already experienced. In addition to being expensive, with the few precious resources economic developers have in their control, this lack of knowledge will waste time. It will create the lack of faith our economical developers need to provide answers and create solutions others feel confident will work.

This economic development leadership's movement toward old age and graying giants also creates opportunities. The industry can morph and learn and adapt to newer ideas, practices, and opportunities that older generations may struggle to comprehend or give credit to the importance of these emerging sectors. Our more youthful troops and leaders will have the innate ability to comprehend this new industry and how it will transform the way people, they included, will live, work, and play. Economic development is going through its own version of the asteroid strike that killed the dinosaurs. Suddenly, deep from within cyberspace, the technology asteroid struck and created a nuclear winter of globalization, and our old herd of leaders has had very little significant success at navigating itself to safety. The economic development profession has been slow to harness technology; thus the lack of dynamic knowledge creation databases such as best practices and community profiling coupled with site location and business assistance capabilities has been passive, leaving many leaders ill-prepared to deal with new economic challenges and opportunities.

However, there can be both winners and losers in this game of economics, and the tactics of the past will no longer be sufficient to its new dawn of globalized economic development battlefields. To prevail in these new times, our warriors must have a new mix of traits not previously required. Not only must they be a road warrior taking their fight to the trenches and the camps in the enemy's backyard, but they must also be extremely technology proficient. The new economic developer must understand the futuristic trends and make decisive moves in the path of progress. The field will be full of those who wait for the knock of opportunity, yet they will never hear this because it will be stole away by the dragon slayer who rides out and vanquishes the odds and brings opportunity home before others are aware of the situation. There must be leaders who see over the horizon and create markets and back market makers as a process of building connections that matter.

Dragon slayers do not worry about being politically correct nor are they patient, and this makes them no one's fool or serf. They see opportunity in the midst of chaos and seize the only pearl sitting in the center of the storm-torn sands. These folks take calculated risks in overcoming the odds of uncertainty. They inspire their boards, their community leaders, and their staff to take these challenges and ride these waves to the beaches of opportunity. They understand that one set back or loss is just one battle in the war of economic development. They will win some, and they will lose some, but they will always show up for the battle, smarter and more agile with each new experience. Each new experience will make them an even greater competitor, a more formidable warrior to their opponents.

Fewer than 10% of our industry's players can ever hope to rise to this rank of dragon slayer. However, those who do will be the knights of economic opportunity on an eternal quest to find the holy grail of deals that will define their purpose for the resolve and sacrifice they have endured during their quest. Economic developers do not take this challenge in pursuit of riches or power, but for the pure thrill of victory. They need to feel as if they have made a difference. Dragon slayers understand their actions affect others who don't even know there is a war being waged in order to preserve and better their quality of life. Each dragon slayer fights to create solutions for the at-risk populations of his or her community, providing the promise for a better future.

Meanwhile, there are many opportunities to renew our growing economy. Some of these are no surprise, yet few communities have the strategy to address these opportunities. I don't care how small a community is, it should have its strategies for no matter how limited its resources. These strategies are as follows:

Pharm/Health—Human healthcare engineering will evolve at a pace that has never before been experienced. Delivery systems, new medical equipment, medical procedures, bio-tech, genetics and pharmaceutical research will burgeon. In a separate but awesome move, the linkage of agribusiness to this venture is even more interesting. The term Bio-Pharming will be a huge movement of specialized crop raised for its pharmaceutical value, and this will greatly affect agri-business in the near future.

Energy is going to be king in the next few decades. The movement away from fossil fuel is already well underway. Future research and development will create new location assets for alternative energy that will be just as blessed as the oil fields of today. Hydro power, sunshine, wind, and other renewable resources will become much more valuable. The development of alternative energy technologies, delivery systems, energy production equipment, distribution systems, and transportation and utility platforms will be transformed. Some communities will see opportunities in staking out large areas of their region for their own alternative energy utility farms (water, wind, solar). This new breed of community based municipal utility will create competitive advantages for those communities that play for the high stakes. No, we can't grow enough corn to off-set our thirst for fossil fuels with the mere use of Ethanol.

Manufacturing will be redefined and more specialized because product customization will be required for every item. This will require enormous automation and technology investments, including massive database profiles for customers and their expectations. This process will be real time, on demand, and instantaneous. In this era, the protection of intellectual property is paramount. In this same vein, the recent growth in China, though it will not stop, will begin to question just how safe such investments are in their communist non-democratic environment. The second wave of manufacturing opportunity could be fueled by the renewal of America's educational focus on excellence in engineering, science, and math. Nanotech will be the wave of manufacturing. Developing a key understanding of the infrastructure necessary to support such facilities while attracting talented folks to a community should be a major focus for any economic development strategy. In other words, shooting a shotgun at everything and hoping to hit anything will not work in this age of niche specializations. We must have our rifles and our sights pointed at the best targets to build our cases within those specialized niche markets and set ourselves apart from others.

Communications, which will include the interactivity of people via the connectivity of telephone, internet, and other mobile and secure infrastructure, will define the value of public locales. The more robust and inexpensive the cost of utilization, the more attractive a place will be to both individuals and companies alike. New infrastructure, such as RFID and other new spectrums, will become powerful venues. Communities will deploy complete boundary to boundary spread spectrum WI-FI coverage and become hot beds for innovation.

Transportation is going to remain one of man's foremost pleasures and needs. We need to ship goods, services, and people to destinations around the globe. In addition, we spend far more doing so today than in the past, in terms of quantity of movement. Today's transportation is relatively inexpensive. Reaching families, customers, and experiences, are a huge part of the human process. The discovery of new methods and support will be a huge boon of opportunity for future economic developers.

Security will not diminish in our value system now that 9/11 and World War III have commenced. Our battle against privacy invasion, global security against terrorism, and domestic and corporate security against crimes will remain major investment opportunities and growth industries.

Entertainment/Media is the fusion of lifestyle, entertainment, and socialization. We will find many new venues, both within the home and external, for creating experience-based fun, relaxation, and education. Electronic games, movies, sports, and theme parks will create new immersion experiences and involve people interested in Hollywood productions extending destination experiences. As such, Hollywood will create linkages that keep this experience linked and fresh, so the enormous dollars spent will fuel new tourism and recreational investment opportunities. These thematic resorts will be a huge business, and locations will fight to the finish to get these multi-billion dollar economic engines in their realm. Economic developers will find that tourism development will become as important to their strategy as their other traditional venues, perhaps more important.

Education/Learning will spawn the most advanced collection system of experience, knowledge, and information mankind has ever been able to access. All of this will be instantaneous and robust. The production and deployment of systems to support and maintain this flow of electronic bytes will be a huge growth industry. Just as it has been in the last 20 years. The development of a new educational system that is capable of producing better prepared students is essential to our economic development strategy. The complete linkage between K-12 systems, community college systems, and university systems will need to become more defined and specialized in order to match business needs, renew our economic capabilities, and compete with other countries that have been investing heavily in these areas. Our innovations factor will be dependent upon new education systems that both modernize and update in order to meet business opportunities for growth.

Knowledge Engineering is all about managing the growth of information and technology based information services that support economic growth, innovation, finance, and distribution and dissemination of information between peers, customers, families, and partnerships. The growth of these specialized companies will continue to unfold at a pace beyond most predictions, and most methods lack the comprehension of this exponentially powerful new medium. Economic developers need to understand the base industries involved in such development and their desired infrastructure and needs in order to create the environment for such growth in their own markets.

Smart Materials are being developed beyond most of our wildest dreams. The fusion known as Nano-Bio-Neuro technology has been incorporated into common devices and materials that will give these artificial objects the ability to react to their environments and the users they are assigned to support. This growth will race beyond the speedometer capacity of measuring, once it becomes commonplace. Today, such research is well beyond the potential stages of conceptual prototyping.

These strategies, and the economic developers that encourage and support them, will cultivate the most powerful economic harvests in the next decade. These awesome industries are no longer the whims of imagination; they will be well established realities by the year 2015. The support, financing, and development of the capacity to commoditize these strategies are still lacking, and therein lay the greatest opportunities for economic developers to exploit early competitive advantages. Even if a community does not have a universal presence or it has a small market, it can develop a strategy to support the focus on these types of entrepreneurial activities.

Then there will be the need to understand the fundamental building blocks for tomorrow's economic development. There will be a need to research companies and industries that will create economic growth and the types of labor and talent they will need. The economic developers, our community leaders, and company managements will need to understand the basic building blocks to these following new industries:

Nanotechnology is the management and manipulation of extremely small matters on the scale of atomic size, and it will enhance the production of new fuels, drugs, materials, and machineries. In some instances, these nanotech bots will be invisible to the naked eye, yet they will function behind the scene, like magic.

Biotechnology is the process of unlocking DNA and the genetic structure within life sciences in order to explore new healthcare treatments, devices, and prevention methods. It will also predict disease outcomes in order to extend life expectancy beyond today's comfort zone; in fact, centurions will become commonplace by 2050.

Neurotechnology is the combination of drugs, devices, and materials created in order to heal, maintain, and enhance our mental and physical performance. The search for the fountain of youth is a reality, and this search is more powerful than ever. These new technologies hold huge potential for the companies and the countries that support these companies.

Information Technologies and Network Connectivity is the glue that holds the new juggernaut of globalization and the economic growth being spawned. This is based upon computing, microchip advancement, mobile communication equipment, and an advanced internet infrastructure. Understanding this advanced infrastructure will become as necessary to communities and their economic developers as electricity and water are today.

Chapter Three

"Community Cycles Usher in Times of Opportunity or the Curtain Call for Sustainable Renewal and Survival is not Guaranteed"

The historical lessons we find for the reasons once great communities and economies failed are intricately tied to very similar traits. Societies destroy themselves from within by making disastrous decisions that implode their economic success, leaving themselves vulnerable to competitors, conquerors, and alternative scenarios that bypass their necessity for involvement and continuation. There are roadmaps to failure that reveal the evidence of such failed societies, communities, and economies. Leaders and decision makers failed to anticipate a problem before the problem was apparent. Once the problem arrived, the decision makers failed to perceive the problem's potential impact on their well being. Once they understood this problem was amongst them, they then failed to act to solve the problem, perhaps because they thought it might pass, with time, and the system and processes that had once served them well would repair itself. Finally, in desperation, they then tried to solve the problem, but failed to succeed, because they waited too long and they lacked the resource, energy, and will to move through this adversity.

But how did these chains of bad decisions change and, at times, destroy these societies, communities, and economies of the past? Empires such as the Ottoman, the British, the Napoleonic, the Spanish, the Roman, and the Greek all had these types of realities confront them. Even their vast resources and technological capabilities failed them as they failed to evolve to the world's progress and its fluctuations in commerce activities. Some of these failures were influenced by climate, religion, commerce, and conquest, but each had its prevalent signs of these arrivals ahead of time and each empire failed to give these problems proper consideration early enough to create meaningful solutions. Many of these communities, societies, and empires drew upon false analogies for these problems, so they fell back to their usual practices, failing to modify these practices each time a problem was unsolved. For example:

Issue: Communities have no guarantee to eternal economic life. They are impermanent or temporal by nature. Solution: None. Real Life Example: David Sweet, the President of Youngstown State University, said, many years ago when he directed the Ohio Department of Development, "Communities have a right to die if they are unwilling or unable to make the changes needed to survive." and he was speaking of Steubenville, Ohio, in the early 1970s.

Issue: Economic health is the function of a healthy economic lifestyle. Communities that fail to exercise, eat right, manage stress, and live joyfully are prone to ill economic health, and they possess any inability to regenerate when they face a serious economic illness. Solution: Listen to your doctor and live a healthful lifestyle. Real Life Example: Portland, Oregon, and Minneapolis, Minnesota.

Issue: Their inability to reinvent themselves and compete for economic opportunities. Solution: Pay attention to what's happening all the time, and adjust to change as they are needed. Real Life Example: Tulsa, Oklahoma, which reinvented itself after Big Oil died in the 1970s and 1980s.

*Issue: Larger economic factors and trends that draw economic opportunity, favoring some locations over others. This is an ongoing outcome of change. Solution: Always work at developing new opportunities and don't rely on the base that there is too much. Ask any economic developer working for a community who has been left behind. Real Life Example: Small communities that depended too long on manufacturing, losing their base to plant relocations to a foreign location. (**Don Iannone**, Economic Development Consultant, Cleveland, OH)*

When it comes to discussing the handling of problems, there is most likely a clash between leadership and what is known as "rational behavior." Different interests clash while some reason they can advance their own interests by recommendations and behavior harmful to the collective society. This behavior is either malicious in nature because they seek to further their own good at the expense of others or they are dug in to protect their current interests and will not yield to modifications, for fear of harm to themselves (greed). In either case, their own interests outweigh their ability to do what is in the best interest of the whole community.

In many cases, these individuals reap huge short-term profits from their activities. They control their situations and cause a negative impact to be diverted to community members. This method spreads losses over a large number, so there is little motivation to fight back, if this plot is realized at all. These selfish acts have played a part in the fabric of our society for centuries, and they still do, today. We see folks who pretend to act in benevolent roles as our wise and cautious leaders, but many times they are actually caught up in their own hidden selfish agendas, whether it be commercial gain, political gain, power and influence, or egomaniacal nature, and the results are the same; they lead us away from confronting the real problems, allowing us to believe our tempo of denial and false bravado, and that this too will pass, until it is too late. But how do we change all this?

> *Training. It's called education. Educating our leaders is our biggest challenge. If our leaders don't understand economic development from the perspective of its practitioners, then how can they know how to implement the programs we tell them to implement? I believe teaching Economic Development 101 to leadership, elected leaders, and planning commissioners will solve this problem. This course will define economic development in terms that they will understand. They will learn to better speak to their staff, understand measurements, and asking the right questions. It will also explain business retention and expansion, and what this means to elected officials, and help them understand that economic development needs some type of strategy. Teaching such a course will make the economic developer's job a lot easier. Education is step one.* **(Wayne Schell**, *President/CEO California Association of Economic Developer's, CALED, Sacramento, CA)*

Chapter Four

"You are Your own Destiny and Best Chance of Survival in Today's Workplace"

There are many facets to this new global economy. Each individual will need to comprehend his or her focus on navigating this journey. There is a rise in importance when it comes to associations, corporations, and ethnic affinities. Individualism is at an increase, and it is now considered the life blood of the new economy. The internet information economy offers us so many choices it blurs the mind. In fact, today's problems range through the necessary and endless array of decisions that confront us daily. Those whose ships or vessels do not seek to master the helm of technology as they navigate this journey will be left behind. Technology and globalization are hinged together, and they rule the new economy and will not diminish in their value. Time is now crunched together, and a 27-7 expectation is in its communications. Time is extremely valuable. Good use of time and the carving of appropriate quality and relaxation time are necessary, or time will be consuming. In the new economy, there are two cardinal rules to self-preservation:

First, individuals must cultivate skills that are difficult and costly to outsource and always have new skills in the silo that explore and teach added value to each individual's brand of operative (each individual is his or her own agent for hire). Second, individuals must acquire skills other people want to outsource, attracting opportunities from companies in search of talent to be addressed by outsourcing. Driving both lanes of traffic in the information highway society will give individuals a double-edged sword.

Consequently, the traditional tenet of our past cultures and societies is family does matter, and this is a very important asset. Individuals need to develop and maintain a support system (family, church, recreational outlets, and professional affiliations) in order to gain the quality of life from opportunities presented. The nature of this support system will need to understand the work model has changed, so flexibility is the key to happiness. Many have said to my own wife I am work and my work defines who I am. This does not mean I allow work to overshadow my family life and other responsibilities, it means my work is second nature to me, so it is on my table and in my thoughts at the appropriate moments. People who take pleasure in perfecting their occupations and professions carry a source of great joy and accomplishment; in fact:

> *Today's workforce is much more aligned with our Great Grandparents' generation than to our parents' or grandparents'. Our immigrant Grandparents moved to the U.S., set up shop on ground floors, and lived above their businesses, so their commute was less than 5 minutes. Their businesses were driven by an interconnected network of relationships that supported one another, and this created economic opportunities. They brought European and other foreign skill sets to a new emerging American frontier-oriented economy that was booming and thirsty for innovative new products and services, just like today's new individualistic entrepreneurial economy.* **(Richard Seline**, *Former Presidential Appointee, Economic Development Consultant, Washington, DC)*

In today's era of globalization, governments are less important, and this not only concerns but confuses them. Those who seek to impede the flow of products and services with protectionist national ideals will only weaken their economy. Just as a powerful river can only be slowed, it cannot be completely restricted or it will overflow its banks and find a new course, so will the global economy. It will bypass barriers and merely flow around governments that create old-world rules and restrictions. The winners in this global economy will be the governments that are the most flexible, open to change and progress, which promote policies that enable the flow of ideas, economic opportunities, and trade. Many see globalization as either the best thing to happen in our economy or the most destructive and vile force of nature mankind has ever conceived.

The end of the 20th century created a frenzied mania. There were orchestrated simultaneous bubbles that distorted our view of new emerging technologies (also known as the internet). People referred technology to business on internet time, and the old rules no longer mattered, just new rules and speed rules. In the end, many made money during the three amigo bubbles: the Dot.com, the stock market, and the real estate mania. Those who used the old rules, cash flow, proper planning, along with a bit of new technology enabled hybrid rules like customer relationship management and just in time customization of products on demand in order to bridge the digital divide and profit in a sustained market. The vast hordes got caught in one or more, if not all, of these bubbles, and they saw their economic horizon pushed out of their reach. Many have not yet and may not ever recover from these bubbles of set backs. However:

> *The best approach to creating jobs is to continually reinvest in small and medium emerging businesses. Once a business matures, it is hard to influence*

them. Instead, we need to invest in the smaller businesses in the community and help them mature within their community in order to capture the net growth of business creation. This will create a pipeline so the next set of jobs comes from newer and emerging companies. ***(Joe Marinucci****, Professional Economic Developer, Cleveland, OH)*

This moved many into the dismal science of blaming others for their own lack of ability. They listened to those who told them the rules still applied. Now we have a vast army of professionals in a position of wanting to find a sustainable employment opportunity, yet they lack the risk tolerance many previous entrepreneurial ages have had. So the baton of opportunity is falling on the technology elite, the technology proficient, and the elite profiteers in this century. The internet technology bubble has created new position opportunities not only for the younger generation but Baby Boomers and Grey Beards alike can enjoy the fruits of this economic era. However, whether one is a dislocated automotive worker, an electrician, a welder, a CNC machinist, a factory line worker, a supervisor, a bank teller, a grocery clerk, a data programmer, a Microsoft specialist, a retailer, an executive manager, or small business owner, success is attainable.

In order to be successful, every individual must think of themselves as a brand and commodity for hire. Each must negotiate every new work opportunity and its advantages. There must be a keen eye on future assignments because a life-long employment with one firm, unless in government or education, will no longer exist. An individual must understand what he or she likes to do and become competent, proficient, and excellent at doing so. Then he or she must evaluate his or her shortfalls and understand these shortfalls. If serious deficiencies need to be addressed to make an individual more marketable, become more proficient in these and break the barriers for the next economic opportunity.

After this analysis, individuals must understand their values and skills in the new economy and match these to their own inventory. In order to reach the income opportunity desired, evaluate the skills that will best serve additional employment opportunities and what is most valued by the employers and contract employment firms. Then understand how to mitigate current situations and what must be done to get back on track. Herein lies the monkey wrench, the evaluation process never stops; it is a constant exercise to add new skills. These forward motions of continuous improvement change with the economic current, and every individual will need to know how to swim this global economy river. The policy wonks call this process a career path, a skills ladder, or core skill competency training. No one can force an individual into this process, nor will it be encouraged because individuals are their own bosses, but when there are lay-offs, taking full advantage of these resources will better the situation because jobs lost will more than likely not come back.

Chapter Five

Fearless Leadership
"The way of the Dragon Slayer the Knight Errant in Today's Context"

Today's leaders are not only called upon to be sages but also broad minded and visionary conceptual out of the box thinkers, on par with avatars such as Socrates(philosopher), Plato (governance), Jefferson (statesman), or perhaps Greenspan (business economist) and tactical strategists, on par with Napoleon or Attila the Hun. In the end, many leaders find their job at the top lonely and full of challenges. They feel their leadership dominance for the realm they benevolently try to rule and benefit under their flag on the field of business and economic warfare is threatened. However, there is a need for fearless leaderships. Those who know me understand my affection for the medieval times, its architecture, and my militaristic approach to economic development and its tactical execution of winning strategies, so this book will not be complete without my own mini *Da Vinci Code* stylistic pearls of wisdom.

First, let's speak of my reality check, my first "aha" moment. I recently went to a Community Development Corporation Small Business annual meeting, in beautiful San Diego, California, and heard the great motivational speaker, Ole Carlson, author of "Beneath the Armor." During the luncheon, several of Carlson's points resonated with me. I have studied many wonderful motivational leaders in order to support my points on fearless leadership styles; successful leaders, CEO's, and entrepreneurs have one quality that is self evident: success is not an inherited birthright, it is earned; thus it is one of the highest forms of privilege an individual can attain. Successful individuals in leadership positions are not timid souls. They do not wait for consensus to form before taking direct and decisive action. As Carlson stated in his presentation, "Consensus says we are all equal, yet, in reality, this is not the case." In addition, Carlson points out that the good of the many will be held hostage by the weakness of the few, or, to quote a business proverb, "the team is only as strong as its' weakest link." The Dragon Slayer leader, though he listens to others' opinions, will not be tied down by timid souls that want to stick their heads into the proverbial sands in order to ignore the chaos and opportunities that flow around them as if they are a rock in a forceful stream.

> *As soon as one cherishes the thought of winning the contest or displaying one's skill and technique, swordsmanship is doomed.* **(Takano Shigeyoshi)**

Fearless leaders set the pace and direction by using a mental compass. They know where to move their troops and the best positions for competitive situations. This is what separates the forceful leaders from the mediocre. Fearless leaders inspire winners to join their legion, and then crusade toward a vision of accomplishment. They recognize winners, and they don't allow losers that lack intellect, mindset, and purpose to diminish their winners' capabilities. The fearless leader constantly assesses the battlefield to see what changes might occur so strategic advantages can be achieved. There is a daily use of knowledge and intelligence, so they can ascertain the best tactics within their strategy to drive home their purpose for following their quest for success, in all endeavors. This is why I have chosen the Dragon Slayer or Knight Errant analogy as my example. These heroes set out on a quest for success defined by their own drive and purpose. 0

> *Nothing can stop the man with the right mental attitude from achieving his goal; nothing on earth can help the man with the wrong mental attitude.* **(Thomas Jefferson)**

Like the Knights of the Templar in the middle-ages, our leaders have to hone their skills as combatants while being guardians of a faith that backs their drive and purpose to their proverbial crusade. These leaders must live their own version of the proverbial, chivalrous knights' code, and they must practice what they passionately promote as an example to those who pitch their camp with them. Fearless leaders also know they have to build a strength they cannot win by themselves; they understand this is too difficult. Dragon slayers inherently feel their sheer presence on the battlefield projects, the psyche that causes others to seriously consider whether today is the day to engage their opposing forces, and champion in the cause, and whether this is psyche or real is left to the imagination of their opponent's fortitude and resolve in their own forces and capabilities. A Dragon Slayer type leader is a force multiplier and commanding tactical weapon, if used correctly in business and economic negotiations.

Dragon Slayers don't dwell on the possibility of defeat because they have a great difficulty in seeing themselves in a losing situation. They carefully calculate the risk of engagement in order to create the most opportune battlefields for their confrontations. They continually look at things from a number of new or previously unknown perspectives. They know and understand that doing things as done in the past is usually not the best option. They are willing, as Carlson points out, to deconstruct their tactical organization in order to reconstruct it in a more efficient and competitive manner, and only if it serves a progressive purpose. In other words;

> *I don't measure a man's success by how high he climbs but how high he bounces when he hits bottom.* **(General George S. Patton)**

Furthermore, powerful people are in their positions because others support them, and they understand this symbiotic relationship. Powerful results come from harnessing and gaining access to the best and brightest people, and the powerful know this. They would rather be small, nimble, and based on qualitative numbers versus quantitative numbers. They will put their elite commando-oriented team up against a slow bureaucratic opponent without fear of reprisal or defeat. They don't view size as a necessary advantage but instead see a larger bounty to defeat.

> *Communities need two things in place in order for them to be able to move forward: a leadership that has its act together, and a decent product. Communities whose leaderships are not on the same page don't allow their environments to change. A well-hired professional cannot help unless this person has the right characteristics to manage the egos and personalities, but then these communities will always be followers and lagers.* **(Jay Garner, National Economic Development Consultant, Atlanta, GA)**

In addition, Dragon Slayers attack the cause of their obstacles to success. They use surprise and stealth as their weapon of advantage. They view barriers as flag—denoting opportunities and venues for new markets and rewards, rather than perilous risks alone. And there is a warrior's code, a Knights' Code of the Modern Dragon Slayer, adapted from the Movie Kingdom of Heaven:

> *The knight's code of conduct: be brave in the face of your enemies (media, corrupt appointed self-interest oriented leaders, politicians); be brave that God may love your benevolent acts for others benefits, pour out his blessing through your acts, speak the truth, even if it brings you personal harm; be faithful and know that God's will shall be accomplished, no matter the outcome of your own efforts (you are merely a cog in the wheel of destiny).*
>
> *Be without fear in the face of your enemies and inspire others (politicians, community leaders, staff, and citizens) to find resolve when they look to you for inspiration. Lead by the example of your own actions. Speak*

the truth, always, even if it leads to your own misfortune. Safeguard the helpless (the at-risk population) and less fortunate of the world, and do no wrong. Believe your actions have purpose, and if you are granted fortune, let that fortune have more than individual purpose to give greatly of yourself to others, so others might find such opportunity in their time (prosperity with a purpose). This is your oath as a modern day knight errant of the Dragon Slayer Guild.

Today's leaders will do well to remember the inspirations that propelled us from the vile corruption of the dark ages and into the age of enlightenment and economic opportunities. We have recently lost sight of prosperity with a purpose and its service to others, and it is not just shareholders and employees who have done so but the collective greater good of our planet's race.

Consequently, there are innate opportunities for all to lead. Every person on this planet has the capability to be a leader if they summon their inner spirit and listen to their own desires. Fear alone holds us tethered to our lack of stepping forward. Leadership is not merely corporate; it comes in many forms and, in most cases, from having learned how to lead by involving one's self with great leaders, following them for a time, and becoming their pupil. Each of us has numerous opportunities to step up and lead, sometimes we are prepared and sometimes we must adapt and learn before we take the helm. Many of us are given ample opportunities to become pupils of sage leaders, yet many don't take the time to do so. We all need to learn to lead in various forms of our experiences, and as the winds of change are always possible and never predictable, our opportunities to do so ebb and flow like a tidal pattern, and we are interrupted by storms that exponentially, for a brief time, alter our patterns and forces upon the landscape. These events can reshape and forever alter our view of personal and professional landscapes. Occupation doesn't matter; they all evolve with time and progress. No person, company, community, family, or organization is immune to change. Change is as constant and as probable as death and taxes and with this in mind, much has been written about change, the human spirit, evolutionary trends, and survival at all levels of man's interaction with each other and the planet. In these books, we are told how we should live our lives.

Leadership advances the approach to effectively reconcile available resources with existing needs. In order to balance the quality of decisions, they must be based upon good information and not necessarily consensus. (**Bill Best**, *Banker, Economic Development Finance, NJ*)

My thoughts on this matter is that In order to survive and thrive in my own existence, I choose to look at life as a holy mission, assigned to me by God and given to me to allow myself to hone my own capabilities to create the best in myself, my family, and those I come in contact with. I know these are greatly emphasized simple words, but they are not easily incorporated, nor are they managed with consistency. I have had fun while applying the numerous teachings of past noble warriors' codes to my modern-life circumstances. As I do this, I try to apply ancient wisdom to today's trials and tribulations. Though this approach may not work for everyone, I find it inspires me to reach deep inside and find a kindred spirit of nobility and chivalry that assists me in melding courage and purpose into my own ideals and actions. Inspiring others and showing that ordinary people can do extraordinary things through determination, focus, purpose, passion, and innovation is best described in this following poem:

IF

If you can keep your head when all about you
Are losing theirs and blaming it on you,
If you can trust yourself when all men doubt you
But make allowance for their doubting too,
If you can wait and not be tired by waiting,
Or being lied about, don't deal in lies,
Or being hated, don't give way to hating,
And yet don't look too good, nor talk too wise:
If you can dream—and not make dreams your master,
If you can think—and not make thoughts your aim;
If you can meet with Triumph and Disaster
And treat those two impostors just the same;
If you can bear to hear the truth you've spoken
Twisted by knaves to make a trap for fools,
Or watch the things you gave your life to, broken,
And stoop and build 'em up with worn-out tools:
If you can make one heap of all your winnings
And risk it all on one turn of pitch-and-toss,
And lose, and start again at your beginnings
And never breath a word about your loss;
If you can force your heart and nerve and sinew
To serve your turn long after they are gone,
And so hold on when there is nothing in you
Except the Will which says to them: "Hold on!"
If you can talk with crowds and keep your virtue,
Or walk with kings—nor lose the common touch,
If neither foes nor loving friends can hurt you;
If all men count with you, but none too much,

*If you can fill the unforgiving minute
With sixty seconds' worth of distance run,
Yours is the Earth and everything that's in it,
And—which is more—you'll be a Man, my son!*
—**Rudyard Kipling**

We all have chances to lead in our daily interaction with others, and these opportunities are our practice sessions for honing our skills, Once we achieve some margin of proficiency, we can begin to mix skills and opportunities and apply them to greater and more dynamic situations. In the workplace, we can run the entire organization, department, division, or work cell with our own initiative. We have the chance to lead in our families. Through elected or appointed services, we can lead in our communities. We can lead in service groups that address special causes or unique affiliations. We can lead in our churches or religious order functions. We can lead in our neighborhood. We can lead in our professional industries. We can lead in our schools and in our personal and professional education environments. In fact, those who lead not only gain greater fulfillment, but they are the ones we deem the most going for them. Service to others before self can only make an individual more valuable.

However, there are disillusions in our quest for the grail. No matter our race, creed, or religion, we at times find ourselves pondering things like "Why am I here?" "What is my greater purpose in life?" "Isn't there more than I am seeing and feeling today?" and "What am I missing and why don't I understand where I need to go?" These thoughts are normal, and each is present in most if not all people, at some point. These ponderings are our search for self-meaning and self-fulfillment.

In my own life, I find this thirst for awareness a sort of quest for knowledge, yet its wisdom is so ever elusive, and this causes me to look at life in one of two ways: an opportunity for abundance, or an opportunity for scarcity. We are what we think. In many cases, prosperity is a state of mind and thankfulness versus the size of a bank account. Being poor, transversely, is not limited to economic power alone, it is the spirit of body. As long as we draw breath, we have the opportunity to change our path, our plight, and our outcome.

There is a school of life, and in my own life, I see it as a hallway in a great chateau with many doors in its corridor. Each time I step through a different door, I find new experiences, and when I find myself back in its hall, I have new choices to make. Do I move forward and find the next door that will open for me, or do I stand in the hall, immobilized by my last experiences? Sometimes I find myself trying to go back the way I came, in search of what I left behind, but this is not a path to progress but denial and fear of new opportunities, so I head toward the next door. Those who do go back, find themselves mired in the all consuming quicksand of denial.

As I eagerly look for the next door in this great hall, I better understand what life has in store for me. My life, in my own professional and personal mantra, is full of chaos and in times of chaos, when everyone else is fumbling about for secure ground and common understanding to stressful situations, I seek the pearls of opportunity and the Dragon Slayer Knight's purpose. It is my choice to mount my steed, ride out, and find my next pearl in the maelstrom sea of change and chaos. No matter how dark the day or how terrible the circumstance, there is indeed something immensely powerful to learn from the experience, and I am always the better person for surviving these experiences.

> *I don't know the key to success, but the key to failure is trying to please everybody.* **(Bill Cosby)**

Understanding is fueled by the intellectual comprehension of acquired knowledge. We apply knowledge to initiative; therefore, we take actions that lead us to our experiences. As Dan Millman, the author of *Wisdom of the Peaceful Warrior* says, "Experience is putting knowledge into experiences." Experiences lead to the acquisition of wisdom, and wisdom cannot be taught academically. I experienced self realization when I learned to understand that my evolution in knowledge is transformed by one simple concept in everything I do, see and feel: we don't know what we don't know yet, and this not only places the acquisition of knowledge and human perfection beyond our mortal grasp, but it also makes life fun and fills it with abundant challenges and opportunities of personal and professional growth. Winners adapt to this lesson, and losers whine and make excuses. After reading Millman's book, I better understood that the ignorant are like stones in the torrent current of a rabid stream, and with time, these stones are broken down by the force of the water. Those who are wise are like water, itself; they retain their balance by surfing the changing waves of time. The wise are like water because they take whatever shape is necessary; thus adapt to the containments or forces of nature. Once they are unleashed from their containers, they continue to flow, with our planet's gravity as their only means of propulsion. Water, like wise people, adapts to its situations and its environments; in fact:

> *Flaming enthusiasm, backed by horse sense and persistence, is the quality that most frequently makes for success.* **(Dale Carnegie)**

In order to find wisdom, we must become responsible for our own destinies. To do this, we must use velocity, just as in baseball, to connect our bats to the ball and send it out of the park. Using the momentum of the ball is the paradox to our advantage because whether the situation is good or bad if we fear the momentum of the ball, we will strike out. Those who know how to use a fast ball against their pitcher will wait and desire that fast ball.

> *As a profession, our ability to positively impact communities will continue to be confined by our unwillingness to impose meaningful professional standards upon ourselves.* (**Jonas Peterson**, *Professional Economic Developer, Mohave County, AZ*)

There are truly good and bad people just as there are fair and unjust circumstances. In order to become responsible, we have to become truly human and comprehend our complexities and how we intertwine with others. Once we have discovered this secret, we can aspire to become warriors. Warriors are not held back by emotions and feelings, nor do they dwell upon negative thoughts or cower away from change and adversity. Warriors know they are accountable for everything they do and say, so they do not blame others for their own actions. This is responsibility.

One lesson I am really quite taken with is the concept of our warrior spirit and its different modes. The art of the peaceful warrior is the introspective conflict within our selves and our higher expectations of belief, principle, and practice. The combative nature of our profession and the acute balance of the physical world allow us to train for the external environment, so our two spirits join to provide us with equilibrium in our times of need. As we progress toward our responsibilities, we can also work more effectively toward solving society's problems. We can lead by our own example, and the inspiration we provide others when we come together to address matters of society or natural circumstances brought on by calamities, man made or natural, becomes our responsibility.

Today's economic developers need to rise to the true needs of our society. We need to become fearless, not politically correct leaders. We must have recommended policies that will lead our society to greater social environmental and economic qualities. We must be the experts when it comes to the truly sustainable development and fiscal realities of how to pay for growth and governance, and a new social contract with our citizens must work well for all participants.

> *It's not enough that we do our best; sometimes we have to do what's required.*
> (**Sir Winston Churchill**)

My book, *Who Moved My Smoke Stack?* Describes the turbulent stresses we face as we transition from the old way of economic life and society to today's modern knowledge-led technology based workplace. This change will devastate many in the workforce, especially its graying members. How an individual faces this eventual turning point in his or her career and how each individual allows it to affect his or her family is really a matter of inner strength and transformation. There is no safe harbor in this turbulent economy. The warrior is well-aware of this danger, and he neither fears it nor seeks to antagonize it. Warriors know they are the masters of their destinies, so they prepare for the next opportunity. In most cases, warriors are not even aware their past positions were abolished or destroyed because they are no longer in this situation when it occurs. The power to change yesterday's skills with tomorrow's demands can be called self loyalty or ME, Inc. I call it reading my tea leaves as each day they are blown by the winds of change. I know every day will bring new situations that must be discerned and acted upon. My destiny and that of my family depend on the cultivation of my inner initiative and my nimble ninja reflexes to each circumstance.

However, in order to gain the focus of a warrior, each day I must reflect and meditate on my own inner self. While some pray, some read or relax, and others meditate, I tend to combine a little of each. Each day, I explore new ideas and concepts that build my knowledge as I listen to my own feelings and thoughts. This reflection gives me time to focus. Warriors not only use a laser-beam focus on each situation, thought, or purpose, they can also deactivate this focus when it is not needed in order to recharge their store of energy and mental clarity. Warriors use their time and relaxation to hone their mental and physical selves. It is their respite from reality, a time to hone the edges of their swords and prepare for the next battle. When warriors face adversity, they use their mental and physical prowess to slash through thoughts that lack substance and stamina in order to physically stay the course until their task is completed. Warriors switch between these moments of battle and relaxation, keeping themselves from getting caught up in anything that will erode or harm their well being.

Meanwhile, warriors must seek discipline while keeping life simple and obtaining happiness. The simple life is the one a warrior chooses. Although it is not necessarily void of material goods or luxury, it is focused upon the habitual pursuit of such. They not only appreciate the finer things, but they also enjoy them. They understand that such things are wants and desires, not necessities, and this separation of the two realms is what keeps them aware and focused on the relevance of staying in tune with their life. Happiness is easy. A warrior doesn't fill his life with a bucket of desires that increases in complexity once he has attained these desires. The pursuit of desire is a carnal weakness. Those who are consumed with the pursuit of more and more discover less and less happiness. Because today's society has built financial systems that compound this problem, most of its members are modern indentured servants, in debt beyond their ability to address reason. Warriors never fall prey to the debt fog because doing so will never allow them to do what is necessary to guide others in matters of fiscal realities.

Today Economic Developers follow two distinctly different professional career paths: one is the soldier or warrior mentality, and the other is the high stakes major league ball player or athlete that is brought in to lead the team to the championship or, at least, a pennant run. We are expected to perform huge monumental tasks and then take the full wrath of our team's fans if we do not win the race. Even if we perform exemplary, we still may be in harms way. In many terms, we are traded (unemployed; at will or by contract) at the whims of management who may not always understand the game or competitive needs to build a winning team. In any case, this makes us both nomadic and self-motivated when it comes to survival in this chaotic profession. Our focus has to be on the higher goals, not merely the telling to others what they want to hear in order to keep our jobs. In other words, we must be diplomatic, but we must never sing for our supper. We must be noble, chivalrous leaders and the principles of our integrity must be displayed in our work and our actions. This is no easy task, especially when this can place our families' economic livelihood in harm's way. A good friend and motivational speaker once gave me some advice that I'd like to pass along:

"May the thought of taking life easy never cross your mind. You're capable of great things, until you are in the grave. We humans are capable of getting much more out of ourselves than most experts think possible. Don't let those who say it can't be done set your parameters for your own achievement possibilities. I never set out to beat the world; I just set out to do my absolute best." (**Al Oerter**, Discus Thrower, 4 Time World and Olympic Gold Metal Record Holder: 1956, 1960, 1964 and 1968)

Chapter Six

"Place Based Evolution and the Power of Progress to Change City Destinies"

Whenever I engage an audience, no matter the topic, I approach my discussion by creating a mental template of what I think my audience might want to gain. I will take this same approach in my discussion of community destinies. I call it the W-5 process of getting in touch with an audience. Each community's destiny is shaped and/or devolved by the actions of its local audience, so these five questions must not only be asked but answered: 1) What is the message? If a community fails to plan for change, it will be consumed without mercy. 2) Why should I care? Life can be positive or negative depending on choices made. 3) What's in it for me? Understanding how to mitigate barriers and exploit opportunities enrich the quality of life. 4) What action should I take? Take command of known skills, pay attention to local decisions, and exert opinions for best interests. Those willing to do what it takes to lead will succeed the changing times, and standing still is never an option. 5) What is my timeline? There isn't one. There must be a constant and current engagement of self-determination in order to survive and thrive in this new global era.

History is filled with examples of how location theory and prosperity is subject to many variables that can change or eliminate a reasonable existence in one locale versus another. First and foremost, we are survivalists and nomadic at our root foundation. As situations change where we live, work, and recreate, choices to move on and find new locations that better provide our needs are made. This process speeds its pace in some cases, such as natural disasters and war, and it can slower its pace due to changes in climate (business or natural) and progress. These chronicled events, from our nomadic beginning to our present day, are very similar to the root of the causes for community growth, decline, and abandonment.

When I discuss today's place based development and evolution with community leaders, most believe their communities are unique and their circumstances are different. This false assumption is the first sign of a community's potential for decline. Communities are more alike in their problems than different, and most face similar circumstances of pressures, relevant to the day (era). At this time, as in the past, there are huge changes in economic forces, creating huge changes in needs, demands, expectations, and opportunities with regard to continued prosperity. Those communities that face these challenges head on, without the normal cycle of denial, will better prosper.

> *My biggest political interference concerns staffing economic development authorities; corporations, or agencies. It is usually a ticket for disaster when either economic development professionals are not hired to manage economic development agencies or when professionals are replaced, over time, with political appointments.*
>
> *It is so important for elected officials to leave economic development to economic development professionals because, over time, politically motivated job placement and successful eco development initiatives can not coexist.*
> **(Frank Mancini**, Economic Development Finance Consultant, NJ**)**

Everyone believes their community is special, especially if times are good. The situation that creates the most chaos for community leaders is the realization that changes are needed. Turning the corner to progress changes the road to prosperity, and this means creating new maps and routes is required. Although many try to traverse this new course using the same vehicles and resources that worked in the past, in many cases, this does not suffice. Potential for success lies in the communities that identify its changes in the natural, social, and economic environments; thus harnessing the resources to create new vehicles adequate to take the new sojourn to a renewed or continued economic stability and growth.

In many cases, the forces that create community chaos are done so by mankind. Aside from natural disasters and wars waged for conquest, domination and pillage are the most destructive forces of our own design (progress). Consider these forces and how they have changed the dominant communities of their time. It is difficult to understand how many communities thrived for centuries only to fade into obscurity when their location situation was no longer a competitive advantage or there was no more compelling quality of life (health, safety, shelter, welfare, trade, or prosperity).

Consequently, agricultural societies located their major cities near trade routes; favorable farming lands, and easily fortified central locations with natural defensive capabilities and an abundance of necessary natural resources. Once these locations were exhausted of these natural resources; climates changes, fallow soil, an opponent's tactics to overcome natural advantages, destroying or harming successful trade routes, their commerce eroded. On the other hand, whenever nature cast its lot; volcanic eruptions, floods, landslides, sink holes, and fires, choices for better locales had to be made. Natural disasters have affected cities such as Pompeii (volcanic eruption), Cambay, India (flooded when the ice caps melted some 9,000 to 10,000 years ago) and our own city of New Orleans (Hurricane Katrina).

Furthermore, many societies have been and still are affected by war and the military prowess of their opponents. Consider the ancient cities of Mexico; Teotihuacan, Chichen Itza, and Tula, all affected by invaders and the aftermath of such military conquests. These cities were in the top five most population in the world. Troy, one of the greatest centers of commerce and an architectural fortification masterpiece (thought to be impregnable), was besieged and destroyed by it opponents, as were Sparta and Carthage. The more modern city of Hiroshima was destroyed, but it refused to die, and its people rebuilt their city's massive destruction and created a more vibrant city. However, many once dominant cities never rebuilt, so their populations were dispersed. Biblical based stories such Jericho (Holy land) and Babylon (near modern Baghdad, Iraq) also record the destruction of major commerce centers virtually over a rapid period of time. Some became obsolete, simply because their empires faded into history, like Hattusas, capital of the Hittites.

Constantinople (modern Turkey), the center of the Byzantine empire and a major religious force, has lost its prominence as a global center, and while it still thrives, it is not at the same stature of world dominance as it was at its peak. Similar examples of this are Rome and Athens because as their empires, led by Caesar and Alexander the Great, faded, so did their prominence on the world front. Still, today's little known places like Ait Ben Haddou, the fortified city at the gateway to the Sahara Desert Region in Morocco, have been lost due to changes in transportation, technology, and progress.

Both in the past and the present, innovation is the greatest threat to cities and communities. Progress has changed the need for many locales and their relevance. Unless local populations seek a new manner to make their location relevant, time and progress will render such places as obscure and, in some cases, totally impertinent. Some progressive failures are still mysteries, such as Machu Picchu and the Colony of Roanoke.

Consequently, there have been recent progressive elements of the global economy that have had an impact on civilizations in the past five or six centuries. Knowing this should give us great cause for alarm when it comes to our future. Technology, more to the point, weapons for destruction (gunpowder), rendered armor and castles fairly useless and immensely changed the face of Medieval/Feudal Europe. Cities that were popular for their natural protective capabilities and major fortifications became not only obsolete, but they also became targets for new competitors wielding such weapons. Castles and the reasons they were built no longer served their purposes. Castles were statements of power. They protected their industry (farming) and trade routes (waterways, mountain passes, and popular trails/roads). Today, these routes are long forgotten, precious resources are no longer economic drivers, and a castle can no longer protect its citizens because they have been rendered obsolete by technology. While many of these great architectural locations still exist, castles are now merely major tourism destinations for history buffs.

For example, cities such as Toledo, Spain, the sword-making capital of the world, never recovered from its peak of prominence because its expertise in weaponry did not convert to the production of firearms and cannons. One might wonder if Toledo's community leaders stood in session at public forums and said things such as, "Swords will always be necessary, and these new firearms and cannons are simply not civilized, so they will not last, and when they fade, our commerce will rebound." Today, if we consider conversations regarding such items as automobiles, ships, airplanes, and robotics, we can understand how discussion topics have changed but not the similarity of how local leadership has a major hand in the decline, renewal, or growth of locales.

Each time a new era is heralded agricultural, feudalism, renaissance, industrial, or today's knowledge-based economic, our locales are affected. Our survival and thirst for thriving and seeking the highest quality of life kicks in, and the migration of location preferences start to develop and cast new lots. For example, Milan, Italy was the center production of the finest and most fashionable armor worn by knights. While armor was a militaristic product, it was also Milan's fashion statement, and the production of this armor was sold to its elite. 600 years later, Milan still recognizes this fashion connection, and it remains the fashion hub of the world, selling its product to today's elite.

When Rome and the Roman Empire ushered in the creation of transportation technologies, paved roads were created, and this speeded access between points of commerce and the movement of people and goods. Transportation technology has been one of the single most prominent forces in shaping the advantages of location-based development. With the advent of paved roads, more cities in the interior of countries can trade with each other more easily, and they no longer depend on a direct access to waterways. New roads shifted advantages from the great port cities to interior cities. Athens lost prominence to Rome and Venice and Constantinople lost prominence to London, Paris, and Berlin. In our case, the US's great interior has been opened through its railroads and its interstate freeways.

All these progressive feats created the first global expansions. Later, national empires like the Spanish Exploration and Conquest and the French and English Empires spread global trade and organized remote governance to the far reaches of the earth. Therein began the first real race to expand economic capacity as an adjoined military and business discipline. The British created the most effective navy, and this has now perpetuated their global trade and has done so for several centuries. Before this, the loosely organized and highly mobile Scandinavian Vikings proved that navies could propel remote people to positions of power and influence far away lands while sending wealth back to their benefactors in the homeland (early economic developers). This site location process evaluated and secured the most productive locations that benefited the conquering hordes that sought out economic opportunity.

For example, interstate highways reduced the value of railroads, further reducing the dominance trains once had when it came to moving people and goods long distances at affordable prices. All of this, of course, hinges on the theory that low-cost energy will propel our transportation modes at both the collective and individual levels. As fossil fuels become more rare and pricey, the access and the use of our current transportation routes may change profoundly. This can and will have a huge impact on future cities. We are just now starting to realize that alternative energies will and must play a major role in energy development. In the future, we will see cities develop in places that were once thought to be remote and backward because of their natural ability to generate alternative energy sources in abundance. Deserts and windy plains will be ideal for solar and wind systems. There will be a renewed interest in rivers as water-borne energy producers. Agricultural centers are already beginning to roll out a massive infrastructure of crop that will not only feed the world but will also propel every type of vehicle. Mass transportation may become more prevalent, and if reliable alternative energy sources are introduced, how we transport may be drastically different.

As transportation has evolved, so has the major carrier of communications. As communication technologies were created, transportation for linkages to delivery were no longer needed. This created a loss of value to these locations that thrived due to their natural amenities and ties to transportation corridors such as roads, rivers, lakes and seas. While the amenities of these natural assets remain valuable, they changed the dominance of many locations. Now, due to the rapid development of communication technologies, communities no longer have to rely on their transportation accesses. Some communities have realized that this new force is an opportunity, so they invested in creating a robust infrastructure, and they continue to do so. Tacoma, Washington and Blacksburg Virginia were among the early pioneers of wiring their locations in order to allow their citizens to thrive in this new environment. Today, many communities are undertaking the expansion of their telecommunications infrastructure, in hopes this valuable asset will position them as a competitive location where residents and businesses can flourish.

Many times, however, the decoupling of market forces or the adjoining of such forces creates new locational pressures. In the past, as transportation evolved and vehicles grew in capacity and capabilities to address the market forces, locations grew in stature. Today's populations grow in more diverse locations, and as such, they need goods and services delivered to them. In the past, major commerce centers (even those during the industrial era) were located near transportation corridors due to their ability to move goods and products from the point of manufacture to the points of distribution; the consumer and the customers. The pressure for farming and sending crops and livestock to market was also a major driver of location development, but the coupling of new transportation technologies, such as refrigeration, has allowed food to be stored longer and shipped further, without loss of value. This coupling has eroded many of our rural, affluent farming communities, not only here in the US but in Europe and all parts of the world.

This same scenario is now playing out in manufacturing. For example, the coupling of automation and robotics into a system allows more to be done with less manpower. It also allows many location decisions to shift from high skilled and high paid cost centers to new locations with low business operational costs and less labor costs. While much debate has been undertaken regarding the affect of over-seas and out-sourcing of labor and production, the greatest loss to labor has been automation itself not labor rate competition. Yet this is not making light the fact that highly labor intensive production with relatively low skilled labor needs are going to seek out lower cost environments such as India, China, and other markets.

We have been cajoled by the media, our corporations, and our own government into believing it is only our blue collar, high skilled jobs that are being replaced (the erosion of the middle class workforce); however, the white collar, managerial, and skilled positions have recently upped the ante. The concern is that the trickle down affect has not produced the jobs it was supposed to produce. Our loss of these lower skilled jobs and now higher skilled jobs has not been replaced by new employment opportunities for those displaced by these forces. Most of these folks find themselves in less dignified workplaces, being paid less and worked harder than ever before. Why? Because our educational institutions are not up to speed.

Countries like India, China, and Ireland and their educational systems are highly focused on the production of better-skilled workers; thus they can now compete for high skilled jobs. Given this new technology for delivering products and services, this will further impact our cities' ill-prepared with a counter offensive. Other European countries, such as Switzerland, Finland, and Sweden, are world leaders in educational attainment, and their economies have benefited from this prowess.

In the meantime, the recent focus on site location has frenzied in order to justify and quantify locations. This form of rankings and ratings and professional opinions make for good reading, but they have little relevance in the actual forces that drive location decisions and create bottom line quantifiable attributes of success. Consumers and their desire for a better quality of life, luxuries, and incomes will buy more or save more, and this has always been the ultimate market equalizer and driver. In turn, we will ultimately decide which communities will be world-class places to live and work through our own decisions to invest in our current choice, or we will move to a better place and let someone else fix the mess at our old location. Today's community leaders face this reality and many of them (probably the vast majority) are ill-prepared to lead their constituents through this tumultuous period.

As fate would have it, men and women have always pondered the perfect place to live, work, play, and raise their families. The need to flourish and prosper in tranquility and garner the highest available quality of life is the desire of each individual. We have created legends and lore around these fantastic places. Camelot, where King Arthur created social order, individual equality, and good governance values during the dark ages (when few could imagine this possible) is one of these places. Plato discussed Atlantis, an island nation that, in its time, was far advanced beyond anyone's wildest dreams. The Tibetan monks created Shangri La, in the Himalayan Mountains. The American Indians and their Spanish conquerors dreamed of finding the fabled city made of gold, El Dorado. Many ancient cultures believed the earth's core held a fantastic city called Agartha. Later, some even added that Agartha was the land were the dinosaurs may have escaped; thus the fables of the land that time has forgotten has driven exploration for centuries. Our basic belief system is deeply ingrained in our conscience, and it all started with the biblical point of perfection called the Garden of Eden. These beliefs drive our affinity with location, so we search for our own version of Utopia, or we create it where we now live and, if this is done correctly, this is healthy for our communities.

Identifying how to remain competitive (relevant) in today's tumultuous environment of market forces in the global economy is an absolute necessity to the survival of our cities. The competition for residents and workers is now being waged, and businesses will follow the talent. Our central cities, while some may be growing and some may be stagnant, are facing the loss of their best and brightest to other locales, with more to offer. Many times, these cities are smaller, rural, and/or Micropolitan cities, where newcomers perceive a higher quality of life.

> *In order to remain viable in a knowledge-based economy, the next generation of economic developers will, by necessity, transition their focus from providing information to interpreting it, from competing to cooperating and from dealing with the present to forecasting the future. (**Jonas Peterson**, Professional Economic Developer, Mohave County, Arizona)*

As we look at the tides of change, we discover a change in prominence and specialties of famous cities and locations around the world. While these locations have survived in a modern perspective, I think many would say they are very mature cities, and that the vast majority have seen their prime and have thus peaked. This does not mean that some of these are not still dominant forces in the global economy but they all no longer garner the same global domination they once controlled in the past: Such ancient global cities were:

Athens Greece—Center of philosophy, commerce/trade and government
Rome—First true capital of the world during the height of the Roman Empire
Vatican City—Center of major religious movement
Constantinople—Center of Power for Byzantine Empire and major religious movement
Jerusalem—Home to three major religious foundations and the earliest major metropolis
Alexandria Egypt—First major knowledge center and major point of commerce/trade
Cairo Egypt—Early architectural and engineering and major innovators medicine
Brugge Belgium—Early European Commerce Center
Island of Rhodes—Strategic fortifications for protecting trade
Gibraltar—Strategic fortifications protecting the entrance to the Mediterranean
Malta—Strategic fortifications and home of templar movement from the Holy land
Carcassonne France—Religious Haven and Commerce Center
Segovia Spain—Commerce Center and capital of Spain's early empire
Toledo Spain—Weapons arsenal and early arms dealers
Milan, Italy—Fashion Center
London England—Finance and commerce center for an island empire serving the world
Paris France—Cultural Capital of inland Europe and earliest sin city
Geneva Switzerland—Earliest banking and quality production center of the world
Augsburg Germany—publishing center of the known world
Heidelberg Germany—Earliest educational center in Germany
Kyoto Japan—Former capital of the Japanese empire

Today's world-class city order might be viewed from the perspective of what we know and understand as values in the current market forces at work in the global economy of 2007. Today's world-class leaders are:

Tourism Capitals:	**Finance Capitals:**	**Publishing Capitals:**
Las Vegas, Nevada	New York (Wall Street)	New York
Orlando, Florida	London, England	London, England

Los Angeles, California
Paris, France
Miami, Florida
Athens, Greece
Venice, Italy
Monte Carlo, Monaco
Rome, Italy

Tokyo, Japan
Geneva, Switzerland

Dublin, Ireland

Education Capitals:
London/Oxford
Boston/Harvard
Raleigh/Durham, NC
(Research Triangle)
San Jose/San Francisco
(Stanford)

Manufacturing Capitals:
Detroit, Michigan
Tokyo, Japan
Hong Kong, China
Shanghai, China
Beijing, China
Chicago, Illinois
Bangalore, India
Taipei, Taiwan

Media Capitals:
Hollywood, California
Atlanta, Georgia (CNN)
New York
London, England

Religion Capitals:
Rome, Italy
Jerusalem, Israel
Tehran, Iran
Istanbul, Turkey
Salt Lake City, US

Technology Capitals:
San Jose (Silicon Valley)
Boston (Route 128)
New York (Silicon Alley)
San Diego

Life Sciences Capitals:
Rochester, MN—Mayo Clinic
Cleveland, OH—Clinic
Geneva, Switzerland

Political Capitals:
Washington, DC
New York, (UN)
Moscow, Russia
London, England
Rome, Italy (Vatican)
Beijing, China
Brussels, Belgium (EU)

Historical Capitals:
Rome, Italy
Athens, Greece
London, England
Paris, France
Jerusalem, Israel
Cairo, Egypt
Beijing, China

Energy Capitals:
Houston, Texas
Riyadh, Saudi Arabia
Dubai City, UAE

Internet/Communications Capitals:
San Francisco/San Jose
Washington, DC
Toronto, Canada
Helsinki, Finland
Geneva, Switzerland

Nanotech Capitals:
San Jose, California
Boston, Mass (MIT)
Tokyo, Japan

Biotech/Genetics Capitals:
San Diego, California
Boston, Massachusetts
Raleigh, North Carolina
San Jose, California
St. Louis, Missouri
Austin, Texas
Phoenix, Arizona

Logistics Capitals:
Panama City, PA (Canal)
New York, NY
Houston, Texas
Chicago, Illinois
Detroit, Michigan
Cleveland, Ohio
Minneapolis/St. Paul
San Francisco, California
Kansas City, Kansas
Jacksonville, Florida

Then there are those emerging nimble place development players that are not population giants but are utilizing cutting edge investments to provide them with a gateway onto the global terrain of economic warfare:

Tacoma, Washington, wired its entire city for high-tech infrastructure
Blacksburg, Virginia, led the nation in developing an internet focus and strategy
Greenville, South Carolina, created a new automotive niche and partnership with BMW that has spawned numerous foreign copy cat deals of even larger size
Napa Valley, California, the leader in wine production and marketing, surpassing France
Branson, Missouri, second home of country music behind Nashville
Orlando, Florida, the home of Disney World, leading the world tourism market
Brussels, Belgium, the seat of power in the new United European Union
Bangalore, India, a challenge to Beijing in its manufacturing dominance
Grand Caymans, challenges Geneva Switzerland for privacy and banking relationships
San Diego, California, leader in Biotech research, surprising other high-tech capitals
Sacramento, California, defacto center in US's liberalism movement
San Francisco, California, linked to creativity, which many attribute to gay activism
Dublin, Ireland, high tech powerhouse and focuses for attracting published authors as a target niche play on intellectual capital movement
Boise, Idaho, a hot boom town for high quality of life and new business growth
Phoenix, Arizona, focuses on winning major genetics center to bolster its high tech focus on emerging industry development

In addition, there are smaller niche place development players. These smaller cities made interesting plays toward creating a sense of place, as well. Lake Havasu City, Arizona, purchased the London Bridge and spawned one of the fastest equity refugee investment markets in the west, now dubbed the new Gold Coast of Arizona. Holland, Michigan, was threatened by a new Wal-mart Super Center, so it reinvested its money and created a more robust and attractive downtown, including heated sidewalks that melt the snow for winter shoppers. Solvang, California, created a unique linkage to its Scandinavian heritage, creating a tourist Mecca for the west coast. This was followed by a linkage with Paso Robles, to form the second most prominent wine region, in California. And finally, Erie, Pennsylvania, faced a major rust belt problem, but by creating a self-help community foundation focused annually on a major catalyst project visibly improving its community, and this has transformed its image from pitiful to plentiful, in less than a decade. This focus not only changed its landscape, but it also reinforced a healthier residential bond.

Finally, there are those unforeseen place strategy windfalls. Among these, community initiatives created unexpected windfalls with positive outcomes not planned for or visualized. Consider some of these other place based projects built for one reason yet created an ancillary industry after the fact:

Egypt's pyramids (tombs to tourism)
Venice (trade to tourism)
Neuwanstein's castle (residence to tourism)
Taj Mahal (religious to tourism)
Great Wall of China (defensive fortification to tourism)
Hadrian's Wall (defensive fortifications to tourism)
Rosslyn's Chapel (religious to tourism—myth of the Holy Grail)
Vatican City (Religious to tourism)
Temple of the Rock (Religious to tourism)
Paris' Eiffel Tower (World's Fair to tourism)
Mt. Rushmore (artistic expression to tourism)
Empire State Building (business to tourism)
Statue of Liberty (Gift of gratitude to tourism)
Hoover Dam (flood control and energy to tourism)
Hearst Castle (residence to tourism)
Alamo (religious to tourism)

Chapter Seven

"The World-Class Journey"

Becoming world-class has several primary areas of concern for cities that hope to make the grade, regardless of what the media hype may say. The key factors are both tangible and intangible by nature. Some can be purchased and developed by economic prowess and others have to be developed and nurtured by creating a belief in the ranks between citizens, instilling focus and resolve toward become what the city envisions and believing in a manifest destiny for the community. This requires more than media hype and political jargon dropping. It requires hard work in the form of a risk-taking leadership that doesn't wait on the consensus but leads people to form such by its actions that instill confidence and faith in the endeavors of their community leadership.

As I have earlier discussed, location matters less as it relates to natural assets in the form of transportation, natural resources, and other industry objectives of value in the old economy. Today's value of natural amenities matters more. There is a pursuit of recreation, and the value of these amenities attracts highly-skilled workers that, in turn, attract new industry opportunities. As Richard Florida once said, "No longer do workers pursue jobs by migrating to them as much as businesses pursue clusters where high value workers congregate."

Furthermore, aside from natural beauty, many other attributes can be man made; thus increase the competitive value of a community in order to bolster its status to a world-class place of prosperity, purpose, and the pursuit of a pleasurable quality life. The attributes most communities, irrespective of size, can focus on that will level the playing field for competitive business environments are not surprising, yet most cities' business development leaders overlook these attributes. Cultural world-class communities develop a performing and visual arts infrastructure that enables expression and viewing of the arts. There are also crossover projects that look at social, environmental, and historical sciences that benefit mankind. This research also acts as a magnet its local economy can use as a tourism play. For example, research such as the Eden Project in Cornwall, England, or the Guedelon Castle Project being built in France that uses the ancient technologies and techniques by artisans and craftsmen, located near the Yonne area in the Burgundy region.

Meanwhile, Green Space and Open Space focus on policies that protect and enhance the natural environment, creating and providing access to parks and recreational facilities. Their focuses are simple; people enjoy green, open spaces, so they will spend their time at these places. Cities that have a green environmental approach focus on implementing energy conservation, state of the art building codes, ensuring the development of high tech residential and commercial features for their residents, and LEED-based incentives for developers that use recycled materials, low energy and water consumption designs, and low-cost equipment. They provide grants and assist residents that improve their antiquated systems in order to meet these new capabilities; reducing energy and water consumption, and using pollution control strategies to keep their air clean. This might include creating hybrid fuel fleets, greater mobility and access for pedestrians and bikers, wider and more rapid light transit systems, or rail-based people moving strategies. They might also consider creating a public/private infrastructure for clean energy stations, for residents who make the choice to purchase hybrid fuel vehicles, just as the US Department of Energy awarded several grants to create such community stations in 2006.

Appearance and historic preservation can be a community's focus toward preserving the cultural and architectural heritage of its area. These communities pay attention to signage, awnings, and facades, and the redevelopment of abandoned historic properties. They may not be able to preserve all their buildings, such as old factories and facilities that have outlived their useful life, but they do focus on significant facilities with ties to their heritage, keeping in mind that if they solely focus on facilities over the highest and best use of the underlying real estate, the progress of their places will be jeopardized. An additional focus on cleanliness and safety is essential to this perspective. This focus makes a statement to both visitors and residents alike; these residents care about their city, and they take pride in its care and use.

Furthermore, education is the most paramount investment any community can make. Raising the bar above what others may think is reasonable pays dividends in spades over the short course of a decade. Boosting graduation rates and holding school districts and teachers accountable for outcomes is essential to this success. Paying for results is not anti capitalistic; it is capitalism at its best. Teachers must be paid better, and a need to attract the best and brightest teachers within their expertise to improve scores is a must. These teachers should promote curriculum expansion to bolster a full experience of youthful, engaging opportunities such as performing arts and band. They will create a major shift in academic excellence for science, math, and literacy. They will include the link to culture and diversity through international exchanges and sister-city visits.

Focus will be provided to lowering administrative expense and increased funding that actually reach the classroom. In order for a community to succeed, it will need to have the best educational system; one that is in tune with the business needs of the community and the economy, and prepares its students to engage in that environment. It will be robust in its outcomes of investments and support continuing education and life long education as its philosophy and practice in its community infrastructure. Its K-12 system, its community college, and its university linkage will align resources and maximize the delivery of the highest quality of instruction to students and workers, both employed and dislocated, in a dignified, meaningful, and comfortable environment.

Business growth is essential to healthy world-class environments. There must be an essential understanding of the driving core industries and the local actions that affect such economic contributors in both negative and positive manners. This is the core foundation of world-class business climate development. Communities that aggressively attack local government and business climate obstacles enhance their core industries to succeed. On the flip side, communities that understand these drivers will create meaningful incentive policies and investment strategies that attract other companies as part of this core understanding. Local governments have to learn how to leverage their assets that can be utilized to grow their economy.

Meanwhile, transportation will still be a paramount issue for communities. World-class communities of all sizes are always improving their transportation corridors and adding capacity and ease of flow to their route designs. This also includes alternative modes of transportation, such as a light rail system, an expanded bus and metro route, bike lanes and trails, pedestrian trails, and alternative energy fueling stations. In rural markets, this means making investments to assure their connections to main-line transportation corridors such as interstates, state highways, rail systems, and air routes. World-class communities understand transportation can cripple their sustained growth and tarnish their reputation if it is not constantly updated.

Infrastructure deployment is another key element for world-class cities. Cutting edge communication, utility connectivity, quality, and capacity is essential to success. Mobility is the key to communication, and places that make sure their visitors and residents have access to such are leaders. Within the physical infrastructure, communities that create multiple energy options, redundancy for quality purposes, and uptime assurances are winners. The next big wave will be led by communities that invest in alternative energy systems and their own alternative energy utility farms to reduce costs to residents and corporate users. In particular, this can offload peak demand and lower rates to users. In the future, wind, water, hydrogen, sun, and agricultural bio-fuel infrastructures will be highly valued.

The underlying reason people choose to stay in one location instead of another is individual prosperity. Communities that focus on giving individuals a higher discretionary income while maintaining and/or improving their access to quality amenities are winners. There must also be visionary investments; there is no substitute for courage and commitment.

Figuring out what catalyst projects will have the greatest advantage in assisting in a community's competing not only today but in second and third wave economic opportunities yet to come is the key to world-class community dominance. This effort takes leadership and outside assistance in the form of experts in process and money. It cannot be accomplished by waiting for grants and funding from the state/provincial or federal governments, it has to be done on the community's own initiative and with its own start-up capital. This is why strategic fundraising and the infrastructure to maintain this is so important for world-class communities to develop. Without a community's will to help itself, why would others want to subscribe to its funding needs? Admitting a community's need for help and then budgeting for and designing place based catalyst projects is the outcome of visionary leadership, and this creates world-class outcomes.

For example, Twin Falls, Idaho, wanted to start an opportunity fund they called Business Plus to assist it in attracting new businesses to its locale. The community really only had one prospect on the horizon: Dell Computers. Dell was considering putting a state of the art call center into one of Twin Falls' former grocery stores. The community raised $1.5 million, but when Dell approached them, they had only about $500K left in their fund. The BP investment fund board was insightful enough to give that entire remaining amount to Dell, to offset their relocation and start up costs. It worked. Dell created some 500 good-paying jobs, with benefits, for Twin Falls' residents, and this will subsequently expanded to around 750 in the near future. Better yet, Twin Falls has done three additional rounds of fundraising, and in these rounds, Dell gave all $500K back to the community as thank-you for the community's initial assistance. Strategic investments not only pay off but build enormous good will, and this creates great corporate citizens. In addition, Twin Falls knows how to raise the cash to help create the future it wants and deserves.

Though it is not easily done at the local level, fiscal innovation and creativity can bring a community world-class. It must operate from the beginning in order to understand how to carve out local resources from revenues to use as investment tools and incentives for growth. As I stated earlier, understating what drives the local economy and how to peel some funds from that process are essential. Locally, this can be done in several ways. An increased Hotel, Restaurant & Beverage tax for tourism and economic development purposes is one way. This has been done where such revenues are shared by the two primary benefactors: the Tourism Agency and the Economic Development Agency, to fund their operational costs. Tourism is a major economic development engine in our country. Most place based strategies need to consider catalyst projects that will draw additional tourism dollars. This will open new revenue centers that are easier to use existing models to capture funding for other purposes for expanding other segments of the economy. Additional sales taxes can be utilized to pay for capital growth projects to grow the business community, such as new industry parks, infrastructure modernization within such parks, major incentives to companies for relocation and business attraction costs, the elimination of obstacles to existing businesses, and the retention of key employers. Employment also drives sales taxes, so there should be some benefit skimmed from such, to directly assist in growing the local economy.

However, leadership dynamics are the missing link in today's economic development and community-level leadership, as well as in our state houses and our congress. We have seen no meaningful legislation to assist economic development in nearly two decades. Most new changes are drastically overdue and woefully below the necessary needs to fill the voids of business and community needs. World-class communities invent solutions and bring them forward. They recruit their politicians to sign on, and then they execute their own dynamic resources by permission.

In addition, a unique sustainable niche development is essential to all and any wannabe world-class community. A community must find something it can do better than most others, and then it must develop it to the max. Stretching to find something no other community has done, or done well, and creating a hybrid solution that will make this offering unique is essential. World-class communities understand that making their place unique is not only paramount to drawing people and resources to their market but better serve those who already live there.

> *Communities need to innovate and draw high-growth potential industries like leisure destinations into their areas. The results in employment, ancillary income to visitor stays, and increased tax bases are well worth the investment—unlike the very questionable practice of financing professional sports team stadiums (high prices for a very part-time attraction). Rather than take a reactive stance in responding to RFPs or other approaches, communities can identify entrepreneurs and invite their cooperation within the community, a strategy that will be much welcomed by creative entertainment businesspeople who are eager to bring their enterprises to a receptive and equally enterprising community. The relatively small amount invested in this reality check will screen out the unrealistic and poorly planned projects in favor of those with great potential economic rewards for communities. Regrettably, few communities have initiated these kinds of searches, which can go even farther toward its conceptualization of projects tailored to their own particular environmental and business strengths.*

*(**Don Lessem**, World Renowned Author & Developer of Placed Based Attractions, Philadelphia, PA)*

Consequently, developing a new place based strategy (opening new markets) is pioneer level work! The places that stand out in the world have all done it and some continue to explore new options and push the envelope; it's their philosophy. These places; Singapore, Tokyo, New York, Las Vegas, Orlando, Taipei, Hong Kong, Austin, Phoenix, San Diego, Vancouver, Toronto, all understand the need to reinvent themselves and push forward into not only the new elements of today's economy but that of tomorrow's. However, choosing catalyst projects is not easy. There are many questions that must be answered before a community can proceed:

> *The trend in tourism and the travel industry continues to increase. Communities recognize that tourism is a relatively "clean" industry. With the exception of additional traffic, noise, and human pollution, which are all easily managed during the community planning process, tourism has a relatively low negative impact on the environment. Conversely, tourism is a strong revenue generator, creating strong direct and indirect economic impacts. Therefore, many communities worldwide have looked within their own communities, taking inventory of products that could be utilized as a catalyst for tourism development. Oftentimes, communities look inward for historical, cultural, or other significant attributes in which a "story" can be developed around. These types of attributes will allow a community to bundle these resources, oftentimes building other uniting programs, such as events and festivals that will promote tourism to the community.*
>
> *In our experience, many communities are not truly aware of existing attributes or product offerings within their own communities that could potentially transform a community into a tourism destination. With minimum investment in marketing and cooperation among independent operators, communities have existing opportunities to bundle tourism product offerings and resources and promote their own communities as a multi-day destination. This is a strong strategy that can be executed within communities that have such diverse offerings.* (**Doug Rutledge**, *International Consultant on Place Based Development, Orlando, FL)*

I refer to this as creating a blueprint for the future, and I refer to it as my seven-step process for community visioning. During this process, world-class communities determine what conditions they want to address with their catalyst project; alleviate housing problems, increase business investments in core industries, grow entrepreneurial and intellectual capital, create funding for speculative investments in new emerging industries, retain businesses, improve educational outcomes, improve the plight of their unemployed dislocated workers, attract foreign direct investment, element barriers to business climate, create a new market, such as tourism, where none exists, create new industry parks, remediate historic downtowns and buildings, and reuse blighted properties. Then these communities have to see what other communities have faced and how they address them. The use of best practices as well as those that failed is essential to the success of catalyst projects.

Once a community has identified a catalyst project, it has to understand that such projects are meant to have a ripple effect in the local economy, and this should create other ancillary positive economic investments because of this leading investment. When a community selects a catalyst project, the criteria should be that such a project will have multiple positive windfalls to the local economy and spur other investments to occur as well.

Catalyst projects should open new markets and reduce or eliminate barriers that have hindered other businesses from entering the market in the past. This springboard effect is essential to getting enough leverage "bang for the buck." This is sometimes misapplied by the old lost leader strategy, and this is not necessarily true or advised in community catalyst projects. World-class catalyst projects are not losers by any shape of the term. They are positive contributors to the economy, creating sustainable market dynamics that enhance real economic return on investment for expenditures over a realistic time period. These projects are initially carried by the public sector and then repaid by the private sector's additional investments. And:

> *Place Creation takes into consideration the culture of community and the character of the people and puts that into the branding of the community. The key is that the branding of a place and the local culture must align. An example; Las Vegas. There was a time Las Vegas tried to brand itself as a family place. After a while, they realized Las Vegas really was a place for adult entertainment rather than a family destination. Hence, they went back to the branding phrase "What happens in Vegas, stays in Vegas". The branding was changed to properly align the message with the culture of the community, adult entertainment."* (**Brad Smith**, *Landscape Architect for Thematic Designed Attractions, Orlando, FL*)

Catalyst projects instill new values in the local economy and increase the positive brand capital of the community. This confidence becomes contagious to others who soon will follow suit with new investments into the economy.

World Class communities understand and launch catalyst projects as a part of their normal business strategy. However:

The first mistake is a lot of communities are targeting their marketing efforts based on desires rather than competitive advantages. Too often the community doesn't properly match its desires to what it actually has as a competitive advantage. To understand competitive advantages, a community needs an outside perspective to tell which industries are competitive; this is what this community has that others don't. For some communities, this is tough, and the message is tough to hear, but if they don't know what they are selling, they are going to have a hard time selling it. (**Andy Levine**, *National Public Relations Consultant, NYC, NY*)

Seeking knowledge through best practices (implementing continuous improvement) is more difficult than one might imagine. It requires some extensive research and networking in order to find meaningful information that can be useful in decision making. The worst thing communities can do is think their collective leadership knows the answer to current problems, opportunities, and/or new challenges. Making such decisions by consensus, and then standing by them, is foolish and reckless when it comes to mastering and growing a local economy. Sounds like common sense, right? Well, guess what? Most communities fail at evaluating best practices because they either don't see the need or they don't understand the cost of failure when taking short cuts.

In the long run, not using best practices always results in increased costs to communities and their citizens. One example of this happened in my own town, Lake Havasu City, Arizona. It was their recent decision to expand and create a city wide sewer system, for all residents. This project had many opportunities to seek out best practices and leverage the investment with other utility provisioning projects, but the city failed to consider these opportunities. The local leadership said why research when we have the voter's approval and enough cash to pay for the project through this referendum. Because of this lack or best practices, many opportunities slipped their attention. First, the project has consistently run over budget. It has also taken longer than expected to finish, and cost creep has eaten up the community's war chest, exponentially increasing costs to citizens. Second, the city failed to use this project to insist other utilities be involved, combining infrastructure deployment such as burying power lines and adding new fiber and telecom capabilities, all of which would have resulted in the reduction of costs to resident's future provisioning and service fees.

Best practices build institutional knowledge, and it is less difficult today due to the recent capabilities of the internet and its world-wide web search tools. Never before have we had so much knowledge, literally available at our finger tips, but this does not mean leadership, staff, and consultants shouldn't pick up the phone and call people and interview those have blazed this trail before. Through this network, discussing a best practice with others who have been involved in similar projects is essential, and there are specific questions that should be asked. 1) What specific problems did they have to overcome to succeed and why? Or, in the case of failures, what caused it to fail and what would they do differently if they had it to do over that might have changed the outcome? 2) A question often overlooked by economic developers, What was the driving force behind the need for the project in the first place, and what would have happened to the community if they had not undertaken this project and why? 3) A critical question: How was the community leadership engaged to build consensus and support and then how was the public engaged to assure their own buy in to the need for the project and underlying value of the possible outcomes?

Once these have been answered, garner what positive outcomes were identified in order to helped them frame what success would be considered at the other end its intended outcomes. Find out if there were windfalls of unexpected positive outcomes unforeseen. What were they? What measurable value did they add to the project?

Of course, benchmarking and tracking results are always crucial to public accountability, so asking what their initial goals and objectives were and how many were achieved is essential. Find out if goals were not achieved and what might have been done to address this. Find out which outside consultants were utilized and how they performed. Would they recommend using them again? How were mistakes mitigated?

Community leaders that go into their analysis of catalyst projects and undertake best practice analysis stand the greatest chance of both succeeding and doing so within the most cost-effective approach. Mistakes are always costly, both in monetary value and political integrity of the community leadership. Egos can sometimes force us down paths that should not be traversed, and best practices can help us avoid these paths. A good way to avoid mistakes is to hold town hall and public forums. These can both educate citizens and allow their input, establishing credibility within the community.

Too many community leaders fail to engage and present to the public their situational analysis and what needs to be done about it and why. They often fear the blow back from the public will be too severe. While there may well be some charged dialogue, it cannot be avoided, and to do so or delay such is simply going to create more issues later. With this said, leaders should be careful not to dive into such presentations ill-prepared and/or without a game plan. They need to let their citizens know how to get from where they are to where they need to be. People need to know there is a plan to get there, and that this endeavor is in their best interest to pursue. It is at this point that setting comprehensive visionary goals and establishing these goals, objectives, and benchmarks that create measurable milestones for tracking progress and recording windfalls from strategic investments can create a community scorecard system.

Establishing a comprehensive method for keeping accountability in the public process is critical to restore faith in our governance system. The best course is to always discuss how we got to the point we are today, and with recommendations, what is causing the need to address these issues. Openly discussing pros and cons and considering their calculated risks is essential. Allowing the public to understand why action must be taken and the considerations that have been given is good business. Community leaders and economic development officials should not allow anyone, whether staff, elected officials, or appointed officials to circumvent this disclosure because doing so will dismantle and further erode public confidence.

A lot of what economic development is about is selling something to a business leader or a business and figuring out what they want to hear. Know what the customer is looking for and make sure not to sell them something that isn't true. (**Steve Budd**, *Professional Economic Developer, Dayton, OH*)

The best manner to assure the public this will be given accountability is to establish clear goals and objectives up front. Determine what success looks like and the best course to get there as known at this juncture. Set strategic milestones for review and determine progress and/or lack thereof. At each milestone, seek independent review and disclose such to the public. If necessary, make adjustments in order to bring the project more light for achieving success or realigning it based on new information or the evolution in the economy and community at the time of review. Be open to change and insight. Understand what decisions to make in order to continue goals set forth, and do not allow decisions that divert the initiative off the course and cause it to creep into areas that do not take it closer to the objective. World-class communities know how to keep their projects and initiatives on track, and they focus on their goals without allowing others to drag a project off the mark.

The biggest complaint community leaders' face is their lack of openness and their failure to disclose their underlying intentions when dealing with the public. This mystique can create paranoia and conspiracy theories, and some of this is deserved. Today, many community leaders act as though they are the benevolent conscience of their communities, especially those in the state legislature and Congress. They are far more concerned with party antics, political action groups, and special interest group's endorsements than serving the real interests of their constituents. I wish I could say there were some exceptions to this, but the exceptions are too few.

Our leaders' misbehaviors have stoked the flames of public distrust. Unfortunately, this behavior does not stop at the state house or in our national capital but occurs rampantly at the local level. Politicians and community leaders hold secret meetings and discuss city and county business in venues where they will not have to disclose it to the media. Their rationale is that this is not breaking the law just assuring the public that their intentions are best served. Though I am no fan of the media because it, of course, creates a sensationalized story about this said issue, but this is no way to handle public business, and it destroys the public confidence in the process. However, this can be changed by addressing the issues head on, with administrative law changes, at our capitals. Business does need to be conducted and can be kept confidential, until the appropriate time, by having sanctioned closed session meetings about such issues and recording these meetings for accountability. At the appropriate time, all information should eventually be disclosed to the public, such as at the point that a recommendation to proceed is being pondered.

> *The best executive is the one who has sense enough to pick good people to do what he wants done, and self-restraint to keep from meddling with them while they do it. (**Theodore Roosevelt**)*

Once, in a county I served, Wayne County, Indiana, the county officials regularly abused and violated the open meeting laws. They told those officials who wanted to discuss what was deemed to be confidential business to meet on their lunch break at their favorite restaurant, *The Old Richmond Inn*, in the upper-private room, coincidentally, of course. This was their common motif of operandi, and they used it, quite frequently, to discuss things they did not want the media and the public to hear.

World-class communities and leaders do not engage in such activities because they understand these actions break down the confidence the public has in their elected and appointed officials.

Chapter Eight

"How Economic Developers Can Create their Own Art of the Deal"

Cities and states go through very huge swings in cycles of their stability, and this is very closely tied to the economy. These community cycles are not always avoidable, but, in many cases, when the storm hits, they can be managed and mitigated better than they are by the leadership at the helm of the ship. Most cities go through these cycles; they are not unique to the United States. Today's impact of globalization has hastened the harmful influences on many cities. The spectrum of how healthy or sick a community is also runs a gambit of levels. Many small towns and major urban cities fall into denial and fail to meet the new challenges head on. When the economic winds shift, the captain has to turn his ship back into the wind in order to catch the breeze from a different direction, but if this isn't done, cities can be racked and shattered by the loss of major industrial companies, causing unemployment, loss of property tax and revenue. An increased demand on the public system and a dissolved public resolve to invest in quality life staples, such as schools and other cultural amenities is evident. Government and its infinite wisdom raise taxes on those who remain and further ignite the fuel behind the problem. Soon, crime and other blight set a path of destruction across the cityscape, becoming a self-fulfilling prophesy. To stop this from happening:

> *Local communities have to make sure their programs are always relevant. They must utilize the monies they get for building and providing the best teaching environment in school systems, best in community college, and access to higher education. They must also keep infrastructure in place, and rebuild it as it changes. Every community has its weak points, such as sewer systems, and they have to iron out these problems. Keep infrastructure current; roads paving, quality of industrial parks, lighting, routing of fiber optics, hot spots for wireless communication. All this has to be considered and kept relevant. Take yearly inventories and look at how quickly local infrastructure is becoming irrelevant.* **(Wayne Sterling**, *Professional Economic Developer, Paducah, KY)*

Many communities lack the resources to launch into recovery mode, so they give up trying to figure out how to tackle the problem. This does nothing to resolve the issues, and the world is not kind to individual or collective quitters. Others wait to see if something familiar from their past might reignite the flames of opportunity. They watch as time and potential for recovery create a bigger problem, expanding their difficulties in fixing this problem. Those that begin to understand they have to redeploy their infrastructure, fiscal policies, and public services, in order to weather the storm and recover, eventually rebuild to better heights than they were prior to the shock of the storm. This cycle is not only inevitable in our historical evolution as mankind but also in terms of the growth of robust and innovative economies that drive our planet. With this said, in order to meet these challenges, communities and cities need to prepare to reinvent themselves over and over again. In addition, these forces can either create real winners or losers. It can also reshuffle the deck creating new winners who may have been prior losers and dethroning old winners for sitting on their laurels.

The forces that are rapidly driving today's global economy are tied closely to the technology/automation of production, the flow of information and knowledge, and the cultivation of new biotech, genetic, and health systems, agri-business, energy/environment, and transportation. In fact:

> *There are three overarching considerations that communities must include to remain viable in the site selection process: the investments in workforce, infrastructure, and the existence of a pro-business climate. A close fourth, which in some ways goes without saying, is a best of class website.* (**Dennis Donovan,** *International Site Location Consultant, NJ*)

Slowly, politicians and community leaders are accepting the fact that economic development is evolving into a powerful new industry within the secret passages that exist between the lines of the public/government sector and the private sector. We see people refer to economic development now as NGOs and Non-Profit Public/Private Partnerships. In fact, economic developers are tied to both worlds of the public and private sector. The economic development profession, which is over 100 years old and has been practiced since location decisions began, is evolving. Today, economic development is broader than the narrow focus of business attractions of the recent past. Economic developers have to be jacks of all trades. They are economic quarterbacks for the community team, understanding what players to use in different situations and what tactics will work best. The tenets include business attraction, business retention and expansion, international trade, workforce development, infrastructure development, and specialized locations such as industry parks, tourism development, and the attraction of investment capital, both internally and abroad.

Economic development is about trying to make a community/city a priority place that is recognized, ranked, and rated as a favorable place to live, work, and play. It is all about the competition to be the best. The problem is most cities really believe they are the best, even though they can't quantify that regard very easily, but, in reality, their townspeople believe this because they live there, and this is their only justification. However:

> *There are three things local communities can do. First, they need updated, meaningful data. Many communities have websites, but they don't have a clue as to what type of information is needed for their different areas. They simply don't know what their product is. Second is their inability to think through relevant incentives for the project. Often, local communities don't have a clue what the implications are for what they are saying; they don't listen to what is important to the business. They need to think through what they are offering and have an agreed upon local incentive program. Finally, there is the lack of a professional economic developer. In too many cases, city leaders will assign a contact person; sometimes even themselves, who doesn't have a clue about economic development. The result is that mistakes are made along the way, and this causes a community's rejection.* **(Bob Ady, International Site Location Consultant, Chicago, IL)**

Meanwhile, the process of forming a new community direction, creating community renewal, or capitalizing on new economic opportunities for a community are really all inclusive to the same approach. In some cases, modern community images are built, perceived, influenced, both deserved and unrealistic.

Perceptions people have, both those who live in and those who only know of the community by reputation, can vary widely. Both the individual and the collective view are widely held. Negative images are tough to change, and many times they are undeserved, but perception is reality in the economic development game of promoting places, and image is everything. Location, Location, Location is directly linked to Image, Opportunity and Leadership.

Some negative images are crime, lack of safety, snobby people, expensive housing, and\or congested highways. Other negative images include communities that are unprogressive, backwards, and environmentally unclean. The alter-ego to these images is the places with positive images. These places are clean, safe, progressive, cultural, highly educated, attractive to employment conditions, affordable in their cost of living, and synched to the wagon of a high quality life that is cost-effectively attained.

Finally, a middle image is full of other issues. These communities have competing, weak, or no image at all, and those with images have no real bearing on their reality. For these reasons:

There are all kinds of reasons why site selection choices are going abroad. First, it is access to markets and getting into markets that are rapidly growing. Second, it is lower costs and being able to out source things in order to be more competitive financially. Third, companies are becoming globally integrated enterprises, so they are operating on a global basis, figuring out the best places to do specific processes like research and development, manufacturing, and back office. And finally, companies are becoming more diverse, so they can do things globally, and as a result, economic developers need to be familiar with other cultures and know how to operate based on these cultures.

The long-term effect is choices are going to grow and grow and grow. The pressures to succeed in terms of creating the right products and getting into the right markets with the right price will continue for economic developers. Economic developers will need to understand the phenomena of globalization in order to compete. We are turning into a more service-oriented economy, and we need to understand who is doing what and what the trends are for operating companies. Businesses are now operating with different business models than they were previously. (**Gene DePrez**, *International Site Location Consultant, NJ*)

The fight to combat bad images, strengthen weak images, contradict unrealistic images, and promote positive images is an annually $50M market within the economic development industry, and this market is growing. Though it does little to change the image of a community, awareness and medium is important to gaining ground on the issue. One of the major problems is such campaigns are waged as business attraction campaigns, not image campaigns. Improving an image is not enough to increase the economic progress of a place and create place based prosperity; image can only play a role in addressing such opportunities, either negative or positive.

> Economic development is about digging in and doing what others think is not necessarily achievable. Economic developers have to believe they can and will make a difference, and then get it done. They are sure not going to win any popularity contests until the achievements speaks for them. (**John Ware**, Professional Economic Developer, Livingston Parish, LA Greater Baton Rouge)

Hence ranking systems have been created. A ranking system is the biggest image and advertising racket in the 21st Century. Many economic developers use facts and statistics to convey a message that can transform an image or create one if none exists today; however, the data and information industry is another sub-industry within the field of economic development, and it garners well over another $100M annually. The onslaught of the world-wide web has greatly leveled this playing field of deployment and sheer size of scope availability, but it does not police the validity of published facts, and this can be a double-edged sword of ubiquitous information fluidity and availability. The technology era has caused economic developers and site selection professionals to rethink how and what information is essential to location. These quests for the "Proverbial Best Place" can take on many variables.

From 1997 to 2002, the International Economic Development Council convened a small task force of industry professionals, and they succeeded in creating an agreed platform of some 1200 measurable variables that are in some instances required to influence location decisions for companies. While the group ardently tackled the variables, they completely lost sight of the bigger issues; deployment, relevance, utilization, and validity of the information. For example, in what technology format would such variables be gathered, disseminated, and updated? How will the data be vetted for validity? What process will be used to build the critical mass of the information infrastructure? How will it be kept current? This problem still remains, and the technology behind the problem, which exists, is yet to be agreed upon and deployed.

> *I have always believed that, as professional economic developers, we operate on the margins. We can't create jobs or direct investment, but we can position the geography we represent—be it a state, region, or city—as a sound place to do business. This involves not only identifying industries for which our location provides strategic advantages but also facilitating the development of the human capital necessary to help businesses be successful.* **(Sue Southon, Economic Development Consultant, Detroit, MI)**

The periodicals in the economic developer's search to carve out their purpose in the new byte era of information have created their own rankings for their readership. Magazines such as *Money Trail* blazed this concept in this research when Bert Sperling created his list of "Best Places to do Business and Live." Other magazines and special interest groups followed suit and new guides were deployed in their magazines and on their web sites. These have all been created because communities around the globe want to be ranked and rated; they need to show their prestige and prowess in the global economy. In fact, not only have they transformed the thirst for image into a new venue, but they have also transformed themselves in the new era. They understand that when these lists run, the communities ranked and rated will want to be advertised in the publication; therefore, they will purchase more advertisements and reprints. This creates yet more advertising expenditures, all veiled behind the curtain of factual rankings.

Special industry groups rank themselves for other reasons; they want to draw attention to their perspective and how communities address this perspective. It is their way of shaping and influencing the image in order to get the message and concerns they feel strongly about entrenched in the discussion process of community buildings and community renewal.

When discussing these well-publicized ranking systems with the top notch professional site location advisors, in most cases, not much weight is used to support their own already arrived at conclusions, and even then, most use them to placate the audience receiving these remarks. In other words, the ranking system matters more to those paying the advertising bills than to anyone else. Even though, in some small sense, these advertisements might reach small corners of the market and influence some opinions, in truth, the amount of money necessary to brand a community and ingrain it into the American conscience is staggering. Most image campaigns run a short amount of a time, some advertise in the wrong mediums, insignificant in their affect, and others are not catchy enough to squeeze out competitors. Perhaps if Budweiser ran a community image campaign and placed it during its traditional Super Bowl launch, then it would get some serious awareness. To date, I have not seen any image campaigns launched during a major sport's event. I do, however, give Northern Virginia credit for gaining some serious headway in its advertising on National Public Radio and doing so for a number of years now. Even this has more possibilities than most advertising campaigns I have witnessed in the past because it reaches a mature and affluent market of very educated and creative folks. If Northern Virginia' goal was to attract this type folk to their area, the target audience was well selected.

The following is a small list of periodicals that enlist the place rating game:

Sperling's Best Places
Places Rated Almanac—economic growth, poverty levels, affordability, population demographics
Grant Thornton—rates business climates
Louis Harris & Associates—Best Places to Locate Businesses
G. Scott Thomas—Life in Small Cities
Corporation for Enterprise Development—rates business climates
Council on Competitiveness—American Cities' Ability to Compete Globally
FBI—Crime-statistics
National Health Center—life expectancies
Brookings Institute—market characteristics (weak or strong)
National Governors Association-rates health and competitiveness
International Association of Mayors-best strategies for resolving local problems

Urban Institute—world class land use examples and protocols
International City & County Managers Association—rates management of change within markets
International Economic Development Council (IEDC)—trends affecting economic growth and renewal and redevelopment of markets

And here is a list of those that have joined in the game:

Money Magazine—Best Places to Live
Inc. Magazine—Best Business for Growth
Conde Nast Travel—most affordable for travel and amenities
Fortune—Best of Business Concerns
Forbes—best for many aspects related to people and business
Corporate Travel—the expense of business meetings
Savvy—best for parents
Parenting-best for raising kids
Zero Population—stress of populations within cities
Foreign Direct Investment—best for investment opportunities
Psychology Today—ranks cities by well-being

By far, this is not a list of all the publications that play the ranking game, but it does demonstrate my points of message and purpose. There is a veil of bias that exists behind the ranking systems. In truth, many communities are simply not rated, so the system is not inclusive, nor does it represent validity. Part of the argument in this case is smaller communities have no responsible party to gather and provide the data in order to be considered for these rankings but, in reality, many communities do understand their locales enough to respond, yet they are simply not aware of the rankings until it is too late. Nonetheless, the media spin creates new images and promotes new hierarchies as a business model not as a basis for pure accountability.

In reality, there are many steps to community growth and renewal, and none of these steps include a ranking system. The process for achieving real results takes time, preparation, and leadership resolve. Leaders must not be bias of their own opinions in such a way that they do not consider the views of the outside world. There are numerous issues affecting a community's ability to reach its potential, but most of these are obstructed by leadership and obstacles at the local level.

The explanation boils down to jobs and wealth; doing things to retain and attract and expand and incubate businesses and other employers that support and generate employment and ultimate wealth; wealth in the community,

> *and wealth that is taxable. The biggest challenge in talking about economic development is getting people to understand the difference between basic economics and the local tax base. Our leaders cannot think about economic development as simply tax development. It needs to be thought of as an "economy" building. We need to get people to think about the real wealth that is being created rather than simply the transfer of wealth to others with no connection to our community.* **(Richard Ward,** *National Economic Development Consultant, St. Louis, MO)*

Again, recognizing there is a constant process of evolution and reordering of our society, economies, and places is a rule of order that must be accepted as a principle of authority. The sooner communities and community leaders pull their head out of the proverbial sand, or out of the proverbial clouds, the sooner they can get about the real business of managing the changing dynamics that drive the influences of their community landscape.

These major obstacles of perspective are the resistance communities have when it comes to gaining outside professional opinions; the almost always widely held in low regard consultants who preach the medicines of community change (visioning, planning, marketing, image enhancement, and all other specialized threats on the horizon). Community leaders view this legion of experts as the carpet baggers of the Old South post civil role era. However, unlike carpet baggers, these consultants bring some objectivity to the discussion. They also have access to other experiences in which they have accumulated some institutional knowledge that can further help their future clients. Once this obstacle is overcome, the secondary concern is that either the consultant will tell a community's leader what they want to hear or the report will hit the mark and live only long enough to get moved to the shelves of Local Government Headquarters, City Halls, or County Administration Buildings. The libraries of these institutions are filled with old reports that were not taken seriously, only given lip service, or never updated to match the movement of time and progress (the evolution of place and the economy).

> *Communities always feel they are unique. They do national talent recruitment to hire the best economic developer to lead them through change and give them sage advice to make them more competitive. Once the economic developer arrives in the market and begins to do as instructed they dub us the Village Idiot, claiming we just don't understand their unique exemption from the realities of today's economy.* **(Mike Kirchhoff,** *Professional Economic Developer, Kansas City, MO)*

Herein lays the many myths of our local leaders and their infinite wisdoms:

Myth #1: Many local leaders falsely believe they, and their collective others, have enough brain power to sort through these immensely difficult problems on their own and without any need of outside opinions. In some cases, they bring outside opinions in simply to validate their own conclusions without bringing any validity to the matter through investigation of other communities' experiences and best practices and their handling of such problems and opportunities. They figure the voters elected them for their opinions, so they must solely express them. The problem is that we voters do not necessarily elect our leaders for their opinions but for their ability to lead and make decisions based upon gathering information (the best available and affordable). Then we expect our leaders to make the best decisions based upon solid direction through others with superior experience in specific areas of expertise related to the problems and/or opportunities.

> *Politics fall into two categories that impact economic development, big "P" and little "p." The big "P" deals with traditional decisions impacted by elected and appointed officials, while the little "p" deals with the politics of local place based pressures, beliefs, influences, interests and how they handle change.* (**Jim Kinnett**, Economic Development Consultant)

Myth #2: In this same vein, we hire staff to manage our community infrastructure and services. We do not expect this staff will be the all powerful Oz on all aspects of their expertise, but we do expect they will know when to seek higher levels of expertise and be able to inform elected leaders as to how to navigate such situations and hire the best professionals to give relevant advice when required. It is our human nature to act more knowledgeable than we really are, and we see this admitted need as a loss of face; thus our powerful posture within the hierarchy of the public system and institutional order.

Myth #3: There is always a major issue in finding the funds to pay for such knowledge. Gaining information is not free, nor is it inexpensive, so argument is made about the expense of specialized opinions in addition to the expense of the work and its process. Yet no one ever spends the energy to determine the expense of ignorance or the non-action of these problems. If the economic plight is going to erode an economy by millions of dollars per year over the next decade, a few thousand, hundreds of thousands, and even millions spent might be paltry to the impact of staying in denial and in the dark. The measurement should always be this; is there a large possibility that such actions would create a positive economic outcome rather than a negative, and if so, should we be interested in gauging what the differential and probabilities are rather than do nothing? Doing nothing is almost always more expensive than acting early in a progressive intervention mode before something becomes a crisis. In the end, this is all just economics; the simple math of plus or minus economic community balance sheets. If a balance sheet is declining each year, there will be no way to cut through to prosperity. I hate to say this but money needs to be spent (correctly and within calculated risks) in order to make money in a positive manner as a community.

> *One of my fears as we work to bring the best and brightest into the economic development field is the compensation ceilings many of our organizations are dealing with, both public and not-for-profit entities. With the shifting demographics and the heated competition for the shrinking talent pool, we are seeing an increasingly difficult labor market. The large organizations can still offer very attractive packages, but small to mid-size markets, and middle to senior management positions are becoming more difficult to fill. And if that is not enough, the private sector is cherry-picking some of our brightest up and coming talent!* **(Robin Roberts**, Economic Development Professional, Oklahoma City, OK)

Myth #4: We don't need to engage government in solving this problem. We are firm believers in less government and the need for the private sector to lead the way in such situations. If we act on this information and become an obstacle to solutions, we might actually be in competition with the private sector. This is all really a charade to convince everyone involved that things will get better on their own, when in reality this is just an act of denial. If the conditions that created the problem have been growing for years and the decline has been unchallenged by new private sector investments, offsetting new business growth and opportunities, then there is a negative private sector response. They don't believe in the community's market enough to take such additional risks or investments, so they will need convincing and probably some shared risk by the public sector to consider such new investments. These scenarios merit the public sector to lead and convince the private sector that the situation can be turned around. In fact, businesses are not built to take enormous risks because such actions would jeopardize profits. In most cases, the risks they do take are measurable and quantifiable. In the case of an eroding confidence in a market, the underlying conditions must be explored so variables can be identified and then fixed. Once this is done, the potential probabilities can be identified for investments and potential outcomes. With the knowledge of this information and the commitment of the public sector to fill the risk gaps outside the control of the business sectors, a community can gain business investment partners for each niche necessary to turn the tide. This process of identifying investments, its necessary gap infrastructure (social, physical, economic), identifying the projects that will create positive outcomes, both ancillary direct and indirect positive economic impact, is what I refer to as developing *economic development catalyst projects*.

Myth #5: The state and federal government need to invest in us to fix our problems! We need our big brothers to step in and perform some much deserved miracles for us. Well, guess what, Dorothy? Every community feels the same way! In short, get real. What makes one community more deserving than another (rhetorical question)? The answer is; nothing. Only communities willing to help themselves, not those waiting for the next train, will get their just rewards. Since we know business is like a competitive sport, those that step out and take the risk of competing and risk their very being to gain the next level are the communities that deserve to win, and they do win. They do not make excuses, or get stuck in the denial that the State and Federal government is going to bail them out, nor do they leave their future to the private sector. Winning communities take their future into their own hands and help themselves. They expect nothing from others. However, other funds are eventually awarded to assist communities, but state and federal governments only assist and invest in winning communities that have already taken their own initiative and do not expect their government to bear the brunt of the burden. It is the old Jerry Maguire slogan, "Help Me, Help You."

In my own experiences at leading change dynamics within communities and regions in the United States, I find a reoccurring process that works well when building the infrastructure of community renewal, growth, and visualization of current and future scenarios. During the *"Seven Step Process for Community Renewal & Growth,"* there comes a time when the targeted audience and leadership finally realize the, what I refer to as, AHA experience! This is when all the intangible elements and variables come together and form an image of what is, what can be, what must be done to get there, and the why of the situation glues together into a salient vision. This vision then becomes a strategic direction and converts to an actionable plan that can be created, agreed upon, and invested in. Once this is known and publicized, the leadership can build awareness within the ranks of the citizens and start the process of building the new foundation for their future.

Myth #6: I can't individually make a difference in my community! This is just not true. I don't know how many public meetings I have attended where a small few vocally opposed or supported an agenda issue, and it was extremely considered by the elected folks. These elected officials do not want to enlist the wrath of the voters, and they never know how such consideration, if ignored, may swell and cause them great voter reprisal. Still, this is not the best avenue to getting things done. The first and foremost objective of the citizens is to stay directly informed. Don't just read the newspaper to get the leaders' spin on what is going on in the public political platform. In every community, there are ample opportunities to attend key meetings, special work sessions, town halls, and public forums. In fact, the law mandates such meetings. In addition, cable television enables our ability to watch such meetings from the comfort of our own homes.

Once and individual has picked something he or she really feel strongly about, learn all there is to learn about this subject and provide an educated address to this subject. Provide an opinion that is well researched, and then present it to the public officers and elected officials. Lead a special interest group and hold meetings on the issue, and others may rally to the cause quite easily. If all else fails and the politicians still won't let this opinion come through the main gate of their castle, scale the walls by force; use a voter referendum item. This will require signatures to submit such a consideration, for voter approval or rejection, and in many cases, the mere thought of this will bring the public sector folks to the table for a helpful discussion. Make the public officials partners in these new ideas and this will build strong allies and a fair chance at seeing these issues addressed and given public awareness.

Every individual owes it to his or her family to take heed in public decisions. Not only this, in many cases, employment, quality life, affordability cost of living, and a child's education hang in the balance. The smallest opinion counts, all that is needed is a visit to the public leaders. With these myths out of the way, we can now look at the "Seven Step Process":

Step 1: *Where are we today and why?* This is what many refer to as the "Audit of Place." In this case, community leaders need to understand what is contributing to their situation (drivers and influencers). It must be taken into a broad account the environment outside the community and its impact on the community; the measurable effect these drivers have on the community profile as a whole.

In this scenario, a community needs to understand its current state and if the pace this impact is having its toll. How long will it be before it is beyond reasonable repair and too costly to turn the tide? What does this future of doing the status quo look like for its residents? The discovery of what can and will happen if things do not change is critical to the commencement of this process.

During this process, economic developers take an accounting of the assets and liabilities of this community. They study its trends, such as housing values, employment levels, earnings, industry mix, local economic diversity, available amenities, living cost, educational attainment, population demographics, government revenues, business climate, poverty levels, housing availability and its mix of housing stock; including affordability, infrastructure availability, sales leakage, capital investments (inflow), new business start-ups, innovation (local innovation such as patents), recreational, and culture and arts opportunities.

As this takes place, the community considers a Strengths, Weaknesses, Opportunities, and Threats (SWOT) analysis. This process identifies the assets the community has and how these can be built upon for renewed success (strengths) and what barriers it has to attaining new growth and renewal (weaknesses). From this list of factors, the community leaders create a list of possible actionable projects that will hold the most merit for making positive impact on the renewed economic growth of its community (opportunities). A list of the community's competitors is then made in order to circumvent its progress or steal its opportunities (threats). This last element is the most difficult because it must also consider the threat of not taking action or only partially carrying out an action. Failing to execute the actions necessary to cultivate and harvest a community's opportunity is a threat to its progress.

The final audit should be realistic and pull no punches. In most cases, it scares the hell out of audiences because they know it is all true. It is scary when a community has to address its real need for change and the modifications for a necessary reality.

Step 2: ***Where Do We Want to Go from Here?*** This process is much more than a visioning exercise. Once the information from step 1 is fully discovered, the veil of ignorance become tattered and torn and a shred of opportunistic light begin to shine through. Understanding the forces and the opportunities being asserted within this community and what lies ahead in its future will make choices easier. Given this information, the leaders and any community participants need to think about where they want to be in the future. What is their best outcome and makes the most sense? Where do they want to be, relative to the future? In this step, there will be questions like, "What type of community do I want to live in?" "What kind of experiences do I want and desire in the place I live?" What will people who move here in the future hold as viable expectations?" "What will our youth need in order to stay and work here rather than move to other places of opportunity?" and "What will make my community attractive to businesses, visitors, and residents tomorrow that we do not have today?" In other words:

> *We need to educate our local leadership to pay more attention to where the revenues of our communities are coming from rather than where our expenses are going. If our local leaders understood who their major customers were, who the local major revenue sources are, they would take better care of their local small businesses. It is our local businesses that provide local sales tax and property tax. Know who is generating revenue for the jurisdiction. Become knowledgeable about local businesses' events. Find a government person who wants to understand his industry's knowledge and understanding.* (**Kurt Chillcott**, *Professional Economic Developer, San Diego, CA*)

This step is the possibilities initiative. While it may seem like a whimsical step, it is critically important to creating a sense of place that will both attract other talented people and retain the current best and brightest to become productive residents. If we all had the nerve to tell the truth, we would admit we desire a great community; one with the many missing attributes of our current model, but we dismiss these absences to the adage we can't afford them. In truth, there is not much a community really cannot afford; it merely chooses not to stretch to attain such new possibilities. In the end, the communities that stretch are the ones that attain the biggest reward. People recognize such actions as valuable and attractive amenities, and they desire to live in such places, and this, in turn, reduces the real cost of such catalyst actions and creates a profitable return on investments to the public. The only time such investments don't pay off is when the community takes actions that are not truly the desire of its residents (not valued) and have no real value to future residents. If truth be told, these community leaders do what they want and disregard the expectations and values of their residents and the trends future residents' desire. It is in these cases that communities must regroup and consider the true needs and desires of the market. Even in failures such as this, quitting is not an option; it is just an opportunity to transform and take a different route to desired outcomes.

During this analysis, a rank of possibilities for what is easily attainable in the short term, what is relatively easy to attain in the next 5 to 7 years, and what requires an obtainable incremental investment for a longer timeline of maybe a decade or more needs to be made. These possibilities are based on assets, resource developments, and a provisioning plan that creates an attainable budget. It also uses the current revenue sources as consideration for this ranking. Don't forget it is important to understand why people want to go to this new level or create this new community environment. These outcomes must be personal to each individual so each can understand why he or she should care how these actions will affect them.

Step 3: *Realistic Outcome Scenarios—the "What If?" Conclusions.* During this step, scenarios for what can be are fully expanded and developed. There will be an understanding of the impact these scenarios will have on the over-all community, society, and infrastructure. These scenarios must be both hard hitting and based on reality, not hemmed in by negative feelings or disbeliefs of attainability. Money should not be the consideration in this step. Avoid making the choices based upon the perceived costs for any possibilities.

We are great at undoing our own best dreams. It is our natural tendency to dismiss ideas as too costly and allow our old loser attitudes to invade the new enlightened territory we have just discovered. If people persist in being instigators for negative feelings about the best possibilities based on realistic and obtainable outcomes, ask them to dismiss themselves from the leadership function. Leaders should always be forward thinkers, optimistic, and strategic creators of tactical advantages.

Step 4: *What Steps and Actions are Necessary to Arrive at Our Chosen Destination in the Future?* During this step, economic developers must visualize a business plan and understand what this business plan must contain in order to receive the greatest chance of success. This is where the rubber hits the road. A methodical outline of all the necessary components is needed to succeed. Who will be the players and what roles and accountability will they be responsible for? What expertise will be required for the various scenarios, what must we garner from outside our community, and what leverage will they bring to the situation? In other words, what will these outside experts bring in the form of their deliverables that will meet our expectations? I always ask people to define their ideas of success.

After these objectives are understood, then we can aim for the mark. When outside talent and resources are brought into the scenario, they should always fill a need that is strategic and exceptionally capable toward the best chance at success. Do not hire one expert to fill all voids; this is simply not realistic. There are specific experts who will need to be hired from various professionals and different niches. These experts must then be required to collaborate on the outcomes, so there is no duplicity. A single expert may claim he or she can do all, but the best desired outcomes may be beyond their real competency. In these cases, I reach for the best, and I expect the best results in return. I call this "best practices."

Many communities, when asked how they reviewed and decided on their fate or on what information they acted upon to make their decisions, fail to produce evidence that they actually looked at a historical project of a similar nature undertaken by other communities. I find that many community leaders just completely fail to explore the path of others. In my experience, there simply aren't too many unique problems that other communities have not once faced. These best practices are very insightful. A good analysis of this scenario can turn up great pearls of experienced knowledge. It helps to identify actions taken by others; professionals with experience in such matters, and participants and leaders that lived through it. Nothing trumps having traveled a path before and having knowledge of what lies over the next hill and around the next bend. In my use of best practices, I find it useful to contact such communities and discuss their view of the process they used. Find out what worked well and what didn't. With regard to these aspects, what would they have done differently? How have these changes transformed or changed their community, and did these changes meet or exceed their initial expectations? Once a few best practices models have been solidly explored, it will be easier to assess a community's possibilities and how to create a new hybrid plan based on the experienced shared by others. This makes the unknown much more understandable. There will be knowledge of the major players and professionals who have experience in such matters that might be useful in assisting this new project.

Now that there is a vision of what can be and what needs will best address this mission in the form of necessary steps, resources, players, infrastructure, and organizational structure, understanding the expectations for these implemented and executed steps is essential. There must also be what I call "catalyst projects."

In most cases, the biggest missing step in these processes is not merely the how to get to where we want to be, but what are the fundamental projects that if undertaken will have the greatest exponential effect of creating multiple other ancillary investments (economic impact analysis at a macro and micro scale). In other words, the best projects within each niche needs to create positive momentum toward other similar investments, related or complimentary to a combined and compounding positive effect on the over-all community, society, and economy. These catalyst projects create ripples that touch all shores of the lake. They create the most indirect economic benefit, not necessarily the most direct economic impact. The indirect will have smaller direct impact projects tucked inside the realm of the positive momentum. This makes catalyst projects tough to define and difficult to visualize because in most cases, the direct benefits are small in appearance and the indirect players are not yet known. This is where we separate the amateurs from the pros of heavy lifting. Kennedy would have called this the projects that when enacted raise all boats.

Step 5: *The Missing Link in Most Communities—Cash Flow Modeling:* Now we get to do the stuff most consultants shy away from and most communities become derailed from progress because of this critical function. First, let's understand the ground rule; there are no sources that can be left off the table of consideration. Second, our own internal staff probably won't have the answer to this equation, so this should be one of those strategic acquisitions of outside professional assistance. Finding models for possible cash flow objectives and sources that can be leveraged to pay for the roll out of our new action oriented business model from step 4 should now be implemented.

This might require new legislative authorization; a borrowing against today's capacity before it is further diminished and then pumping up our revenues as the positive outcomes kick into financial windfalls. It might mean new fees for desired services not yet funded. It might mean the linking of negative drivers to financial models in order to resolve negative aspects. Many things might be perceived as negative but, in reality, they are in fact positive opportunities and their solutions are not as painful as some might think. The trick to this exercise is thinking way over the horizon and out of the box, and there are many examples for these types of investment tools.

For instance, a community wants to create a new sense of place to bring tourists and visitors to the area. It will require some massive amounts of public investment to create enough synergy for the private sector to invest the risk capital.

To level the playing field, the community creates a special tax zone that acts like a super Tax Increment Financing (TIF) district. In many cases, TIFs are used by local governments across the country to capture the future tax impact of a project and lend it to the project or abate the payment of the tax to create better cash flow during the first 10 to15 years of this project. There is also what is called the *"Super Destination Zone Tax,"* but this works differently. A super zone allows the community to capture sales tax. Special taxes on visitors (tickets, in some cases), hotels, food, and beverage are issued within this zone, and these taxes pay-off the necessary investments for this project. In a sense, these funds are paid by the visitors, so there is little or no real negative impact on its residents.

Furthermore, let's take growth as an example. Some are for it and some are opposed to it. However, growth in places that are pleasant to live in and have vibrant and healthy economies is inevitable. Think about it, dirty, out of the way, backwards, and depressed communities never discuss how to attract residents to their communities. However, growth is painful because it causes congestion, strains on the existing physical infrastructure, and crowded schools. It sucks through the straw of additional government services like fire, police, emergency services, and water. It spawns new ideas in the community for change and progress that may not have been desired. It brings in a diversely new set of values that does not necessarily follow the established protocol of the established status quo in the existing balance of the community leadership. Much of this debate is healthy and good for the community because it causes the community to stretch and discover more possibilities for progress. From the aspect of the demand for costly improvements, the answer is usually mathematically predictable. Newer residents, if truth be told, are willing to pay their fair share, taking the burden off its existing community members. This creates Impact Fees, and they are the impact per new household on the growth costs necessary to continue meeting the healthy expectations of community residents. Such fees, if utilized correctly, create enough windfall for the government to pay for its increased demand in the deployment of new infrastructure, services, and education, and they can be far reaching, as well. They can be utilized for construction permits, utility hook up fees, road improvements, special property taxes, and contractor licensing for those who work the projects. When all this is combined, it creates the economic energy to overcome the negative financial aspects of the new population from a monetary standpoint.

Another example is *Economic Development Incentives.* These are some of the most controversial topics in both today's liberal and conservative media. Nobody wants to dole out corporate welfare at the expense of the taxpayer. However, this is mostly myth. Most incentives, if properly done, are based on the direct economic contribution received by the jurisdiction from the massive injection of private sector funds. The funds extended to the project, in the form of inducements and incentives, are simply tax representations and the direct economic impact the private firm is projected to have on the local jurisdiction and economy.

There are several forms of such incentives, but most are paid for by another created revenue stream from the outcome of a business. In our industry, we refer to this as "Found Money." Found money lowers the initial expense to the company for entering the new market; it also lowers this company's risk level. In addition, found money creates a returned investment that is high enough for a private company to accept the higher degree of risk for the investment decision. All this boils down to shareholder returns. If the shareholder return is higher than the risk projects return, this will entice the investment decision. In the site location and business attraction business we refer to this as the "Gap Analysis." During this exercise, economic developers try to determine if the incentives offered will be paid back by the benefits received, both directly and indirectly (will the public sector make a profit on this deal?). Then these economic developers must determine if the risk of investment is going to occur in a reasonable timeline; one that will negate their public risk. If the resources are present to provide the incentives and the public leadership supports the use of them; then the economic developer creates a proposal referred to as a "Development Agreement."

In this agreement, the economic developer will have certain conditions that must be met so the company won't go into default, forcing the repayment of its incentives (claw-backs). These measurable items are the direct drivers in the ROI model, and they can be used by the economic developer to arrive at the value and offer of the incentives in this model. Protecting the validity and provision of these variables from the private firm protects the validity of the assumptions made mathematically in their economic impact model. Each time a model is used, the economic developer takes credit worthiness and market conditions (is the company in a growing, mature and/or declining industry?) into account. Despite the criticism economic developers receive from the media, uninformed residents, and many elected officials, these incentives are well thought out and protected in order to assure the public their monies worth. The key to remember is that incentives are considered, in military terms, a force multiplier. Incentives level the playing field against other competitors and create competitive advantage, so the represented market gets its fair chance at being awarded the deal.

These deals have many suitors, and as such, the company and their hired gun; the site location advisor, have many other options. When communities decide not to play in this process, they are choosing to be bypassed of its opportunity. One has to buy a ticket to win in the business lottery of attraction deals. Incentives are considered a major decisive factor in creating distinct differences between markets. In many cases, companies look at incentives as their means to offset some of the possible negatives of selected markets. After all, there is no Utopia; every place has its blemishes of some sort; some more than others.

Some of the best examples of major incentive deals involve both local and state incentives. In many cases, states use their legislative process to create specialized stimulus packages to attract business deals. Most of these incentives are also based upon some form of value that is being injected into the economy, such as quantity of jobs, quality of jobs (earnings/wages), physical property, machinery and equipment investments, and the type of business being attracted (high growth specialized niche industries that meet the shortage of such industry mix in their existing economy may get a larger incentive consideration).

Step 6: *Creating Measurable Objectives, Realistic Goals, and Milestones of Progress on the Horizon.* The process of creating this matrix of objectives, goals, and milestones is to create not only accountability to the public but also allow for correction and modifications for the unforeseen to the plan as changes in the economy and environment occur. As changes and new circumstances occur, they are taken into consideration and modifications are made to the original course, accommodating new information, influences, and opportunities that arise during the roll out.

Measuring should always be done in a fashion that is comparable to others striving for the similar situation. For example, base these findings against the current national averages, industry averages, state averages, or other community peers and/or competitors to gain a perspective of how these outcomes are playing out. Goals should be created based on realistic and attainable results. If the goal is to capture more knowledge based jobs, create a weight for what success looks like. For example, if a community currently only has a mix of maybe 4% knowledge employment or industries and the state average is 9%, first try raising the state average within a decade, and perhaps surpass the state average if the national average is 12%. In this case, a community might want to use the national objective, not the state, as the benchmark because the state's average is lagging behind already. This same example can be used for the workforce wage levels and the necessary skill levels in competing for new business development opportunities. Create realistic goals that, at a minimum, meet today's standards. It may become more difficult to visualize exceedingly high goals, but when this happens, many times a community begins to succeed in its own endeavors.

The use of these milestones and benchmarks is useful in making sure progress, along the time horizon, is on course and not delayed. If momentum is lost and benchmarks and milestones are missed, the cause must be found. Once this cause is found, an acceptable mitigation must be addressed. If it is being caused by new drivers that were unforeseen, adjust the project and take these into account. If it is being missed because of poor execution, resolve this; then it will be time to get serious about roles, responsibilities, and reassignments (the three R's).

Step 7: *Communicating the Plan to the Community.* This requires explaining the justifications and factors that drive the process and vision for where a community needs to be. Both the bright side and the downside must be discussed. The community should be told the trends and the cost of letting the course run in the status quo. They should be told the positive outcomes of the plan being implemented. They should be told how this outcome will more than pay for itself and why it is in their best interests to act immediately. Show worst case scenarios, best case scenarios, and most probable middle of the road scenarios. Discuss the adjustments to new challenges and future concerns as they arise.

*A leader is a dealer in hope. (**Napoleon Bonaparte**)*

Because there are many shortfalls in the current leadership void of our political halls, there is a destructive approach many current leaders take when it comes to the sharing of detail and truth with the public (these facts are not confidential). The public is never given the benefit of understanding the true scope and nature of the issues that face their communities, states, or their nation. People do not want benevolent dictators telling them what they want the people to know under the guise that it is for the peoples' own good. The best approach is to always tell the entire story and all its relevant facts, both pro and con. The economic developer must above all tell the why and the best direction of a community's full spectrum. In other words, allow the public the knowledge of all seven steps. Most of the time, residents will understand their situation and appreciate the candor and honesty. If the economic developer practices this approach, there might begin the restoration in trust for governmental leadership and a start on the path toward correcting so many other fiscal policy issues that hold our country's future hostage.

Chapter Nine

"Gaining Perspective on What to do and Why and How Others have Faced Similar Issues."

There is no excuse for not knowing how to cultivate intelligence. There is no excuse in not acting to create events that will positively shape the local economy. It all begins with primary fact finding through delving into best practice reviews and looking at catalyst projects undertaken by others. The process of this analysis increases the probability of success and preparedness when recommending decisive actions. The first rule is to create some order or rhyme and reason to this sleuthing of the proposed subject matter. What is the issue or idea being investigated? This is the underlying focus for and intelligence gathering analysis foundation and its entire endeavor. This might be community based, individual, or organizational in nature. What are the perceived outcomes of the project or consideration known and what is known about the basis for how the decision will be made and supported from a justification basis? This is where assumptions or biases come into the intelligence gathering efforts. Are there any others that have faced similar situations that can be the starting point for this search for relevant and useful information? A casting of nets, to find knowledgeable examples, works here; therefore, seeking out industry examples by asking professional organizations affiliated with these scenarios for leads is essential.

Once there is a list of opportunities to pursue, approach these opportunities with a set of open questions, always apprising the audience of the situation with an introduction that sets the tone and environment as a friendly request for assistance. People love to be useful and provide their own expertise in assisting others in such matters. The economical developer might then ask these seven following questions and direct them to other economic developers: 1) What were their lessons learned and how will these lessons help? 2) How were their projects designed (analysis, justification, expectations, consensus, milestones and benchmarks)? 3) What worked well and why? What did not work and why and how would they do them over again? (This is where their pearls of wisdom will either help in the creation of hybrid solutions and/or knowledge of avoidable efforts.) 4) What windfalls and outcomes resulted from their experience? 5) What was the time line and milestones for their own project and how close did they come to making those assumptions in the end? 6) Who did they assign key roles to perform during the project (consultants, industry leaders, community leaders, organizations, corporate affiliates)? Of this group, how pleased were they with the work and deliverables from their partners? 7) Who or where did they consider when doing their own analysis and can they provide this original research that supported their own decisions?

After these questions have been asked and answered, there is a solid basis to compile in order to create enough information to do a fairly compelling analysis before recommending or making a business decision to proceed with an action. Once there is in-depth information, tough decisions are easier to dissect and allocate into a real frame of risk analysis and definition of successful outcomes that are the potential for a well executed plan of attack.

Then the economic developer must understand the catalyst project design parameters. What does the underlying objective project and aim to address? How does this project address strategic goals; as a community or organization? Will it better position achievements over-all objectives, and if so, why? Is it understood how the project creates additional benefits and return on investments that will leverage initial investment? In other words, what additional windfalls will this investment spur for the risk? From the public sector's standpoint, this area is crucial to understand. What barriers does this project reduce or eliminate and what bridges does this project create to attract additional private sector investments once completed? How will this project benefit the public and what realistic outcomes will be derived from this investment? How can the risk of this investment be best managed and still provide the maximum benefit to those taking the risk along with the public sector? Is it understood the necessary amount of risk and exposure, and is this enough to create and attract others to join in this risk by investing in complimentary components of the project? How will measures and track results be reported to the public? Are the calculated risks sufficient to allow flexibility in changing scenarios as the project evolves and unfolds and matures to sustainability?

Once the economic developer has completed this analysis, he or she can begin to understand and rank the considerations for the projects responsive to the community's needs. Every community should be undertaking a series of such projects if they want to thrive and survive in this fast-paced metamorphic economy.

Chapter Ten

"The Great Debate to Incentivize Deals or Not..."

The misinformation that has been printed with regard to the dark science of economic development and the site location industry has created a distorted perception of the battle for new economic investments and the jobs they create. Many one-sided and jaded media folk, political pundits, paid soothsayers, and economists have misled the public into thinking this economic war would be better off if allowed the businesses to make such decisions, absent the full-scale competition to woo them to the chosen location. Again, just like Camelot, Utopia, and Valhalla, it all looks great on paper, but the reality of this foolish rhetoric will be devastating to the local economies. Before I go through and debunk these one-sided myths, let's start with the first problem and make the assumption that their theory is correct, which it is not.

In our county, there is no way to create a level playing field that restricts the powers of the individual states on such an issue. Because of this, there will be some who might volunteer for this love-fest (mostly those who don't participate much already) and the rest will prey on those who do de-escalate. In our capitalistic society, such artificial controls on market forces normally backfire.

First and foremost, when a business begins to make such considerations for relocating, closing, and, more often than not, simply expanding their operations, these considerations are based upon market forces within our capitalistic system; lowering operating costs to stay competitive and continue to produce shareholder value and return on investments. Expanding its market and gaining competitive advantage costs money to finance, and such moves should not put undue pressure on its enterprise so the company has the most potential for success. This process dictates the necessity to gain as much up-front advantage as possible in order to offset these start-up costs:

> *Globalization is a very real force of economics which each community and state will have to embrace or suffer the consequences of community decay. A significant challenge for today's economic developer is recognizing the early signals and having the vision, fortitude, and support to proactively adjust*

> incentive policies to adapt to the changing business landscape. (**Karin Richmond**, Economic Development Consultant, Austin, TX)

Many cities, counties, and states want to know what they are competing against, but such information is and should be proprietary and confidential. When shopping for the best deal, create parameters and objectives, reducing and eliminating variables that don't work. It is highly unusual for a corporation to outright tell other corporations exactly what they need to do to get the deal, and though they might modify their proposals based on input, they will never show their exact numbers.

> I am a big admirer of Sir Winston Churchill, and my favorite attitude he reflected was give me the tools and I will get the job done. This is how economic developers feel in the face of adversity when trying to do what is necessary to win the day on the field of economic competition for community jobs, business climates and quality life for residents, which many times is not supported by the actions of the political leadership. (**Don Jakeway**, Professional Economic Developer, San Antonio, TX)

When companies tell a community it needs to do something to reduce their operating costs and environment or they will have to lay off their employees, they are not doing this to threaten their employees, they are giving the community a well-advanced warning; a warning that their market forces have changed so they can no longer make enough money to sustain their business model at this location. They are asking for insightful help to cut their expenses and stay open. Even if the incentives are paid and the plant inevitably closes, this does not mean the deal was done maliciously, it might be as simple as it just didn't work and it just couldn't turn the tide. Many nay-sayers, media folks, and union-backed political action based special interest authors want the public to believe such stuff, but it is usually not the case. Companies can't control the market force; consumers drive this, "Give me more for less and exactly the way I want it, when I want it." This drove automation, customization, just in time delivery systems, and point of sale controls for our modern landscape. Most business school experts believe companies can no-longer plan for more than about 3 years because change happens almost 100%; turn-over and maturity in less than 24 months. This has much more to do with failed economic development deals than premeditated schemes to debunk the public. Companies do not enter deals for the upfront cash; they enter such highly visible transactions out of necessity. They can't just run off with the cash. Every deal invests almost all of its incentive money into the region in the manner of wages, physical infrastructure, facilities, construction costs, machinery and equipment purchases, and maintaining support operations.

The idea that money just gets up and leaves the region is absurd. Even failed deals have considerable positive impact as they spin forward in its initial stages through employing contractors, sales receipts, and capital investments.

> *Incentives are critical to successful site location. Certainly the required project parameters must be met if an area is to be considered as a finalist in any site location process. But it has been my experience that most site location consultants will identify at least two sites that meet all project relevant criteria. In other words, they are exactly the same from a site location perspective. It is at this point that incentives come into play. Companies place varying levels of importance on the types of incentives offered. Some are more concerned with their up front costs (i.e. land, infrastructure, utilities) while others are more concerned about their constant costs (i.e. labor, workman's compensation rates, utility costs, taxes), but all companies are concerned with the bottom line; where their incentives can make a difference.*
>
> *American manufacturing is not dead nor is it dying. It is undergoing a profound series of changes that will fundamentally alter the way manufacturing looks and operates in this country. Intense competition from around the world has introduced new players into the global manufacturing community. Low price point is no longer a viable market strategy for manufacturers in the US. US manufacturers must consider improved productivity, innovation, and niche market development to stay competitive. While manufacturers race to control costs and enhance their means of production through the extensive use of new technologies, they must have a supportive local and national environment to stay competitive. High taxes, escalating labor costs, runaway utility prices, and the pressures of over regulation negate our manufacturer's best efforts as they seek to compete with manufacturers in other countries who do not have a similar cost production profile. The National Association of Manufacturers has shown that it costs the US manufacturer 32% more to produce products in the US than in other locations around the globe. If manufacturing is to prosper, we must, on a national, state, and local level, do all that can be done to lesson this cost differential. Finally, to be attractive as a market for manufacturers from around the world and to support our existing manufacturers, we must enhance the resources available to train and retrain our workforce for the jobs of the 21st century. A highly skilled workforce is the fundamental element that we must have in this country to secure a strong manufacturing climate.*
> **(Jay Moon**, *Jackson MS, Professional Economic Developer)*

There has been much debate about the difference in the states incentive wars. Again, these decisions are made individually, not collectively, as our state leadership. Governors know that if their state cannot maintain a positive balance in jobs and economic growth, the over-all quality of life will be reduced, and this will create a potential trend of decline.

States have chosen to focus on creating predatory legislation to one up their neighbors instead of working on business climate changes that will enhance their business operating costs in the global marketplace. Even economic developers believe the state's short-sighted approach to predatory economic development incentive policies should be shelved in favor of meaningful economic development policies. Even though some jobs move from one state to another, causing some people's blood to boil, the alternative might be far worse. If economic developers don't create such regional state options, these jobs might move overseas. The most compelling reason a plant relocates to neighboring states is because it knows the region and this is a comfortable decision versus moving somewhere completely foreign to them.

People claim new jobs are less lucrative than those that have been lost, and this is sometimes true, but it is not the fault of the business it is the transformation of the market capabilities that drives these newer jobs. If a high-skilled job is necessary, highly-skilled people are what they will hire, and their wages will be comparable to the wage levels for the skills in that market. For example, a welder in Los Angeles and New York will not make the same wage as a welder in Tampa Florida, and this is just a basic tenet of economics not something the company is responsible for. This does not mean the value of the wages paid is of any less consequence to the welder in Florida than those in the two other coastal markets; it is merely the cost of living differential. Companies move to create wage advantages so they can afford to continue to compete for the sales of their products and services.

These same pundits also misquote the economic direct and ancillary effect of deals on regions and local economies. This is called economic impact; the multiplier principle of a dollar exported or imported into an economy, creating additional dollars within the market. Each market has different multipliers based on federal and other highly expert research done annually by numerous professional and governmental agencies that take into consideration housing, labor, transportation, and energy costs. These are highly tracked issues not subjected to a considerable amount of inflated projections; however, they do create a ripple effect similar to a thousand stones simultaneously hitting a lake, creating waves across the entire lake. These models are useful to economic developers because they use them to determine how much a project is worth to our region and community. They do not merely guess at the level of incentives paid to attract a company; they back it with the value these incentives create. Even when they calculate the risk, they do so conservatively, so there is a windfall to the community (a margin of additional profit to the community beyond the cost of the incentives). It is very insulting to know there are people out there who believe highly-devoted economic developers merely make guesses; this is not at all true.

I must now touch the subject of unions. While I have no hate for unions, I will say that their numerous examples for being inflexible have not saved many jobs and, in most cases, have cost their communities jobs. They become entrenched on saving face rather than jobs. In times of reduction, unions, just like businesses, have tough decisions to make, and they cannot please all their members. Instead, they hold fast, at a cost to all members and their jobs. With all the business laws in this country, the time and need for unions has come and gone. Free markets blow through them when they need to and all this really accomplishes is an added cost to the employee and an artificial safety net that does nothing in times of severe economic trauma. A union's collective bargaining is not done in the scope of reality. Knowing this is the case, unions create an agenda that tells its members what they want to hear without trying to solve this problem outside its input. Unions can't comprehend the necessity for change. Unions become entrenched in their short-term position and posturing at the long-term expense of their workers. In the end, whether unionized or not, the market forces always prevail and the union barricades and fortifications that are alleged to be there to protect its members crumble like the walls of Jericho.

Union safety nets are similar to the great French folly that was constructed after World War I; the Maginot Line. This wall of fortifications was supposed to make France impenetrable to future German aggression. The French public widely believed this to be the case, and in addition, the wall created a great economic boon. Yet, in the end, when World War II started, the Germans merely jumped over this wall, using technology (airborne forces), making the wall irrelevant. In less than a month, France fell to Germany (even faster than in World War I). Unions are the modern day version of this same scenario. We build complex fortifications, processes, and systems only to see them easily defeated or by-passed by new and innovative approaches. The Chinese built the Great Wall of China, the Romans built Hadrian's Wall, and both these failed when the forces of change challenged them.

In the Medieval times of the renaissance, my favorite legacy of human endeavors, great castles were built to protect communities, resources, and people from other marauders, raiders, and invaders. These great masterpieces were impressive to the eye. They allowed their people great confidence in their power and place of residence, but when the forces of greed, power, ingenuity, and progress combined against them, bringing new siege weapons into the spectrum, these beautiful works of human architecture crumbled and succumbed to the well organized assaults of their feared oppressors. Gun powder was the final blow to these castles just as technology and automation have been the downfall of unionization. Add globalization to the equation and the playing field has evolved so much that unions cannot field any means of an adequate force in order to stop their demise. Union incentives have succumbed to the sieges of change.

Incentives are very often misrepresented. For instance, Bob Ady's interview was distorted in Greg Leroi's book, *The Great American Job Scam*. While the author describes taxes as irrelevant to site location decisions as prophesized by Bob Ady, a former Fantus CEO and the most successful living site locator, Leroi fails to convey what forces will turn the tide of change in favor of communities. Though Leroi cites that labor, transportation, utilities, facilities/occupancy, and taxes are the prevalent factors amongst the possibility of some 1200 measured variables, depending on the nature and complexity of the site search (IEDC created a list of 1200 typical and agreed upon variables for such consideration), he offers no pearls as to what could be done to influence these in a positive manner, without incentives.

Later, Leroi cites Dennis Donovan (of Wadley-Donovan) about a 30 point checklist in *Expansion Management Magazine's* article, "Trade Secrets Revealed." Leroi takes an insider's look at incentive negotiations "as if they are deceitful." This is rubbish! The tactics used are common sense; for example, negotiating on multiple fronts, what Leroi calls the "Prisoner Dilemma." However, negotiation on multiple fronts makes sense. Many localities promise the moon in early RFP responses, and when pressed for actual techniques as to how they will fulfill such commitments or whether they actually have the ability to do so, these places or communities fold under pressure. No business would place its entire outcome in one basket. The due diligence process site consultants utilize to weed out these ill-conceived promises are put to the test. It is the consultant's job to eliminate all the places, only then can he find those most suitable for the deal. It is much less about finding the right place as eliminating the wrong places.

Leroi quotes yet another site selection consultant, Bruce Maus, a veteran site location consultant from the great Scandinavian land of Minnesota, "When the deal is incentive driven we lose our objectivity." But this isn't true. What is true is when Ady once said, "The single most critical factor to a successful business is the quality, availability, dependability, and cost of its workforce in general." The biggest contributors to these factors are family upbringing (many times linked to economic security) and the holistic educational and training systemic environment available to each individual at affordable means.

Companies want to be and individuals want to live where there are great schools and institutions; however, they don't want to pay for them. Though individuals may purport their support, in the voter booth, they reject anything that has to do with the betterment of their school systems, especially those in our retirement ranks. This should beg the question, "Would they be willing to pay for them if the manner in which they are being asked to do so changes?" This leads to my analysis and its conclusion that in order to combat the negative effect of change on our communities, there needs to be a totally new approach to situations. There needs to be new policies, practices, principles, and protocols that will be based on realities and driven to reach new outcomes with new resource deployment methodologies.

In his book, Leroi also discusses tax increment financing (TIF) as if this is an assault on school funding, again playing to the pundits of education and its being harmed by corporate America. Leroi's slant is that economic development is corporate welfare, but nothing is more removed from this reality than his novice one-sided explanation of one of the most proactive and positive economic development tools: TIFs. Leroi says that these diverted property tax dollars rob schools of their funding in order to pay for corporate investments. What Leroi, and most pundits, fails to explain is that TIFs come from new taxes created not existing taxes, and these taxes have never been a part of the school budget in the first place. These funds are used under a timeline, and even when there is a surplus, they do not come from the current funds; therefore, school districts see no reduction in both their current funding and the indirect benefit of residential property taxes preserved by the new economic growth (jobs and employment retention and creation) creates a windfall that is never given any credit. In lieu of what Leroi believes in regard to the use of TIF, the opposite is true for school district funding. This is not to say that property taxes and other real property type taxes are at all the appropriate manner for which schools should be funded; however, this in itself creates biased funding formulas where rich districts have much more than poor districts. If the federal government wanted to approach education from a realistic standpoint, it would create one formula to pay the necessary amount per student nationwide, funding education properly. This would level the playing field in education, so no child would ever be left behind. Incentives like TIFs are essential to a community's wealth. In addition:

> *A community must continuously monitor and encourage the expansion of its "primary employers" and recruit new primary employers to the area. A primary employer is one which sells its goods or services outside the area, importing wealth to the community. Unfortunately, most community and government leaders do not understand the "dynamics" of a local economy. They believe a growing retail, consumptive sector will cause an economy to improve and erroneously focus economic development efforts on these types of businesses.*
>
> *In reality, a growing retail sector is the result of a strong economy, not its cause. Many times the effort to promote the retail sector comes from local government officials as retailing is a direct source of additional tax revenue. This is "local government finance development" not economic development. Ironically, if local government would instead focus on true economic development, the size of the economy would increase, causing retail sales tax to increase.* **(Bill Fruth**, *National Economic Development Consultant, Hollywood, FL)*

Given the nature of the black art or dark science of economic development and the site location matrix of economic combat, it is no wonder there is such covert and clandestine treatment of information. The media (who allege to enlighten the public) spreads its harmful stories and misguided concepts; then it creates an absolute oath of silence when it can do little or no harm to sensitive negotiations. Economic developers use claw-backs and other contractual obligations to bind corporations to the deals they have made, but just as the old saying goes, a contract is only as good as the intent of the person signing it. There are no absolutes in this war of economic combat. Deals evolve and change because the battlefield shifts and never stops. In this economic war, there are no cease fires and peace talks. What seems to work for now may inevitably fail later, but this does not mean the men and women who forged a deal did so with any intentions of such failure, nor does it mean they intended to defraud the public. Business moves like a wave, and this changes the shore when each wave lands. Time may prove to make some deals irrelevant before their horizon has had time to play out, but this does not mean this irrelevance was done in bad faith. Sure, irrelevance makes for sour grapes, but business executives merely have to start over find a solution for staying in business when this happens, and so do economic developers.

> *In South Africa, economic development is virtually driven by the consultancy of private entrepreneurial folks, like me, who are dedicated to improving social and economic conditions. There is not the same formal infrastructure in North America and Europe that there is on the African continent. (***Claire Patterson**, *Economic Development Consultant, South Africa)*

Armchair economic development experts like Greg Leroi have never had to actually create jobs for communities, so their opinions are backed without experience. Leroi's book is filled with the absolute most anti-capitalism concepts I have ever heard. Some believe school boards should decide their own TIFs, but this is absurd. Members of a school board know nothing about the business side of the economy, and this has already been proven in the handling of their own matters. Put them in charge of the economy and the economy will suffer the same, if not worse, fate. This is just pure Utopian folly; sensationalizing a topic that could actually harm the residents of any community that does so. So, how can incentives help and not harm a community's residents?

> *There are a variety of local incentives available to manufacturers. The problem is they are time sensitive and generally discretionary to local governing authority. These local authorities should extend their benefits (such as property tax exemptions beyond ten years) and the incentive should be absolutely available to the manufacturer that meets the established*

criteria. This should also apply equally to existing businesses that expand. However, there is the need to move away from incentives based solely upon job creation. With more technology in the workplace, manufacturing will need fewer employees, yet these employees will be better skilled and earn more. Manufacturing is undergoing a change and those in the local community must recognize and respond to this change.

The name of the game for manufacturing in this country and its foreseeable future is workforce. Businesses will expect states and local communities to provide a trained or trainable workforce as a given. **(Jay Moon**, *Professional Economic Developer, Jackson, MS)*

When Leroi later speaks of placing deals on the ballot to be voted on by the voters, he only assures communities with such initiatives no economic growth. Companies will simply not subject themselves to such a naïve process. They will, however, seek greener pastures; ones with a more friendly business climate and the voting citizens will lose the opportunity they might have gained because of this folly. Have these kind of absurd concepts and ideas ever worked? Why don't we ask people who come up with these types of scenarios to show us where they have worked and what the outcomes have been? These social and economic scientists want to use the citizen's life as their test tubes and experimental test grounds. I myself have not seen these wild concepts work anywhere, and I will stay with the foundation of what works and I will seek to improve upon these grounds. There is no doubt progress can be made and new policies, practices, and protocols should and will be explored and implemented, but this should only be done without causing economic and social chaos.

Leroi also compares James Renza (Location Management Services now affiliated with the National Association of Manufacturers Site Selection Network) to Ed McMahon for his marketing of his services to business clients. Leroi believes consultants like Renza should be tagged and recorded so the government can track their whereabouts and their activities. Obviously, Leroi hasn't read George Orwell's famous novel; no one wants this type of "big brother" scenario!

For years, some economists and politically-oriented action groups have produced theories that economic development is counter productive to our society. However, collective denial when it comes to choosing not to compete within the realm of economic development will lead to exploitation of the weak or non-competitive. In other words, a non-competitive economy is one that concedes without firing a shot. This soft revolution of complacency is the most destructive force facing this nation and its communities, and the revolution of invisible change and degradation has been underway for some time now. In order to win this economic war, we must train our troops, and education is our only hope of doing this.

Chapter Eleven

"Education Matters in Economic Development Matrix"

One thing we all share in common is we all have some place we call our primary area; one we associate with as our home town, our place we reside, and the place we work. Sometimes these places are one and the same, and sometimes all three are different. Nonetheless, this place, or places, locks us into a perceived opinion of who we are; where we are associated with in a physical sense. This creates some small link to our own image conjured by others of our image and personal brand. For example, I am Don Holbrook, and I live in Lake Havasu City, Arizona. When I say this, people conjure up their own vision of my lifestyle and my place of employment before or while making an opinion of me.

In the United States, the term "world-class city" is commonly referred to as a community that has established a competitive advantage in the new economy and its competitive advantage of place. For example, a world-class city will most likely have most or all of the following attributes; a superior physical infrastructure (utilities, telecommunications) and public services (water, transportation); a superior workforce that is both highly skilled and productive; a highly accessible educational system which produces superior results through student attainment, research, and development activities; a highly competitive cost of business structure for doing business (taxation, licensure, public fees); and finally, a world-class community has strong and vibrant arts and recreational amenity that creates a positive quality of life for its residents.

When all or most of these attributes are coupled with a strong support in the economic development sector for small business, finance, and entrepreneurial efforts, and a strong focus on safety and crime control is maintained through local leadership, results are a place highly competitive in the world economy. Such places are highly regarded by employers, workers, and residents alike. In the new drive for economic advantage, it is believed that today's employers follow highly-skilled workers, and no longer do people move to a place for work. Today, employers move to a location where its workforce is focused on world-class economics, creating a magnet for job growth and economic wealth for its citizens and government, jointly.

Those related to and concerned about quality education may sometimes wonder the role economic developers play in the creation of an established world-class place and the positive brand this gives a community's outsiders. How does what economic developers do create a positive association with the places he or she lives, works, and plays? Again, the 5 W's I mentioned earlier is essential to the kick-off for needed action and reaction to this matter. In 1996, I heard Bill Clinton's speech writer tell our organization (IEDC) that in his own life, President Clinton related every speech and discussion to this simple mantra, and it served him well.

Economic developers play a critical role in the great divide between those who will go on to contribute highly to the new economy and those who are at significant risk to be more vulnerable to its perils. The economic developer needs to realize that the United States' prominence is slipping in the global economy, especially from the perspective of products made and ship to others (Manufactured and Exported products). Our nation faces enormous challenges in its need to reassert its world prominence in the new global economy. In the 1950's, manufacturing represented 40% of our GDP, today, it only represents approximately 9%. The nation must return to its higher levels of economic prowess:

> *The biggest challenge is to find ways to capture and foster the best ideas, discoveries, innovations, and, perhaps most importantly, the "Meta Ideas." These are the ideas that act as catalysts to support and to develop and distribute ideas. Education is the largest contributor to this scenario and the cultivating socio-economic environment where this cultural metamorphic exchange occurs. We must draw the best and brightest together to interact, network, and discuss new concepts and challenge what is considered the norm versus what could be.* **(Paul Romer, *a Stanford Economist*)**

In addition;

> *The seminal shifts in the global landscape have been linked to an acceleration of trends emerging that impact us in both our individual economic security and national security. Technological superiority is paramount to the establishment and continuance of national security and thus sovereignty. Countries now invest heavily in education to gain economic and military advantage in the new world order, and this is a fact. This is also dangerous because it is not imminent as the "Quiet Crisis." This is a threat that if not corrected will erode our intellectual security, economic well being, our national security, our global preeminence, our multi-lateral opportunity,*

and our ability to provide proactive leadership to new threats and new Meta ideas. Each will surely come forward in the future; this is a certainty. **(Shirley Ann Jackson**, *President of Rensselaer Polytechnic Institute)*

Though our community colleges are working to bridge the social and economic divide to the new global pressure to compete, they have so far only been able to do so in two primary areas: creating new entrants training in preparation for entering the workforce through highly specialized training, certificates, and occupational specialized courses designed in collaboration with business, and addressing the ever-changing needs of the incumbent workforce by upgrading skills and providing career-ladder understanding that matching known skills and the attainment of new highly desired skills to the employer base of its communities and its over-all economy.

Furthermore, the Secretary's Commission on Achieving Necessary Skills—(SCANS) set the standard that the progression to move from school to work is imperative in the continuous strive to stay competitive as a nation. This standard embraces certain attainment building blocks such as reading, writing, mathematics, listening and speaking (important because English is world standard for business language), and science and technology, now combined with soft skills

These soft skills involve social ability, self-esteem, self management, honesty, and integrity, and these are primarily learned through experience and accomplishment. People possess some of these qualities inherently, but they are nurtured in the educational system first, and then built upon by further educational attainment, whether academic or learned. To be competitive in the new global economy, focus needs to gear toward attaining results in the areas of science, technology, engineering, and math (nicknamed STEM). This is the base-element formula for a knowledge-based economy. Those who start with these elements and then apply fiscal investments in core research will create business friendly environments, and embrace entrepreneurial innovation. These are the people who will thrive in the new global economy.

> *I tell everyone that their kids must learn a second language. But it's not Spanish or Mandarin. It's science. The genome map will be as important as the internet. I wish I knew more about lab science ... or at least got better grades in chemistry, but at least I'm smart enough to KNOW that this is where the future lies. Remember, the Rules of Citizen Attraction and Engagement are simple; 1) Discover what the market needs and wants; 2) (Re-)Design your community to meet those needs and wants; and 3) Deliver the products and services through the communication and networking channels they use.* **(Rebecca Ryan**, *Author & Cool Communities Consultant, Madison, WI)*

Consequently, life long learning has now been established in our economy as a primary requirement for workforce excellence. Individuals, industries, and educators need to fully embrace this. The Late President, *John Kennedy* stated; "Let us think of education as the means of developing our greatest abilities. Because in each of us there is the private hope and dream which, if fulfilled, can be translated into benefit for everyone, and greater strength for our nation."

The heart in our nation's limitless potential for greatness lies in our educational system; still the greatest and most adaptive in the world, today! Yet our forefathers made no mention of education in the *Bill of Rights* because, at the time, education was limited to the wealthy and privileged few. It was our national conscious that drove education to the common folks, and as it grew more important, we flourished as a nation.

> *It was making education not only common to all, but in some sense compulsory on all, that the destiny of America was settled. (James Russel Lowell, a 19th century writer)*

Today, more than ever before, we need to use our community colleges as far more than just bridges. Not only are they a less expensive entrance to the formal four year education system, but they are also the tip of the spear in developing our new highly skilled workforce. Educational attainment increases economic opportunity for those who finish the ascending levels of educational attainment, and this gap is increasing today versus the past. In other words, today's employers value a highly skilled and educated worker far more than those with less education. Today's employers want specialists not generalists. What an individual takes in school matters much more today and both new entrants and incumbents need to understand and embrace this now more than ever.

In Fact, the United States Government has taken a position that post secondary education is the most successful and effective method of preventing crime, as well. It costs roughly $200,000 for each new police officer deployed today and the net result has been attributed to a net economic positive impact of $600,000 on our local, state and national economy. This same equivalent investment in education, especially if targeted to the at-risk populations (those most likely to fall through the cracks of society and be incarcerated), will have an impact of $800,000 annually. Education, crime and the over-all quality of life are interlinked; therefore, the best investment a community can make is in its furthering of its educational infrastructure; one that reaches the most at-risk populations. Two thirds of the inmates behind bars have less literacy skills than the average citizen, and this is proof that our educational attainment impacts our community's competitive advantage, our own economic ability to make a significant and meaningful living, and our enjoyment of life in general.

Furthermore, the U.S. Education Department states that $1.00 spent toward job training creates a $1.66 return on investment, $1.00 spent on academic completion creates a $3.53 (ROI), proving that job-training and preparedness are highly valued but not the single answer to the equation; students of all ages who complete their education still earn significantly higher wages than those who attain certificated education.

In addition, when education is measured, the economic impact is enormous in communities.

> *The creative class lives and flourishes relative to its perceived perception of the amenities created and available in communities and the diverse range of choices available. There is a need, in economic development, to alter our approach from measuring competitiveness in economic terms to a measurement of a well-being index.* (**Richard Florida**, *famous author and economist*)

Economic impact models are measured by their outputs. Outputs are measured through; 1) Total job employment and income (wages and economic growth of personal income), ranging from those without high school to doctoral and professional attainment $20,000 or less to above $90,000 on average. 2) Business value added and output; the production value of the business infrastructure and the economic value created for the shareholders and government benefactors for their activities. Normally this is significantly higher in locations with superior educational infrastructure. 3) Property values are increased in areas with high educational attainment and, in fact, many choose their place to live and are willing to pay higher taxes and property purchases to gain this superior educational infrastructure. Again, the economic developer can stake a major case with local policy makers that investing in educational systems and infrastructure, if held accountable for outcomes, is the single biggest determinant as to the communities' over-all success.

Educational attainment also impacts both wage and employment rates. In fact, "Less than 2% of the people with less than high school make more than $20 per hour, while more than 30% of college graduates make more than $20 per hour." (**Charlotte Keller**, Mohave Community College)

> *Those with less than high school have an average unemployment rate of 16.3% and those with a college degree or higher have an average of only 3.3% unemployment rate.* (**Stacy Margolis**)

In other words, as our nation looks at the means to get people out of poverty and reduce social welfare, it is apparent that investing in education is the most significant potential for combating this scenario. Our policy makers have failed to understand this powerful paradigm to utilize education properly and shift this from burden to enormous opportunity. There is some inherent policy and perception issue with the value of today's education, and despite all I have preached, only about 25% of our population has attained a four year college degree.

However, economic developers can make a greater impact. In the past 15 years, community colleges have been moving towards an interlinked educational system, an Individual empowered and entrepreneurial community college system, moving away from the "Regular College system." They are broadening their roles in ways beyond just providing degree and certificate programs, workforce preparation, community services, and cultural amenities. In other words, the new entrepreneurial community college is evolving to meet the needs of the business community in a very specialized manner with regard to their new entrants, incumbent workers, and dislocated workers. As our country and society retool away from economic development strategies focused on smoke stack chasing to the more intellectual property development and highly skilled workers (human capital), our community colleges have to lead the way.

> *Globalization has increased the wage inequalities around the world and displaced the labor market at a phenomenal pace, and this will only continue to increase and sharpen in severity. Time to react will get shorter for individuals impacted by these trends.* (**Lester Thurow**)

Many of our current intervention models were created in the industrial era; thus these models are ill-prepared for today's problems. Thurow believes that, in this matter, the four year universities have been slower to respond than the community colleges, but this does not mean community colleges have risen to the occasion or their full potential. Thurow says some community colleges have risen to the challenge, but many are still entrenched in their role of being a catalyst for transferring students to four year institutions. However, partnerships between the business community, specific employers, community colleges, and K-12 educational infrastructure are important to managing our supply and demand of talent for the workforce. A recent example of this is that while there has been focus on increased high school graduation rates, 1/3 of companies have to provide remedial education to their workforce in order to render this workforce competent to their needs (Council on Competitiveness, 2005).

This role, of course, is generally falling upon the community college system for assistance. However, it is the K-12 issue that remains ineffectively addressed by its methods. Many businesses blame the focus on educators teaching to the test rather than knowledge cultivation and the instillation of soft skill qualities. Educators counter that this is mandated by the government leadership. Our workforce is being latent in its ability to address business needs. This, in turn, is eroding our ability to compete with business environments from our global competitors. This also forces us to look externally to our borders to fill our workforce needs (immigration), which places yet more pressure on our educators to intervene with the business community and train these new entrants for its labor pool.

As a whole, economic developers are not blameless in this situation. Economic developers have not focused on the development of partnerships between the business and educational worlds, nor have they forged meaningful working relationships that are truly interdependent on each other and proactive in response to real world needs. It is sad to say that many of my economic development colleagues are simply out of touch with this new reality. While most economic developers merely give lip service to the coined statement, "Knowledge and workforce skills are the true source of wealth creation in the new economy," yet the few realize:

> *Communities must understand that they must compete on quality not price and they must also target their efforts to particular industries that are in line with the business targets a community wishes to recruit. India, China, and other countries will remain a force in the global marketplace; however, the data suggests that the original lure of lower wages is eroding as other transaction related costs have escalated. Communities should also understand that the US is not the only target; Europe, as well, offers these countries excellent opportunities for markets.* (**Jim Beatty**, *International Site Location Consultant, Omaha, NE*)

Economic development must shift from strategies focused on the competitive advantages of place assets and resources in the physical sense to values based upon the advantages based on knowledge, creation, and human capital. This is outside the comfort zone for many current economic developers and political leadership because much of their institutional knowledge and experience base was developed in a vastly different era. In addition, many face enormous challenges in today's technology, which only compounds this problem.

In 2006, **Michael Bloomberg** (Capitalist and Mayor of NYC) spoke to the IEDC, at their annual meeting, in New York City. In his speech, he mentioned the 7 habits of highly successful cities. His measured goal for attainable success at the city level are; fight crime, focus on small business, provide measurable accountability, sustainability is a local issue, invest in the spirit and soul of a community, green space and amenities matter, and invest in the future (out of the box opportunities over the horizon timelines for results not caught up in instant results). Bloomberg's final statement on this issue was that, "There are no socio-economic problems that more and better education cannot eliminate in our society."

Each and every economic developer matters in this global economic war of survival, more than he or she understands or dwells upon. Each is extremely relevant in his or her opportunity to address societal needs. In many cases, some are unsung heroes, but each is appreciated and very needed.

The foremost reason more people do not understand and embrace the benefits of higher education is a lack of communication. People need to continuously be reminded that these opportunities are attainable to the common person. They also need to understand positive benefits in wages an education can instill. Education will impact not only their lives but those of their family.

It is easy to get caught up in the psychology of reduction as budgets get tightened and policy makers make unwise cuts and investment decisions, but each economic developer must raise the bar of not only our own productivity and out-put in addressing these areas, but also strive to raise the awareness of decision makers and the common person with regard to this higher value received from the investments in a broader educational infrastructure spectrum.

Today's average individual is more paranoid about his or her economic future. There is good reason to worry. According to the Progressive Policy Institute, average income wages in real dollars is down by 15% today versus 1975. This gap is widening, and now there is the term "shrinking middle-class." Traditional jobs are being replaced by higher tech jobs on one end and lower cost jobs on the other, and, in many cases, middle-class jobs are being shipped abroad, to new locales. To combat this, our policy makers need to invest in areas that create measured growth, and education is a significant contributor to this potential model. There is no evidence that local production of graduates, in and by itself, will be an effective policy for a new economic development strategy, so investments in education alone to address our many problems in creating world-class communities is not the answer. Instead, a portfolio approach is more probable. Focus on higher education that is linked to quality workforce cultivation, quality public infrastructure, emphasis on quality life and amenities, and an effort to maintain and bolster the business climate that is conductive to the employer's ability to be profitable. All these interlinked and interdependent strategies should produce the highest yield for return on investment.

Yes, economic developers can help. Each can make a difference in a meaningful way. Each can help to expand workforce profiling and high school new entrants to guide students and make them aware of their opportunities and possible options related to their own desires so these desires are attainable and known to them more rapidly. Each can help to expand interaction with a broader spectrum of the business community and thus the creation of more customized training programs based upon business needs. Each can create an earlier communicate with high school students with regard to today's workforce realities and how to get the best shot at their desired occupations.

Each can help to expand high school, community college, and university shared curriculum partnerships for remedial folks, incumbent and dislocated workers, and students alike. Each can help to create linkages within the workforce investment boards (WIB) to create work skills testing, profiling, and counseling for students and current workers.

All this will reduce financial strain on today's independent structures and allow those costs to be borne by a wider array of financial support, improving the market for its users, as well. An economy of volume and costs control will arrive at delivering useful and meaningful initiatives, and education is the essential key.

Chapter Twelve

"Political & Fiscal Policy Reform Considerations"

While there have been great debates on the states' time zones, whether or not new anti-genetic research such as stem cell and abortion should be allowed, blue versus red states, and Presidential conduct, the necessary debate and then its decisive action to renew and rebuild American economic competitiveness has been lost and forgotten. We have allowed today's new corporate masters to create, in an indirect and undisclosed fashion, a financial and social debacle in America, and this threatens the very foundation of Life, Liberty, and the Pursuit of Happiness; its republic democracy and the ability to sustain itself as a nation of united people in a dignified and responsible manner. This century is in a serious threat of collapse. Make no mistake, all the blame cannot be placed on corporate America or politicians, but they do deserve a huge amount of this blame.

Each individual, through apathy, greed, and the lost sense of being a great society have been the underlying root cause that enabled this silent takeover of collective will and welfare. Because I myself try not to represent these qualities, I have drafted an exact structure for policy revisions, and I have outline, in common folk terms, some insightful debates and outlooks that need to be given serious and decisive consideration.

> *Open your eyes and see what is happening locally and globally. That is the main message our experts had for our local leaders and those involved in local economic development. Given the state of many of our economic development organizations, and the way our local cities are running, we are due some real troubles even 5 years down the line, let alone 20 years down the line, in keeping ourselves competitive on the global basis.* **(Cathy Katona**, *Chicago, IL)*

First, there is a need for Political Reform: We must take back the legislative process from corporate America in order to win the necessary sway we need in our Town Halls, State Houses, and Congress. To do this, we must insist the following:

1) Term limits for all elected offices (no more than two terms).
2) Restricted ability to influence and lobby for a number of years thereafter.
3) Consider voter campaign federal funds for support of our individual causes we deem as important enough to raise the stakes on PAC money.
4) Clean elections to level the playing field against rich and affluent candidates that try to buy their way into office and common folks can stand a chance in the election process.
5) Strict corporate and individual donation limits (no loopholes).
6) Restrictions against hiring family members of elected officials to influence special interest political considerations.
7) Make corporate junkets for politicians deemed as travel for education and meetings illegal.

and government must become more transparent and hold a higher accountability for responsible governance, ethics, and responsibility to its voters.

There must be Trade: Free Trade as well as the theory of Trickle Down Economics are no longer areas of great debate for their impact analysis. We must move on and now fix the problem we allowed corporations and government to create. Trade and Trade Agreements have not proven to go well for the average working-class American; in fact, this has been quite the opposite. These agreements have been good for multi-national corporations and the upper 20% of our society that have made enormous profits from their structural nightmare. These now failed and false doctrines need rapid repair in their diplomatic and above board unilateral discussion with our trading partners. We can no longer tolerate unfair treatment in the global economy at the expense of our workforce any longer. To do this, we must insist the following;

1) Create responsible and equitable tariffs that level the playing field for American industry within our borders to make and sell products.
2) No more subsidies for multi-national companies that do unfair labor or human rights business with trading partners at the abuse of human dignity.
3) Expand free trade zones for incentives to foreign direct investment manufacturing products in America.

and the focus of our trade agreements needs to be on the American working-class and high tech jobs, not on over-all shareholder profits and capital flows. Capital flows do not pay the bills; they just boost the ultra wealthy into even higher wealth brackets.

There is a need for Education: This is what first made our country great, but our roots have been forgotten. We were first to make education obligatory and available to its common folks, and for this drastic shift, in those days, we as a nation have been blessed beyond our forefathers' dreams. This deserves a most serious remedy consideration, so we must insist the following:

1) Fix the under-educated and broken school districts by supplying them with top teachers. Create a "pay for performance" merit pay and hold teachers accountable for their knowledge and expertise within their teaching areas and student outcomes. Teachers deserve a targeted pay increase of 25% or more to attract the best to this profession. Teachers should be allowed to make a dignified wage because they have more influence on our future than any other group outside the family unit. Contrary to Teacher Union media, this is not anti-capitalism it is responsible business and governance of our most precious asset; our children.
2) The Federal government and state governments need to reinvest in the facilities and curriculum of our school districts, both uniformly and equitably, so there is no favoritism played. Our youth need exceptional facilities, curriculums, and k-12 social experiences in order to evolve into responsible well-rounded and very capable adult members of society.
3) Students need more time spent in citizenship and community works, as mandatory school obligations. In addition, students should have proper knowledge of the economy, its workforce, and the competitive and stressful road ahead and how their choices matter infinitely to their possible success and welfare.
4) Standardized student testing with realistic high level of mandatory standardized curriculum, including science, math, and English.
5) Standardized per pupil stipends and vouchers for each school district that is least affected by property taxes.

There is the need for Immigration: This country was founded on the works of immigrants and we are all, by nature of our ancestors, immigrants. The ridiculous focus of blaming immigration for the demise of the American workforce is ludicrous. Just as in other policy modifications, this policy needs a balance and fairness of necessary enforcement, not a media-driven frenzy similar to no growth tactics used in real estate development by NIMBY (not in my backyard) folks. We need healthy immigration rules for all socio-economic levels of society, for a healthy growth in our economy. This does not have to come, as the media would have us believe, at the expense of our tax payers or homeland security; rather it is our current lack of attention to reality that has spawned the problem. We must insist on the following:

1) Expand legal immigration to allow enough people to come in and fill the needs of employers in all job categories (low skilled and high skilled).

Give those coming in 90 days to find gainful, fulltime employment before they are gradually forced to leave (no benefits). Include expediting the application process and proper security screening and tracking while in the country. Require immediate citizenship classes and make these classes mandatory for continued residency.
2) Secure our borders 100%, without question. I don't care if we make it the biggest public works project in our history, it has to be done. This could be part of the New Deal of 2008.
3) Illegal immigrants will face an automatic deportation after the amnesty period for registration has been put into place. No driver's licenses and/or banking accounts of any type for cashing checks, unless valid legal identification is available.
4) Make the companies' officers who employ illegal immigrants subject to jail time and massive fines and upon follow-up violations, confiscate machinery and equipment, or close down their business.

There needs to be focus on Energy/Conservation/Next Economy: Energy is no doubt today's greatest problem, and its greatest opportunity, and America faces this problem at a perilous time. Every dollar of petroleum purchased sends a portion of its funds to fuel some terrorist element. I am not saying all Arabs and Islamic people are bad, but I am saying some of their religious groups and ethnic races have their bad apples. But our own ability to dismantle the fuel behind this radical extremist threat is based on our ability to reduce and/or eliminate their funding. This would allow for a civilized, non-violent way to address the long-term threat of terrorism in a realistic and attainable manner. This reason alone should give us the basis for a massive retooling of American ingenuity and infrastructure to capitalize on in this Next Economy opportunity. My point? Energy touches everything we do (live, work, recreate), so it is the very fabric of our interaction and commerce; therefore, new alternative energy innovations will be the biggest economic boon ever experienced on our planet. America should and could lead the world in inventing new, clean energy sources (non-fossil fuels and renewable fuels), distribution systems and production systems, as well as the transportation platforms that will use them. The repercussions of this advance are far more than just economic and homeland security, they have enormous environmental positive outcomes that protect everyone on this planet. We must focus on the following:

1) Federal funding, research, and development grants, exponentially for this initiative, giving absolute use reduction guidelines that affect all energy use of fossil fuels to make sure all corporate citizens are forced to get involved with this innovation initiative.

2) The Leadership in Energy and Environmental Design (LEED) initiative for all building codes and alternative energy tax credits should be exponentially increased to offset the cost of the transition to better and cleaner materials.
3) Creating tax credits for hybrid highly efficient vehicles equal to 50% of their purchase price and allow such tax credits to be sold for equity to use, when purchasing these vehicles. Provide energy vouchers for the reduced cost of fueling such vehicles for a 5 year period of time with each purchase. Vouchers may be redeemed by the vendor for cash. This would not only be paid for with increased gasoline taxes, but it would also transform the majority of the U.S. fleet within a decade.

There is the need for Intellectual Capital/Innovation/Piracy: While I am a strong advocate for the working class, the highly skilled, and the low skilled workers of our country, this does not mean I will forgo the focus on the high-tech entrepreneurial sector of our workforce and corporate enterprises, yet I hold the opposite view. Our country needs to apply massive focus on the Small Business Innovation Research (SBIOR/STR) and other research grants for small businesses. We give far too little to this initiative while we allow corporate big business much greater flexibility. Support for innovation, large or small, is absolutely necessary to invent and grow the Next Big Opportunities in the global economy. My approach requires we rethink our broken taxation system and instead of making it less complex as a focus or flattening it irrationally (both of which I am in favor of, if done rationally), I would call for creating incentives for proper and prudent investments into tax credits, to offset income taxes for corporations and individuals (both of which need to be adjusted back to allow for financing the cost of doing business in our country). Here are some attainable starting points:

1) Increase SBIR/STR grants by at least five fold.
2) Create a tax credit market for R&D credits to be sold for equity to conduct research and commercialize products.
3) Allow tax credits for the formation of local and state innovation and opportunity funds so states and communities can raise monies to grow these sectors of their own economies.
4) Give tax credits for the award of patents so inventors can raise capital to promote their product for commercialization and seed capital funding.
5) Strictly enforce piracy issues through the world trade organization (WTO) and create tariffs for companies that have been found guilty of such violations.

There is a need for Big Business Employer/Employee Relationships: Yes, the pendulum has swung too far. While debating issues like presidents, abortion, gay rights, time zones, immigration, voting systems, and war, the more important debate was axed. This is not to say these topics are not worthy of debate, but we needed to also take care of our businesses while we engaged in this improvement to our society and governance situations. We cannot be fooled any longer; corporate America has little interest in our citizens, and in our hearts, when they recommended policies, we should never have expected this. Their job is to make money, and lots of it. The Governments job is to protect the welfare of its people. Big business did their job exceptionally well, and government failed miserably at their job, at all levels, especially in the last two decades. Government must realize that healthcare must be made affordable and accessible to all members of its society. The following must be put into plan:

1) Dislocated workers (those laid off or wrongfully terminated) shall be paid 50% of their average wage of their past year of employment if they have worked two or more years for a company. No funny business with lay-offs and rehires to avoid this should be allowed. These benefits are the responsibility of the company and such wages shall be income tax free for the period of 18 months or until re-employed at a greater or same level of wages. Benefits shall not be reduced until such time as the employee has surpassed the 100% of previous wage levels.
2) Companies must pay for required mandatory job skills testing and curriculum to improve the scores of dislocated employees during the benefit period. Employees have to make progress at improving their skills scores by at least one level during this benefit period, and they must demonstrate adequate progress throughout this benefit period.
3) Employer must pay 100% of an employee's healthcare costs, not only during employment, but also during dislocation.
4) The unemployed and under-employed shall be provided healthcare benefits vouchers to purchase family coverage, and these funds shall be paid for by the use of tax credits sold to healthcare providers and systems. This would allow the system to reduce the tax on their own profits and equitably allow all members of the workforce access to healthcare.
5) Expansion of R&D tax credits and workforce tax credits for new jobs created at above the state average wage for such occupations, by more than 10%. These tax credits shall be commercialized, so they can be market-based and allow the creation of cash to offset hiring and retooling costs for innovative new business opportunities.

6) Make mandatory 401K contributions for all wage earners. The corporate employers 10% must require a matched 5% pre-tax contribution from its employees.

There is need to rid ourselves of Corporate Subsidies, Pork Barrel projects, and Industry Abuses: There is no doubt the general accounting office (GAO) has done a better job of addressing contract-awarded abuses. Today's blatant abuse of pet projects and industry subsidies bears need for our biggest reforms. Subsidies are given when none are necessary and not given to industries that suffer these needs. Subsidies are given to rock stars, movie stars, and big business for their investments in industry, farming, and other areas of the economy. Family farming, a once stalwart enterprise and dignified profession, has been eroded and destroyed. There have been bridges built to nowhere (in Alaska), funded antiquated telecom industries, rewarded poor cropland use, and federal land abuse, by big business. We must insist on the following:

1) End Subsidies for domestic industries, unless they are family owned, small in nature, and not abusive to the environment or economically unjustified.
2) Reinstitute farming subsidies for family farms with tax credits instead of cash, when performance is poor. Issue tax credits for cropland rotation, new equipment and machinery purchases, and facilities and operating debts, only if economically deemed necessary (hardships, crop failure, new crop introductions such as BIOPharming).

There need to be changes in our Federal & State Taxation & Budgetary Processes: This is the red elephant in the middle of the table nobody wants to discuss but everyone knows is necessary. We are now a huge debtor nation, driven by an insane amount of too much personal debt and corporate irresponsibility, from pensions to taxation. There should be a transition from an income and wealth accumulation system to a more consumption-based tax system, allowing incentives for savings and investments into areas of the economy that will build prosperity and economic growth. This will flatten the tax code, but it won't necessarily reduce taxes to individuals and corporations unless they invest in areas that actually create jobs for the working-class and other members of our society. The greatest success we have had in the last 20 years is the housing tax credit program, and this should be the model for creating markets that do good things. This new system will not penalize higher earners who invested back into tax credits that actually create funds for new jobs and open new markets for economic expansion. Some might look at this as a Draconian approach, and it is a major shift, but to continue today's denial will be far worse. The premise of these tax code changes will focus on reinstituting deductions against income taxes to some level for middle-income folks, and eliminating them for the lowest wage earners. This would spread the wealth more equitably among a far greater percentage of society while still fueling profits within the corporate sector from the investment of tax credits and new expanded markets. These changes should include the following:

1) Increase Use and Licensure taxes for occupations in conjunction with certifications and business licensure. Include toll roads for interstates outside the metro areas, airline taxes for introducing and supporting other high volume expansion of transport, such as a more European and Japanese style passenger rail systems, and light rail in metros increased visitor taxes for people entering the country.
2) Flat Income Tax (15%) on all individual and corporate earnings and wages including dividends. This will be offset by tax credits and mortgage interest deduction up to $2M in income, annually, and it will limit housing deduction on the median value of homes adjusted, annually. The first priority for these funds will be to incrementally pay off our national debt and provide solvency to our retirement systems. This will include allowing social security to be capped and adjusted annually, but it will not limit the percentage paid in by wage earners, so such taxes will have to be paid through the extent of wages.
3) Implement new transportation and utility taxes to improve roads, bridges, utility grids, and physical infrastructure.
4) Eliminate the inheritance tax on any inheritance below $10M, and adjust this annually to reflect the consumer price Index (CPI).
5) Create a 3% to 5% National Sales Tax on consumption to better and more equitably capture the affluence of luxury and other expenditures (use exemptions for clothing and groceries). We are a rabid consumption-based society, and this tax will cause discretion when purchasing luxury items.
6) Incorporate Sin Taxes in areas of that cost enormous amounts of money spent on healthcare and abusive behaviors (tobacco, alcohol, gaming).
7) Modify Internet Retail Sales Systems that provide local sales tax revenues, and make them mandatory, paid to the zip code local government jurisdiction of the purchaser, so local and state governments get their fair share of ecommerce revenues, leveling the playing field for brick and mortar retailers.

There is the need for a change in Student Loans/ Education and Aid for Schooling: Every individual in our society deserves the proper and affordable right to attend school after K-12 is completed. We must retake the lead in creating highly skilled, useful, and productive graduates from our educational systems. Again, our system can use vouchers backed by education tax credits, to pay for promotions and incentives in order to spur interest to continue and improve educational outcomes at the individual levels. The following will help:

1) Provide every graduating senior with a voucher for continued education worth at least the average cost of community college. When this $3K (estimated example) voucher has been given, each student must use it within 12 months of his or her graduation. Provide science and math vouchers equal to the average cost of tuition for state universities, during four years of undergraduate study, and increase the cost for graduate school costs if a maintained 3.0 grade point is averaged, annually.

2) Create a voucher ATM card that has rewards redeemable at stores and restaurants worth $4,000 for all students who stay in school and graduate without any jail, drug, or extreme disciplinary issues during school. This can be paid for through voluntary inclusion and stores that support education, and it can require other purchases, in some major cases, equal to the expenditure being used, perhaps a 50% one-time reward system. Kids love gadgets, clothing, food, and technology, so such a card will make them aggressive at taking school and school behavior serious.

There is a dire need for change in our Foreign Relations: This one is complex. See below:

1) Here is where the world's cop is our biggest out-of-country issue. We must step up and become better world citizens by signing on to serious environmental legislation in order to reduce and eliminate pollution and the greenhouse affects. We must pay our real freight for being the leader in the United Nations, and as such, this is where our aid must flow, to and from, and only there. Lending our experts to resolve poverty, disaster, and wars is critical, but, if at all possible, it must be a teaching role, not an enforcement role. This means we must be a strong, vigilant, and prepared militarily but not so easily involved in military conflicts, unless we are provoked or directly threatened. In the case of terrorism, if any country harbors terrorists, and we find they do so, and as such, these terrorists threaten our nation, we must punish this nation to its fullest economic capabilities. If these terrorists are directly linked to any action that harms any U.S. citizens, we should take swift military action to destroy such movements and cells, permanently, and let all nations be forewarned of our intentions in advance.

There must be a change in our Military Policy: While I may be an economic warrior, I am certainly not a soldier, and I have the utmost respect for today's nation's elite men and women who provide us with our freedom and safety. No words can express my gratitude to them and their families for their hardships, courage, and dedication—case closed. But there are better ways to support our troops, and these are as follows:

1) Our troops must have, whenever thrown into harms way, the absolute best technology, hardware, weapons, machinery, logistics, and safety and welfare benefits available, without question. There must be investments, at all platforms, that will improve these factors, and they must be the best possible in the world. There must also be an increase in pay, in order to attract and retain the best soldiers. Along with this boost in pay, wages must be income tax free for a lifetime (those earned from military service including pensions). I do know that military prowess goes a long way with diplomacy; therefore, I love the Teddy Roosevelt approach.

There must be focus on Homeland Security: Separate from our military issues is the points necessary to safeguard our nation's homes, borders, and residents. This will also be a huge boon to commerce, through job creations. It will require new and additional massive security measures in the form of infrastructure deployment and inspections technology. We need a Sig Sigma quality control approach to individual and national security. First, put Agent Jack Bauer in charge of the program (I believe every avid *24* follower will agree Jack would do anything to keep our homeland secure). This is how we should approach homeland security:

1) Raise the 5% Inspection of all today's cargo shipped into this country to 100%, paid for by the shipper. This is the reality and cost of doing business due to today's terrorism elements, and this will keep all members of the world focused on this situation. Any company and/or country that compromise shipment must be severely penalized, and if the situation merits, must be embargoed from further trade with our nation, period! This is the defacto cost of negligence for endangering even one American life.

There is the need for Economic Development and Capitalization of the Economic Growth Opportunities: People who choose to represent the interests of our citizens should do so with one arm tied behind their back. However, when and if they fail, others publicly embarrass and ruin them for their alleged lack of success. I have watched countless quasi-civil servants become targets of political abuse for events not at all within their control. These folks continue to do their job, if possible, but under extreme emotional and economic stress. I know such is life in the fast lane, but these representatives deserve the best tools when sent into economic combat, on our citizen's behalf. Most the major reasons for failed economic development initiatives are poor community leadership, poor, or lack of, state and federal policies, inadequate leadership when it comes to addressing the needs of a situation, and lack of will to capitalize projects that build and bolster local economies, which, by the way, do then trickle down and bolster state and national economies. To this extent, the addition of new incentive zones for focused industries such as Biotech, Genetics, IT, Nanotech-advanced manufacturing (robotics), and alternate energy research must be created and funded at each state level and backed by state-based tax credits. These zones must also receive global trade zone status and then become exempt from certain taxes, such as property and other state and local taxes. An economic developer must focus on the following:

2) Creating Tax Credits for local economic development eligible purposes (operations, infrastructure development, workforce development, industry parks, brown field remediation, business incubation, micro credit, small business revolving loan funds, opportunity funds, venture and seed capital funds, downtown redevelopment and expansion, cultural and performing arts centers, and catalyst economic development projects of their unique design).
3) Expanding government guarantees for new SBA expanded programs, including more intellectual capital and micro businesses. A major focus should be on mezzanine level debts and gap funding of capital needs of small to medium businesses and index the levels to the CPI.
4) Expanding the availability of private activity bonds by adjusting and indexing cap levels to annual levels so they rise with costs. The lack of this has unreasonably restricted business and there are no negative repercussions for doing such modifications.

My list of policy changes is by no way 100% inclusive of all the things our nation needs to do to fix its problems and exploit possible opportunities. However, this list would go a long way toward fixing the plight of the individual worker and our national economy while protecting the sovereign security of our Republic. It also has a healthy dose of economic stimuli and additional realistic tax-based fiscal responsibilities. We cannot afford to allow our local, state, and national government to be a debt-ridden system, so we must restore fiscal discipline while sharing this burden with every corporate and individual member of our society. We all know he who has the gold makes the rules and money is power, so the lack thereof is the exact opposite, and we do not need to get into that situation with less than friendly economic competitors, such as China.

Chapter Thirteen

"Retooling Business Retention & Expansion Strategies:
A Lost Art that Deserves Rediscovered Focus and Purpose"

For decades, economic development agencies have touted the need for substantial commitment to the efforts of retaining and assisting in the expansion of local businesses. Much of what they promote for such media and politically correctness does not actually transfer to their operational scope of consistent work. More cases than not, business retention and expansion production do not receive the actual staff attention it merits. There are so many more attractive and sexy conversations with prospective new clients and deals looking to come to the area, so the existing prospective are left unattended until there is a serious situation. This famous phrase is bandied but largely ignored, "80% of new job growth comes from local, established, existing businesses." Far too many economic development efforts are reactionary versus proactive. In addition, there are far less innovative strategies being infused into our traditional business assistance retention and expansion efforts (BARE). Economic development itself is as much a science of knowledgeable attributes as it is an art of skill sets, and business retention and expansion is the absolute underlying magic behind this concept.

The onslaught of globalization and its fast-paced economic competitors from overseas has created an even greater strain on local economies, and the need for much more strategic BARE efforts are essential. This powered, 24/7, always on economic and business climate, is driven by the internet and other enabling technologies. These same forces also create an opportunity for advancements in creating more out of the box, over the horizon, hybrid BARE strategies for progressive-minded economic development organizations.

In the past, Economic developers have had a maverick almost caviler attitude about bringing in enough new business to offset the loss of existing ones, but this rule no longer plays in today's economy. In more and more cases, communities are facing sustained net losses, not net gains, in the ledger of gross new economic investments and jobs created. This is especially true in the nature and quality of jobs being created, when a business is successful. Higher paying existing jobs are being replaced by lower paying new jobs through business attraction deals. Many economic developers and local community leaderships are missing the real message in favor of the more attractive media attention and community awareness given to new entrants to their economy due to business attraction deals.

> *We, as a profession, in working with companies, need to enhance our ability to understand the technical needs of companies, especially those engaged in international projects. Even though consultants are usually hired to perform the due diligence and specific requirements with regard to a business, we need to, at a minimum, be able to understand the technical aspects and its workforce expectations. This will increase the effectiveness of measuring international alliances.* **(Ed Nelson**, *International Economic Development Consultant, Atlanta, GA)*

So the message is clear, start fixing house by spring cleaning its own industries and uncovering pearls of opportunities to grow local economy from within, first and foremost. Incidentally, those successful in this effort will spill over, and positive ramifications will affect the local business attraction efforts. Local businesses often cite they feel neglected locally, and sometimes this leads to their looking to be a business attraction client somewhere else in order to garner the attention they really desire from their current locale. In addition, state and federal incentive and investment programs are skewed toward business attraction deals, not business retention deals.

The economic development's mission must be a clear best practice design. It must find protocols, procedures, and systemic practices that will allow it to cultivate this existing crop of business opportunities and challenges. However, there are several obvious issues that need fundamental addressing. First, communication needs more attention than currently given new business deals, from the external to the local economy. This is more than lip service, it is a paradigm shift. Admitting to this shift means not making excuses or claiming a procedure has already been done. Listening to our local businesses is essential to more than just retention. This effort can spur new growth and investments that create jobs and increase the local tax base. These efforts can uncover new markets and sexy new technology applications that have innovation and entrepreneurial opportunities a community can exploit to its advantage. This process creates a spirit of partnership in developing a competitive intelligence network that can systematically turn up new opportunities within the ranks of companies that already believe in the strength and quality of their local community. These companies are already converts; thus they don't require the normal sales pitch. Once the economic developer knows this is all true and readily admits to this, year after year, the question that remains is, "Why do we continue to fail to capitalize on this knowledge as economic developers?" Because it requires change, and fear of change, especially coupled with the need for advanced new technology tools, can be daunting to many middle-aged economic development leaders.

BARE is at the root of our new, hybrid model; a technology-driven adventure. Economic developers need to think and utilize technology, just as a private sector business would do if they were developing its own markets. This means economic developers have to have a customer relationship management (CRM) approach that will make local businesses feel valuable and listened to.

In the past few years, we have seen new technology-driven models introduced to the BARE market, enabling economic developers to keep in touch with their businesses. These efforts, once established, created a 1 to 1 market analysis capability. However, this still requires a personable relationship in order to manage and cultivate this information source and do the data-mining that spring from these technology enabling seeds. Once we populate our technology with our core industries through our initial product launch and outreach marketing efforts, we begin to see the power of these new tools. This 1 to 1 role creates opportunities for our assigned BARE representatives a creative knowledge of local business trends, business cycles, and barriers to growth and challenges that might affect existence if unmitigated. These business intelligence factors will lead to a greater, more positive, economic development outcome. Every client is unique and as such, each should feel so. In the business world, one would not set out with untrained professionals to conduct such business intelligence efforts, so this must not be done in the economic development realm, either. Economic developers must teach their SWAT team members how to garner the nuggets of critical information with face to face interviews, without making them seem like a check list of fill in the blank questionnaires, so prevalent today. The most critical factor is disbursing this information into a useful database system, so the economic developer can study and react to individual and community-wide trends and needs. In these efforts, there are steps to success.

First, select the best technology platform to perform the task of remote interview, constant contact follow-up, and additional information input, from both interviewee and interviewer, at their own pace, and then use data management and trend analysis in the form of critical reports and follow-up tracking.

Then, craft the strategy that will tactically put in place, sustain, and fund this effort. It is critical to understand that many core businesses are driven by decision makers outside the market. This means a large part of a travel budget should be spent, calling on home offices, to make them feel their importance through the conveying of locally owned businesses. This step should also create reportable metrics for public reports, building both public awareness to the importance of BARE and the local benefits being derived from these efforts, much like creating business attraction client projects. This should include jobs retained, jobs created, the payroll and wages related to those efforts, new economic investments and the positive indirect and direct effect on the local and state economy due to these efforts. Accountability to today's public is critical.

No technology strategy or tool can supplant the need for human work teams, what I refer to as our own economic development SWAT teams. These teams should be led by our core paid professional cadre from the ranks of the economic development agency and closely intertwine; the key staff of various local economic development savvy partners (chambers, utilities, telecoms, workforce boards, community college, and university staff). These teams should then add key local subject matter experts to respond to critical new business opportunities or responsive needs as they are identified. This subject matter expert (SME) intervention has to be done on a voluntary basis. The addition of local politicians and state officials, with regular familiarization tours, can be a critical element in not only gaining better political support for BARE efforts, but also making businesses feel more appreciated. These VIP tours can also be used by the private sector, to show clout with the home office. These key personnel visits help the community that wants added local attention.

Follow-up to these efforts and managing the work flow created by these efforts with paid professionals, volunteers, and subject matter experts and their realistic capabilities is essential to world-class business assistance, retention, and expansion programs. Using an automated flagging system to alert this staff of actionable expectations is both simple and useful. Red Flags are those issues that need immediate attention and mitigation, from the professional staff to the critical situation. Yellow flags are situations that require additional close monitoring. Green flags are situations where an opportunity to create new investment or jobs exists and needs actionable solutions or incentives. As difficult as it may seem, a professional economic development staff has to create the posture, or belief, that its organization and its leadership are the Oracle of business intelligence resources; thus merit critical inclusion into the discussions that address each flagged event and its discussion points. In other words, this staff must be capable of bringing value to the equation in order to build such a belief system.

It is important to realize that the involved volunteers and staff members in this 1 to 1 CRM process need to be trained for economic development expectations. In addition, the economic development agency should understand and purchase third party data and information on their core industries' markets, to allow all parties to better understand what is driving the core industries to be visited. In other words, go in informed yet not too informed, allowing them to openly know the preparations for these meetings. Each time these volunteers meet, they should be debriefed, either face to face, or through a technology-driven template. The initial report created prior to each meeting is what I refer to as a corporate "Dash Board Report" on the key known facts about the company. Here is an example of a Dash Board template wizard; Name (division or HQ): Ownership structure (public or private): Management team; local and top management and their locations: Number of local employees: Gross employment; company wide: Years in the community: Changes in ownership during that tenure: Previous situations that merited economic development intervention.

Secondary to this information should be the purchased data on the company's industry. Is this industry growing, maturing, or declining in the national and global market? What role or market share does it currently hold? Is its market presence growing or declining? Who and where are its largest competitors?

Similarly, there are four simple pieces of intelligence one must gather in these face to face interviews. During these interviews, the conversation will try to match known but not stated industry trends to its conversational intelligence openly disclose posture and position in these same factors. The SWAT team member must then judge, on his or her own accord, if the company is in fact, growing, stable, or declining. This is a major category to the report, and it will be derived from the follow-up report to the BARE committee and team. The second part of these interviews is the uncovering or the perception of the current local business climate (is it positive or negative, and why?). The third focus is to understand if there are any issues or barriers beyond the local level that the company needs to mitigate and/or address to sustain healthy business operations from their current model or new ventures (flags). Finally, there will be the discovery of what actionable follow-ups will be needed addressed through what has been uncovered during these interviews. This is the action plan that needs to be brought back to the team for proper focus and development of solutions to instill the value of this time for both the volunteers and the business executives. Keep the following in mind:

> *The missing elements in economic development and its technology can be looked at from two different standpoints: the internal process standpoint, and the external customer standpoint.*
>
> *Internally, there are three levels of technology competence. First, many people running ED organizations are old school and don't see the need or have the ability to assimilate technology. Second, those who recognize the need for change and assimilate technology, but they are unsure how to take the next steps because it is not their expertise. Finally, there are those who buy the cutting edge technology, but then do not use it to its fullest extent.*
>
> *When it comes to customers, the biggest deficiency is someone trying to serve the private sector that is not tech savvy. In today's global market, the difference between the have and have-nots has been the ability to assimilate technology into their own products or services. When we look at economic developers, to be viable, to be relevant in global economy, they too have to ratchet up the use of technology in the products and services they provide the*

private sector and in the dialogue they have with the local business owner.
***(Laith Wardi**, National Economic Development Consultant, Erie, PA)*

Today's business retention, assistance, and expansion have a myriad of new opportunities that demand yet even greater knowledge and expertise from the economic development community. Because of this, hybrid business retention strategies have to be created. Strategies like the New Entrepreneurial Research & Development Needs might include patent development and the pursuit of grants to fund such efforts. This can often include using and connecting university led professionals and other like-minded local entrepreneurs to a company; thus allowing a creative synergy. Sometimes, just knowing who to speak with is important to local companies. Even more valuable is the knowledge that local funds can support some of these efforts. Examples might include **SBIOR** consultant funding and matching funds through low interest loans when grants are received. Sometimes, allowing the spin-off of new entrepreneurial efforts in incubator space is important. In addition, some communities develop local seed, venture, and angel funding to further promote local entrepreneurial efforts and having these uncovered and linked to an already existing local business makes this investment more comfortable.

Furthermore, there is the need to generate bridges to small business succession. Some companies go through succession issues. This might arise either from the loss of a key leader and/or owner or the disinterest of their heirs and the want to continue the business at the time of their desired retirement. In this case, many scary situations can arise, and economic developers need to get out in front of these issue. First, the business might be sold to a disinterested non-local and consolidated into his or her other ventures, elsewhere. However, the business might have the opportunity to sell to the employees and as such, the economic development group can assist in financing such a transaction, hiring a new paid professional leader to carry out the on-going operations; or the business might be attractive to a local entrepreneur who desires to own and operate this business, so the economic development group can match an entrepreneur with an established business, again helping to bridge its financial concerns to go forward. None of these situations gets much real focus in today's economic development, yet each is a very cogent situation that readily occurs without our knowledge. Without local economic development leadership playing a role, many businesses fail to understand what is available to them in the form of options, so bad decisions might be made through lack of knowledgeable decision. Many smaller businesses merely close their doors because they haven't a successor for their enterprise, and this is readily apparent in today's smaller communities, just take a drive down Main Street America.

When our economic developers help in mitigating and brokering small business transactions from a knowledge perspective, they cultivate high growth, locally oriented business leaders. In many cases, this proactive approach can prevent unnecessary shutdowns and closures. The missing element is in the current dinosaur model used to address business workforce needs, both from the educational system and from our transition and mitigation system of dislocated workers and continued support for workforce training and preparedness. Economic developers have to link educators, workforce resource providers, and businesses into meaningful conversations that are held accountable for actionable outcomes, linking them directly to the same metrics used to measure success in our basic BARE program (jobs created, retained, and business investments resulting from such efforts). Holding all sides accountable is not only fair; it is realistic in order to continued economic support of such efforts within the community.

As I have mentioned many times, today's communities want to be recognized and appreciated as great world-class places to live, work, invest, visit, and recreate. Every community should decide to find some niche it can carve out as an area it can dominate, creating a branding value around its local flag, for global recognition. Communities have to ride the wave of innovation in such a way that they are in a state of equilibrium with the market. This requires intelligent design within the halls of economic development to accomplish. There are many key assets that need to be in place to create a world-class business climate that grows more than its fair share of local businesses into even greater successes. These key assets cross over and further support many other areas of traditional economic development, business development, and attraction models concurrently while helping local businesses expand and grow. Some of the basic business transfer models are:

    Innovation support for entrepreneurs and entrepreneurial companies

    Infrastructure upgrades and cutting edge development and deployment

    Intelligent logistics and transportation design in multi-modal scenarios

    Enhanced local capital (traditional debt, seed, venture, and angel)

    Enhanced buildings and sites improvement and shovel-ready sites for new facilities

    Easily navigated business licensure and permits

    Competitive and low cost business climate management (plus incentives for growth)

Reductions of front-end risk required for new operations to start-up or expand

Support of innovation research & development efforts

    This approach can build a very positive brand for its local efforts. As in any other marketing effort, this brand should be cultivated and marketed both externally and internally into the community. There are several really well-established branding activities that can assist in accomplishing this, and at this point, my intent is to focus on the not so common. Needless to say, there should be printed and electronic media to support this effort and distributing this should be part of the everyday operation of the economic development agency.

    The real value comes in cultivating networking functions that allow businesses to engage lively conversations regarding growth and new opportunities while also gaining a keen awareness of new tools, resources, and other like-minded experts who might result in further collaboration to nurture and grow the desired ideal outcomes. The most successful venue is a diverse venue of meetings scheduled and marketed to the community, such as niche roundtables within special industry circles, angel and entrepreneurial presentations for local funding, research and development training shops, and specialized topics on business climate issues, such as globalization, trade, immigration, workforce development, skills training, and talent recruitment. These networking opportunities, when coupled with an aggressive and well placed technology driven CRM system, can allow economic developers to connect the dots of business development opportunities within their local markets.

    World-class is a state of mind, and I have continued to state this in my economic development publications, speeches, and consultations. Those communities that will prevail in today's global economy have a "let's get it done and help ourselves" attitude, first and foremost. Once this paradigm shift and recognition of realities is founded, a willingness to build investment strategies that allows the creation of funds to carry out its mission, and a vision begins. Communities create and forge new opportunities through focused focus on these efforts and they sustain their support.

    Most importantly, this focus spawns self confidence not bravado, and it builds a community spirit that makes others want to engage and interact in the process. The visible belief in a healthy and vibrant future becomes contagious; thus there is a self-fulfilling prophesy. Communities that believe they can create a world-class community allow nothing to distract them from their purposeful and strategic direction. They tie all their decisions to this strategy, making sure each decision builds additional capabilities that enable growth to come to fruition. The secret is the power of positive thinking and acting, and this convinces others that this is where they should tie their own future to the proverbial wagon train to make their way to the next great frontier of new opportunities just over the horizon.

Chapter Fourteen

"Understanding and Managing the Technology Paradigm Shift: *Catching the Wave of Transformational Technology Critical to Economic Development Information*"

Information drives economic development because it is what is always sought by key business decision makers in order for them to determine whether or not to make an investment into a local economy. For many years, the economic development industry has severely lagged behind its private sector counter parts in its capabilities to provide relevant, useful, accurate, and up to date information that is not subjective and biased by local opinion. Site selectors claim this is a critical area of road improvement, necessary in the deployment of a current information superhighway. During a critical period of the information boom, the International Economic Development Council convened a special task force comprised of the leading site selection consultants and leading economic development thinkers, to address this pitfall in this 21st century technology bloom. The task force recommended approximately 1200 critical information elements be agreed upon as the new standard utilized by site selectors in formulating their requests for information from community, regional, and state level economic development agencies. These open standards are commonly referred to as the "IEDC Data Standards."

However, there is still a critical area of need; finding a way to provide hard to get information sought by corporate decisions makers and site selection consultants and measuring its accuracy and validity. Because the private sector corporations have agreed upon open standards allowing information of this similar nature to cross corporate boundaries, this information can now be utilized by many rather than the few. The end product justifies this collaboration. This created the data-mining and data-warehousing generation that has resulted in a prolific growth of commerce. There are now numerous commercial platforms that operate in what is referred to as "semantic grids" or "metadata environments."

> *In order to compete, communities need to have knowledge of their comparative, competitive analysis for where they stand in the global economy. An economic developer should know where his or her regional community stands in the global market place. From this information, economic developers are then able to make quantitative decisions on investments for more development of a product. It helps guide the spending of money. I call this "deathenomics." It is not important to be number one in each industry, but no one wants to be number 10 in any industry area. World-class communities strive to be number 1 or 2 for each industry.* (**Steve Weathers**, *Professional Economic Developer, Toledo, OH*)

This scenario was partially addressed in the early years of this new century when economic developers and site selectors created and published the aforementioned standardized set of data measurable variables. This effort provided the foundation for this problem to be addressed.

Now, a few years later, we are faced with implementing these data standards amongst our local economic development communities. Some larger cities, of course, have significant resources, but the small and rural communities lack such resources. Even with significant resources, the key to getting the Data Standards ubiquitously woven into this information infrastructure is not an easily understood process; in fact, it has been made more difficult than it needed to be. However, there are two remedies. First, the inclusion of any new technology and software vendors into a special task force at our professional gatherings. The time has come to discuss the implementing of these open Data Standards. Both the formalization of this task force and the eventual formation of what I would call an "Economic Development Technology Guild" are inevitable in order to continue its focus on all vendors providing their wares in formats that cross the spectrum of the needs of its users.

After figuring out how to gather, validate, and distribute such data between economic developers, technology vendors, demographic and information brokers, and private sector clients, this can become the top discussion point and, more importantly, the expectation of their clients to make this process open to choice and competitive pressures. In the software and operating system world, this would be called a "dynamic distributed database." The common meaning is that it grows as it is used, and it acquires more information as transactions and volumes of use allow it to define trends and fill information voids as necessary to conduct and fulfill requests for information (RFI) or in support of proposals responded to by communities in pursuit of being included for consideration in a site location decision (RFP). The really useful part of this is that as information changes, through added or made available information, the system updates all points within the grid so everyone, simultaneously, has access to the most current information in the supply chain after it is validated and accepted by the appropriate local administrator it pertains to.

The second remedy is the already built-in capacity for the more common database operating systems because they now have this capability built into them. This capability is what used to be referred to as an "agent-based technology" (ask for something, and the agent finds and supplies it), now more commonly referred to as "embedded data tags" (variables). These systems are smart and metamorphic in their ability to constantly provide an ability to refresh data such as licensure, permits, sales tax revenues, populations, and buildings and sites availability that change frequently.

Though these remedies sound complex, they are really simple. Their solutions reside in the same currency used in today's computer software world, known as open sourcing of critical data elements (variables and functions). By taking the IEDC data standards and adding critical data tags (agent based smart markers), relevant information that resides in a computer can be garnered equally by all who have access or seek access legitimately. This creates a viable two way stream of information providers and seekers. Here is the really great part, by creating this dynamic distributed database format as it is sought and then provided, the collective knowledge of the entire system adds and grows from the learning and sharing process. In other words, knowledge can start out with basic information, and as economic developers and business decision makers continue to seek more information, redundant information will no longer exist. Even more attractive is the eventual inclusion of the information primary sources, such as the US Dept of Census. As new information is added through research and tracking, it can be made available to the public, and this system will automatically acquire updates, so it will always be current and accurate, allowing real estate records and transactions, populations and demographics, business licensure, and permits to all be filtered to the economic development systems and instantly available to those needing such information. It would vastly improve the value of economic developers, especially when it comes to business decision makers. It resolves the quantity problem of not only how to move such huge blocks of information but also its management.

Given the technology creep that has occurred within the economic development industry over the past few years, it is very reasonable to expect that most offices have a budget. Even the modest budget will allow for a technology infrastructure, such as web sites and customer contact management software. Some may budget in a more robust web enabled database for available buildings and sites, community profiles, business assistance programs, workforce, permits, licensure, and a plethora of other economic development-related business climate management tools. This has caused the annual budget for technology to increase within economic development organizations, so even small economic development agencies can begin to address this new concept by requiring future modifications to their websites. GIS systems, contact managements, specialized databases for community profiling, buildings and sites, and business retentions are incorporated in the IEDC Data Standards as necessary embedded data tags in their own modules. The cost for this is relatively inexpensive, and IEDC makes it readily available for technologists to download and utilize, via its web site (*http://www.iedconline.org/?p=Data_Standards*), which leads to an excel spreadsheet that hosts the set of data tags.

Why haven't these remedies occurred already? Because it requires some upfront investment and, in many cases, we Americans are not at our best and finest when faced with adversity. For example, let's speak of New Orleans. The storm in the gulf coast, in one day, changed the entire information profile of that region. Now, in order to rebuild this area, there is a severe lack of relevant and up to date information. Where are the utilities available? How many workers are available? How many businesses are up and operational? How does one go about getting a permit and what is the current zoning?

Nothing is valid any longer. 40% to 60% of the population has shifted or is gone. Housing and infrastructure is obscure. How do business decision makers and politicians make critical decisions when, at best, such necessary information is a guess? The Greater New Orleans Inc. economic development partnership had to move rapidly in order to address this huge problem. Now they are faced with rebuilding their entire information infrastructure and profile; who they are, and what they have. In the process of doing this, if they would very inexpensively add in the new data elements, they could begin to share this information between the 10 parishes of the greater New Orleans area. The windfall of this project, for the mainstream of economic developers, is that these new data elements could be available for use by others across the nation. In addition, vendors and software technology companies could quickly add these new open source capabilities to their own products, and as such, the boon would be realized by all those that desire these improvements to their own local information infrastructures. Then, by 2010, we could have a greatly enhanced national economic development information infrastructure as a windfall of the Katrina Hurricane in the Gulf Coast.

However, there are further steps to implementing this recommended course of action:

Step 1: As economic development agencies address upgrades in their new or existing software and web based tools, they should choose the correct vendor to tweak their systems and make modifications that make dealing with information and clients more expedient, reliable, and friendly usable for all, both internally and externally.

Step 2: Economic development agencies need to make sure their underlying software platforms support the ability to utilize meta-tags and distributed database elements. Today, most of the more common database foundations do, but some vendors have little or no experience in utilizing these features, so they essentially remain in the proverbial sense "turned off" and in the dark.

Step 3: In the scope of work for upcoming technology contracts to build economic development organizational infrastructures, economic development leaders need to incorporate these requirements and introduce the vendors to the IEDC data standards as part of the expectations from the project outcomes.

Combining all 3 steps in technology, work, and budget will be the beginning of a naturally transformed economic development industry and a true grassroots effort in an open environment. Essentially, these new dynamic data points will light up the grid of the new emerging economic development specific semantic grid and provide much greater accountability, for both economic developers and their clients' information exchanges. Most importantly, this new capability will greatly expand the economic developers' capabilities, information dissemination, and retrieval management practices.

Chapter Fifteen

"Technology-Led Entrepreneurial Business Retention Efforts: *Planning for Succession and the Economic Development Team*"

The root or core principle in economic development is the growth of a business base in a local economy. This lost and fading art is beginning to regain its importance. The resurgence is due, in part, to the exodus of companies through overseas and outsourcing of the traditional manufacturing base, due to globalization. Because of this, there are several key elements to business retention and expansion (BRE). I refer to these elements as entrepreneurial, and they include innovation-led development of new products and services, new niche markets for emerging business opportunities that are hybrid for existing economy products and services (capitalizing on market-led opportunities), knowledge-based applications that replace traditional products and services, acquisitions for competitors to acquire new products, markets, and services, and finally, successive transitions for family businesses that develop new entrepreneurial owners in the local economy. I am now going to concentrate on "Tech-Led Succession Transitions," the economic developers play in these transitions, and the known facts of these transitions:

Fact 1: 70% of family businesses do not succeed in transitioning to the second generation
Fact 2: Management and Ownership do not have to coincide with a healthy business
Fact 3: Children do not have to be the successors and may not be the best choice
Fact 4: Taxes, Management, Ownership terms and value attainment are the main issues
Fact 5: Family discord is the number one killer of business successions (unrealistic expectations and frozen sunk costs that are easily recoverable)

Economic Developers know the stats on BRE; 80% of new job creation comes from the existing expansion of businesses already in the economy. Yet this remains the most under funded least creative focus for most North American Local Economic Development Agencies; furthermore, it is relatively ignored by most state economic development agencies. It is just not sexy and news-worthy compared to the big new deal on the horizon that no one yet knows about. Economic developers seek their version of the Holy Grail; the proverbial homerun they all wish to hit in their careers. The big deal they can land and bring home to their constituents. Most economic developers will work their whole lifetime, lucky to get one of these deals, and many will never get one. So, my friends, I ask, where are the successful odds? BRE might not be sexy, but it pays the bills and forces our economies to hum. Let's now talk about adding some spice to BRE. I have several rules that will add this spice to BRE:

1) Know and understand the core industries in your community and the ancillary support businesses that depend on them.

   a. This is achieved by creating a tracking system and inventory of as many businesses as possible. Use contact management and simple database technology to build this base information foundation
   b. Track, record, and contact all businesses through their licensure, announcements, chamber of commerce notices and logs, and other business information resources such as D&B, and Hoovers
   c. Contact all businesses via a blitz and get as much primary information as possible by using call center style tactics. Collect emails, phone numbers, and names of key executives, industry NAIC code primary description, ownership structure, and market information (local, regional, national, international)

2) Recruit and train a cadre of SRT/SWAT team members of local experts on the various subjects necessary to discuss key business issues in the community.

   a. Capitalization
   b. Human Resources
   c. Marketing
   d. Management
   e. New Product Development
   f. Taxes
   g. Retirement planning
   h. Business Valuation & Sales

3) Understand the growth, no growth, and emerging growth sectors of the general national economy and how these may realistically relate the local economy and core businesses.

   a. Growth related businesses need different tools than no growth and mature businesses
   b. Some mature businesses are not capable of succession unless they reinvent themselves (let those unwilling souls rest in peace until the end)

4) Understand the mindset of the ownership teams and their long-term vision for the continuation of their business or eventual sale and retirement.

   a. Family ownership single tree (generational mix of management or not)
   b. Partners different than family (generational mix of management or not)
   c. Corporation held by many investors (not publicly traded)
   d. Corporation held by institutional investors

5) Understand the Matrix of the SWOT analysis on a company.

   a. Diverse and always improving to meet the market with increasing market share
   b. Mature and struggling to remain stable and find new niche with flat and/or stagnant market share
   c. Declining market share and no vision for turn around
   d. Plans for the eventual sale or transfer of the ownership and/or management of the business in place and executing strategy to implement such expectations (understands the business value in market terms)
   e. No succession plan in place and no idea how it is going to handle the sale, transition, or retirement from the business (no idea of real market value to an outside unbiased qualified buyer)
   f. Ability to cash flow business sale internally without the owners remaining involved in the business once new management is properly trained and adapted to the business
   g. No ability to cash flow the sale of the business and meet the sale expectations of the business owner(s)

However, economic developers commonly fail to understand how to match resources to needs; thus the great failure of their efforts in BRE. Yet they can change this by advertising, via communications and web sites, the great business expansion and growth opportunities as possible receptors of inward investment oriented folks looking at our communities and categorize them; retail, services, manufacturing, knowledge-based, logistics/distribution, back office, or tourism/hospitality (recreational services, hotels, restaurants; the most overlooked in this area)

> It is important to first gain an understanding of the communities one is working with. Just what are the 'truths' its residents hold? How does it perceive its future? What indeed are its problems? Does it have any, or is the economic developer imposing problems upon it? Just what comes next after SWOT Analysis is important to grasp. Often, impositions are made on a community, and although these are often timely and well meaning, if the community hasn't the knowledge to utilize these new opportunities; then the opportunity is met with mistrust and opposition. (**Peter Kenyon**, *Economic Development Consultant, Australia & New Zealand*)

Then, develop a network of connections to entrepreneurs in the community seeking new investment opportunities, and then catalog and track these in a technology database. Cultivate knowledge for the difference between a start-up, an acquisition, and the odds of success in each case. Understand when each is relevant. All this can be done with the help of community college sponsored business development courses, entrepreneurial networking functions (budding entrepreneurs), interviewing those identified and ranking their skills, knowledge, and resources, university related R&D participants and SBIOR applicants, and patent applicants, and sponsored angel and seed capital network systems and events.

Now that we have the basics, we have to incorporate these sets of data standards into our technology platform and incorporate these key elements by doing so; the second most common overlooked area because we have no technology platform to do this work! This platform will help trigger customized questions that will uncover this information given through discussing with the potential interviewee(s); develop an alert system status (Red Flag, Green Flag, Yellow flag) for various businesses and each situation; match resources to needs, and then do follow-ups to make sure these needs are carried forward and acted upon; discover reoccurring issues that affect the ability to retain and transition local businesses that might a need broad level of attention and specialized economic development tools; and track results and report them for accountability purposes and outcomes measured (jobs retained, jobs created, new investments, new markets, entrepreneurial ownership, transition accomplished).

According to Gregory K. Amundson (GKA Consulting of Louisville, KY), it is always about the W's and the L's, and these must be accounted for in our Net Gain analysis and what was learned from each experience so that best practices can be honed and worst cases avoided in the future. Generally, setting up a successful business succession plan involves seven stages:

1. **Survival**—once the business has survived the start-up stage, the owner should consider a business succession plan.
2. **Commitment**—the owner must be committed to the concept that the business must continue creating opportunities. This commitment must be communicated clearly, extensively, and often.
3. **Recruitment**—recruiting good people always pays dividends; it is a key area of importance for any succession planning.
4. **Development**—investing time in developing family members, key employees, and management team members, and allowing them to exercise authority and control, will be vital to success.
5. **Selection**—after developing a transition plan and recruiting the right people, selecting a successor or successors becomes easier. By empowering a broad range of key people, the selection process is simplified and an owner's options are enhanced.
6. **Announcement**—once a succession plan is in place, the owner should communicate this plan. Such communication gives key management people and/or family successors a clear understanding of the path to the future, as well as any role they may play in that path. This also allows them to set future goals and objectives.
7. **Implementation**—in implementing the succession plan, an owner must be ready to step aside and allow the successor(s) to take over. This owner must be prepared to take on new challenges in retirement, knowing his or her financial future is secure.

This is the semblance of a real market-oriented BRE entrepreneurial approach; one that addresses the many interwoven elements that commonly affects the eventual succession of local businesses in an economy. If this is applied, the real time and resources on this subject economic development will spawn many very sexy outcomes, commonly thought only possible through new business attraction. This approach will also build tremendous value for the economic development organization within the existing business community; thus creating a sustainable force to continue proactive economic development within this community. In order to be affective, monitoring and tracking various resources and matching these to the proper needs of the business community is essential. Gaining knowledge for this process is step one. From this, gaining understanding and finding a track to build experience will bring success while navigating these waters.

Far too many businesses are closed and liquidated because economic developers did not do a proper job of identifying the issue of succession needs. There was no building of the appropriate assistances to address such needs. This has been a real local travesty that many times could have been avoided.

Chapter Sixteen

"Hybrid Capitalization for Economic Development Purposes: Cash is King in the Global Economy; it Builds Flexible Capabilities and Mitigates Growth Barriers. Those who have the Gold will make the Rules . . . Do you have the Midas Touch in Economic Development? Can you develop it?"

The rules for engagement, in the global competition for economic development deals has not changed, but make no mistake, it has been exponentially intensified. No matter what is heard from corporate executives and site location consultants, it is all about the bottom line and how the economic development packages can adjust in a positive way, the net profit a company has for making, distributing, and developing its products. The best business climates all have their shortfalls, so each must be looked at uniquely; thus economic development incentive plans have to be flexible and customized in order to fit the needs of each end benefactor. This does not mean local economic developers should blindly throw incentives on the table; this would be like throwing paint against a wall, covering some spots but missing others so it looks sloppy, and this will not meet the expectations for any client.

The first rule is to create a realistic basis for an approved jurisdiction's incentive policy. This policy cannot be set in stone, but it should better provide guidelines for how and what is to be considered when considering the use of incentives, mitigate economic growth barriers, or close key deals by lowering risks associated with the new project in the locale. This is the "cost of opportunity model," and these funds should not be reserved for new business attractions alone but also the retention and expansion of existing local core industries.

Common Metrics for consideration are as follows;

> ***Job creation***: not just the quantity but the quality of jobs being created. Are they higher than the average wage for the area, and will they provide key benefits, such as healthcare, retirement, and daycare?

Economic Investment: perhaps the most important measurement is how much and of what type of facilities, machinery, technology, and equipment is the company proposing to invest its monies into? How does this create a competitive advantage for this company, in the global marketplace?

Economic Impact: is essential to truly understand how and in what manner this company will positively impact the community as far as employment, enhanced tax bases, leverage in the growth of other ancillary industries, and the diversification on the local economy. These are measured in both indirect and direct fashion; direct being directly connected to the company, and indirect being caused by the company in a ripple-type effect on all other industries in the local and state economy.

ROI strategy: is the most important equation to figure. How does this company create real accessible cash flow within the coffers of the local and state government, and how would such funds be extended, paid back, or absorbed back into the economic development stream of cash that affects its constituents? This is better when it is not intangible but actual cash flow benefits.

The second rule is to understand what types of industries and basic economic development activities should receive capitalization assistance, incentives, and inducements, and how these are important to the local economy. The trick is to address the key sectors of business growth from the rudimentary base level. Understand first who owns and makes local decisions with regard to the existing companies in this economy. Which companies are controlled by outsiders from afar? Of these companies, which are what we refer to as "Core Industries"? These types of industries make products and perform services that are utilized and delivered primarily to others outside the local market, so there is an in-flow of cash to the region that is then spent in the local market. It is not that other industries are not important, but Core Industries are the most critical; therefore, they deserve the largest share of focus. Sub-section to this second rule; economic developers cannot be all things equally to all people, there is a hierarchy and discriminatory basis to when and what actions deserve incentives, inducements, and capitalization risks.

Furthermore, it is a myth to believe the state is the deciding factor in most economic development deals. Except for the extraordinary large transactions, this pressure falls to the knowledge and resourcefulness of the local economic development leadership, so waiting or depending on state or federal assistance to address capitalization, inducements, and incentives should be made explicitly for the community by the economic developer's own innovation and ingenuity.

Then there is a basis for action. This is where the question of needs versus expectations and the role of philanthropists versus traditional capital takes place. What is the right relationship between philanthropists and investors while bridging the traditional chasm of doing good (philanthropy) with doing well (business/financial markets) to enhance the quality of life for our residents? Is there a need for "smart subsidies" where philanthropists subsidize for-profit socially beneficial enterprise development to address the most pressing social, economic, and environmental challenges? What is the basis for such private sector-led initiatives and how do benefits flow from both sides of the equation so there is an equilibrium achieved for economic justification?

There needs to be the ability to provide those with money a real reason or basis for investing in activities that have vague or indirect benefits to their over-all preservation of their own economic well being. To create hybrid capital in a market, there is a need to know the tipping points for such decisions, and providing realistic motivation that involves raising the cash to fund economic development activities that benefit the community and its investors. Since no community is an ideal cookie-cutter candidate for these remedies, this approach has to be well developed and thought out from a community's unique perspective and willingness to accept some risks and embrace the uncomfortable process of change and paradigm shifting.

Return on Investment Philosophies:

Premise

The model for future economic prosperity has changed in this global economy. In the previous model (Old Economy), the production of goods was based on proximity to raw materials and limited distribution channels. Abundant labor chased growing businesses to whatever location these businesses set up their operations. Capital supplanted labor in order to increase productivity and, in turn, profits and wages. The brawn of men and women created the economic advantage for these industries, within the realm of the local workforce. Geographic location mattered more than it does today.

The new model (New Economy) is based on ideas, creativity, innovation and an interconnectivity to the vast worldwide marketplace. Political borders matter little in developing, deploying, and delivering products and services. Today, successful businesses chase a scarcity of skilled, available workers. Skilled workers are attracted to places with high life qualities, and rich cultural and recreational environments. The importance of location has shifted to the worker and away from the industry. New economy communities are experts at shifting paradigms and reinventing the current reality while not being mired in past practices and failed methods for creating economic growth.

The first thing to being an entrepreneurial community that grows and develops, that creates worth, that generates higher standards of living and good jobs is understanding this doesn't come from big factories, big assembly lines, or stocks of raw materials. There is only one asset: people. People are core to economic competitiveness. Places that harness the creativity of their people, mobilize the creativity of their people, develop and attract creative people will win. In this sense, place (community, city, town) is critical.

Prosperous places need functioning ecosystems, habitats, or an environment that not only develop creative people but also attracts, retains, gives reason to stay, and gives reasons to engage in the development and building of new businesses. (**Richard Florida**, Author, Economist & Creative Class Consultant, Washington, DC)

Old Economy

The Old Economy was based on a competitive cost race to the bottom in order to secure and hold a market. It was driven by bottom line profits at the expense of human toil. The competition has become so fierce that it has constricted community wealth and its means to supply government services. At the same time, maintaining a high quality of life was nearly impossible. Because of global competition, the equilibrium of equitable wealth is at risk for its citizens. New models need to abandon past economic development practices and embrace innovative risks of adverse models that will level the local playing field.

New Economy

The New Economy is based on knowledge and its abundance, or on an economic opportunity worldwide theory; the concept that collaboration will grow the pie sufficiently large enough to serve an ample piece to everyone willing to participate by adding their skills to the equation. A skilled workforce is imperative in this economic model to attract and retain economic investments in a community. Creativity and innovation, coupled with entrepreneurship and risk capital, generate high value-added products. These products yield higher profit margins, better pay (livable wages that exceed old economy jobs), and more community wealth, if executed properly so as to impact the dislocated and incumbent workforce. New world-class communities need to understand and embrace this economic development model if they want to succeed and thrive in the global economy.

Socio-Economic Gap

New economic development models lack a sufficiently skilled workforce to operate optimally in this new economy. New workers must acquire and master both basic and advanced educational skills, and a skills-based professional training. Furthermore, because of inherent demographic forces and trends (loss of the best and brightest to other realms), new economic development models must attract skilled workers to the region and repatriate those who have departed earlier, leaving family and friends in the region behind. Skilled workers are attracted to culturally enriched environments that are economically rewarding, fun to live in, and provide superior amenities for their lifestyles. New economy participants, though highly mobile and risk oriented, do not have an image of such an environment, so their minds can be swayed by media and tourism oriented experiences. Though it is difficult to make the transition while communities struggle to pay for services to existing residents, there must be a stretch to invest in a new infrastructure amenity that will not overly burden these residents for those being sought. In order for a world-class community to be capable of maintaining its cherished high quality of life, it must respond to such capital challenges without ducking the issue. Many politicians do not want to make these difficult decisions on their watch, and they hope the answer will come from some other source; the proverbial market forces so called upon to solve all of today's public problems. The New economy has already shown its response for how businesses flow to the most favorable location with the easiest access to operational success and lowest cost for production, distribution, and sales.

> *America's workforce will begin its journey without a map. Some roads will be superhighways and others will be dead ends, causing American workers to embark on a mysterious voyage. They will travel along roads with many pitfalls and unexpected diversions, and many workers will be stymied by these pitfalls and baffled by these diversions, causing their standard of living to become stagnate or to decline. The American workforce is in need of a map to its best destinations.* **(Richard (Dick) Judy,** *Author & Workforce Consultant, Indianapolis, IN)*

Task

There must be a move toward a new economy model. In order to do this, a community needs to: 1) raise the skill level of its workforce, 2) create high value-added products, 3) collaborate across all sectors, 4) plan economic development for its region, and 5) promote an image to retain and attract skilled workers and new economy businesses. This new economic model not only needs to build new economy industry clusters based upon the existing industry set but also create new industries in the region.

Challenges

The New economy has three primary economic challenges: a tightening labor market, a falling relative per capita income level, and an unfavorable educational attainment level for new workforce entrants. There is a global scarcity of talented labor, indicated by the increasing spread in earnings for education attainment between the "have and have not." Given this, the new economy, one based on knowledge, is dependent upon talented workers, educational attainment, and realistic workforce skills, and this will become increasingly important in the future. Higher skilled workers command higher incomes, and these skills are not easily transferred to the recently dislocated workers. Skilled workers are attracted to communities with rich working and living environments. New economy economic development models need to attract skilled workers that meet the needs of industry and raise per capita incomes. This is a different economic development paradigm than has ever before been developed.

Recommendations

- New economic models must abandon the economic strategy of a cost race to the bottom and embrace the concept of future economic abundance theory. This is best and most efficiently accomplished through proactive collaboration across all sectors in the region; business, labor, government, education, and the general populace. Building awareness must be done, not in a fear-mongering mode, but one of leadership to the next level of success for all residents.
- New economic development models need to reengage the very things that made the regional economy vibrant in the past to make its economy vibrant in the future. This will mean risk-taking capital, technological innovation, individual entrepreneurial activities, advanced cost-effective infrastructure, and desirable workforce members will be the fundamental building blocks of the new economy.
- In order for disparate groups to work together, they need a common vision. However, developing consensus can be slow (sometimes too slow), so fearless leaders must know when to act and lead with decisiveness. This vision should be bold and all encompassing in order to raise the bar for the

entire economy. The region should initiate an economic development plan that brings all facets of the region's resources together while maintaining the quality of life and not risking further decline or stagnation.
- Proactive collaboration in world-class communities requires an opening of the region's mindset, both socially and culturally, to take calculated risks in the growth of their economic opportunities. Cultural diversity is the key to the melding of fresh ideas, best practices, and collaboration, but it requires a realistic approach to immigration. This diversity has worked in the country and the regions of our country in the past, and it will work in the future. Once again, attracting the best and brightest from abroad is a beacon to those who seek a higher quality of life.
- New world-class economic development models must also develop both an internal and external image that promotes their economy's resourcefulness, their high quality amenities, and their lifestyle benefits in its region. Inventorying and promoting the richness of a region's assets will help to retain and attract businesses and workers to the area.

Concepts

The unifying concepts that underlie the economic development strategies involve a movement to new economy building blocks and proactive collaboration across new world-class economic development boundaries. Initiated together, these concepts will set the foundation for economic prosperity in any region executing such tactics.

> *The Global Entrepreneurship Monitor tracks seed and venture investments. $21 billion of private venture capital is invested annually in approximately 2,500 businesses. In contrast, $107.8 billion is invested per year in millions of new ventures started by family members, work colleagues, and friends. Five percent of the general population is an informal investor business development. Savvy states and forward thinking localities are working to harness and nurture that much larger source of capital through angel networks, venture forums, and investor training. Localities with limited capital can use their capital where it matters most, by filling gaps in the financing chain, correcting or compensating for market failures and inequities, building the capacity of local investors, and increasing the success of investments.* (**Diane Lupke**, *National Economic Development Consultant, Evanston, IL*)

The new economy building blocks are brain power, risk capital, technological innovation, advanced infrastructure, and entrepreneurship. These new economy building blocks must be incorporated within the mindset of local economic abundance theory in order to be successful. Business, labor, government, education, and the community must all work actively together under a common vision in order to harness the resources available within these regions (and some outside these regions), and this will drive future economic growth and create world-class economic outcomes. There should be five strategies developed for the new economic development opportunities model, and the following should incorporate these basic tenets:

- *Strategy I—* Move to a New Economy Blueprint in order to construct the necessary elements.
- *Strategy II—* Move to a Collaborative Economic Development environment with all associated agencies in a region and share the workload in an accountable performance-based model where roles are defined and expectations managed.
- *Strategy III—* Change Social and Cultural Mindset to Calculated Shared Risk and Collaboration for improvements to shift the paradigm for future abundance.
- *Strategy IV—* Change Regional Image to nothing less than positive and world-class expectations that will improve everyone's plight, not just the elite or those in control of today's governance. Everyone must believe an abundant economic wealth will flow to them when they accept today's risk for the tomorrow's promised awards. Being accountable is essential in this step.
- *Strategy V—* Promote Diverse Core Industry focuses on the necessary drivers of the local existing economy that can and should survive and thrive and those that are missing and necessary to grow additional economic diversity in the future.
- *Strategy VI—* Develop a quarterly and annual report card system that can be used as part of the public relations campaign to educate the general public of the elected and appointed officials in the progress of being made. This should include realistic and measurable metrics and milestones tied to goals and objectives linked to a time-line. This will build public and organizational trust for the endeavor and provide insight when mitigation and modifications become necessary.

Execution

Installing and instilling these strategies will not be accomplished quickly, suddenly, or without cost. A long-term action plan needs to be developed, and the pieces should be developed as a blueprint of budgeted expenses and accountable metrics and milestones that can quantify a return of investment to the citizens. Adhering to the plan will not mean it can't be altered as situations in the region change. Developing and executing such plans requires constant evolution, a willingness to be flexible and open to new knowledge gained through experience, adoption of best practices, and the avoidance and mitigation of worst practices. It means continual and lasting effort must be applied over the course of the next ten to twenty years, to monitor an economy, comparatively assess its trends, and take proactive collaborative actions to adjust the path of a world-class community's and/or region's success.

First and foremost, there must be a recognized necessary targeted capital intensive area of need that a sustainable economic development model must address; a Locating Funding Sources for specific uses. Types of Core Economic Activities that need Hybrid Capitalization are as follows;

Small Business loans to retain and grow existing businesses in the economy:
    Best practice example—*Revolving loan fund* leveraged with national pools for leverage of local capital. Instead of investing precious funds in a few deals, have an exponentially larger net to cast and greatly enhance markets gap capital, secondary collateral capital, or mezzanine capital needs by using such tools.

Innovative knowledge-based new economic models for business development that are cutting edge and emerging business concepts with unproven markets for commercialization purposes:
    Best practice example—*Community Seed & Venture Funds* that invest in the expansion of patentable knowledge-based products and also qualify for SBIOR funding. These funds can hire expert consultants to best assess and assemble the business model for presentation to additional funding sources as well as patent the concept legally.

Entrepreneurial individuals who wish to acquire, expand, or start-up a business endeavors in the region that is within a core industry and help further diversify the economy:
    Best practice example—These deals are the most difficult to fund; however, they can provide the most rewards to both community and individual alike. Grown at home businesses tend to stay at home. The development of an *Angel Fund or Network* can be a very attractive asset for the local economy. Such activities can be coordinated and designed at the cost of the local economic development organization and participation can be matched on a case by case basis, along with other angel investors, as deals become ready for funding approval.

Retention and expansion of existing businesses that need to retool and rework their business model to evolve and succeed by today's global standards:
   Best practice example—Targeted incentives such as low interest loans, tax abatements, and tax increment financing for new investments made by the company. This requires the use of several pools, such as a revolving loan fund, and other incentives; perhaps tax credits, employment tax increment funding, sales tax abatements, fee forgiveness for permits and property tax rebates, and abatements in unison. In addition, funds can be created to address local workforce recruitment and training such as work skills assessments, key employee recruitment, and employment needs profiling in order to match available workforce members who may be currently dislocated or under-employed and seeking employment.

Attraction of new business investment for projects and core industry opportunities that will create quality jobs, economic expansion, diversification, and global outreach to commercial markets:
   Best practice example—This needs a full arsenal of tools, but at the nub of the matter is the need for flexible cash response to unique situations that might enhance the attractiveness of a deal to a prospective client or mitigate the risks relocating to a community. This does not normally fit the traditional revolving loan fund model, so it will need a unique approach. This can be achieved by developing what is commonly referred to as an "Opportunity Fund." These funds provide cash to purchase various elements that are very necessary in attracting new deals, including such amenities as land grants, workforce recruitment, skills testing and profiling, key employee relocation, low interest or cash grants to offset start-up costs, environmental, architectural, and engineering design of a site, and proposed facilities, including technology and automation processes. Relocation and financing of new equipment and machinery as well as transport of such existing machinery and equipment into the new location for relocation is essential. Additional enhancement might also address the sale and disposal of older dinosaur facilities, if their relocation and expansion results in the closure of another, or several other, location.

Physical Infrastructure and Facilities for the attraction of new business opportunities is essential in developing a world-class economic development strategy:
   Best practice example—Creating shovel ready land (fully improved with infrastructure at the curb and fully permitted sites) and, in some cases, speculative facilities for certain niche industries such as manufacturing, warehousing, call centers, and business incubators with a low, front-end risk cost of acquisition to the company are key catalysts for attracting

core industries to a community. If these types of scenarios can be done in conjunction with land grants and/or leaseback purchase incentives, they could attract some highly viable industry clients. Speed in the marketplace and quality actionable physical assets are key decisive factors. The use of opportunity funds in conjunction with local non-profit and/or industrial development bonds can be a decisive advantage; a path to profitable economic development.

In order to level the playing field of competition, there needs to be an understanding of economic justifications; what drives an economy and why. The age-old theory is compete or don't compete. The choice, for some, is to set the resolve to none-participation in such ploys to attract new opportunities, and as such, show a disdain for such uses of funds. Over-all, those that choose to take this course have not seen their economy grow as robustly as others, not now, nor have they realized the positive economic benefits of such resolve, and this is especially true in many Northern and Plains States. Their failure to address business incentives and retention strategies resulted in two major outcomes over the past two decades: an increased outsourcing and over-seas deployment of their traditional business base causing severe hardships for the working middle class, and the flight of old core businesses to new growth and investment opportunities into the "Business Friendly Southern States." Again, the citizens in these states are indeed less well off today and financially stressed, and many experience increased family pressures and additional strains in our social and governmental infrastructure.

Have these States' staunch resolve or failure to react appropriately been worth this posture to those who matter most? Do they feel that the refusal to raise the bar was worth their plight today? I think most would say, in hindsight, work should have been done to fix the situation and remedy the need to relocate. Again, cash is king in building a competitive response to threats like these to our local economies, both today and in the future, and the war chest needs to be filled, utilized accordingly, and sustainable through ROI strategies to re-circulate such investments as the funds return to the local economies.

No longer will the trickle down affect be effective. Focused pinpoint targeting now has the highest positive affect on local economies. Today's entire military doctrine is based on the pinpoint accuracy of the necessary force and the lethal dosage of might to crush opposing forces. To implement economic development, there must be an approach to goals and endeavors with this same pinpoint accuracy and focus. There must be focus on the catalyst opportunities that simultaneously reduce or eliminate barriers for economic growth, reduce entry costs and risks to new investments, and produce responsible outcomes for the citizens, such as economic opportunity to quality wages and jobs. This focus will then determine which investments will spawn the greatest over-all leverage within the region to grow ancillary investments resulting in the same. The final evaluation is whether the investment is one that is sustainable and environmentally suitable for the community. These parameters are the basis for how responsible world-class communities determine economic justification for the use of hybrid capital, publicly endorsed and supported inducements, and incentives for business development.

If the investment cannot be measured in such a way that these opportunities out weigh the risk of such investments and/or the cost of doing so undermines the ability to deliver and maintain other critical quality of life elements within the economy, then they are truly not well thought out. There must be the utilization of hybrid capital needs in the maintenance and improvement of local infrastructure, educational systems, heritage and cultural amenities, recreational outlets, and green space.

In order to win the economic war for deals, there must be lots of capital for different venues. Sources for growing and supporting local economic development infrastructure and paying for the cost of new investment opportunities is based on creating accessible readily available pools of capital that are at the discretionary control of the local economic development leadership and their partners. While many economic developers know these following actions are truly necessary, their normal response for not creating them or implementing such a Hybrid Capital structure are very similar; there is not enough cash to sufficiently do the job, there is no political support, nor is there the understanding of the necessity to implement this approach, and because the situation is different, there are assets and amenities that overcome the need for such capital.

However, these responses are somewhat based on the naïve understanding of the global market place or a lack of today's realities. In addition, there is the fear of change and professional risks for trying to lead a community and its leadership through these perilous times. Nonetheless, focus on leadership, tactical executions for well honed strategies, and flexible risk funds for investments are the key to survival in today's global economy.

There are many types of economic development funds, but these are commonly over looked or inappropriately used through impractical practices. These are a few of the sources for potential funding:

- Revolving Loan Funds-

    o Banks pools of capital and grants
    o Federal grants
    o Loan and application origination fees
    o Interest rate surcharges

- o Municipal/County grants/loans
- o Fundraising campaign for investor models
- o Bond surcharge on IDBs

- Micro-Enterprise Innovation funds-

  - o Bank pools to gain CRA credits
  - o Private foundation grants
  - o Municipal/County grants/loans
  - o Fundraising campaign for investor models
  - o Bond surcharge on IDBs
  - o Origination/application fees
  - o Interest rate surcharges

- Community based Seed & Venture funds-

  - o Federal and State grants
  - o Private foundation grants
  - o Municipal/County grants/loans
  - o Bond surcharges on IDBs
  - o Interest rate surcharges
  - o Exit strategy equity recoveries, in addition to preferred dividends with exit clauses
  - o Fundraising campaign for investor models

- Angel Funds-

  - o Municipal/County grants/loans
  - o Bond Surcharge on IDBs
  - o Interest rate surcharges
  - o Exit strategy equity recoveries, in addition to preferred dividends with exit clauses
  - o Private Placement Memorandum with qualified investors
  - o Fundraising campaign for investor models

- Business Expansion Funds (M&A partnerships)-

  - o Municipal/County grants/loans
  - o Bond surcharge on IDBs
  - o Fundraising campaign for investor models

- Opportunity Funds-

    o Municipal/County grants/loans
    o Fundraising campaign for investor models
    o Employment payroll taxes
    o Special use economic development sales taxes
    o Tax Credit programs (if applicable)

- Speculative Land & Facilities Funds-

    o Non-Profit bond allocations
    o Municipal/County grants/loans or underwriting of debts
    o Investor backed public private partnerships
    o Private Placement Memorandum with qualified investors
    o Fundraising campaign for investor models
    o Tax credit programs (if applicable)

- Public Policy advocacy Funds-

    o Private Sector donations and political awareness events
    o Fundraising campaign investor models

Furthermore, there are many tactical strategies for victory. Those who want to be the victor in this high stakes game need to look over the horizon and anticipate where others will go and why. Once there has been the anticipation for the desires of others, roads of needs can be built within the community. Success cannot be achieved while remaining rooted in practices and mindsets of the past. World-class communities look ahead and make strategic investments in order to create competitive advantages that separate them from the mire of other communities that lack this same forward thinking vision, focus, and resourcefulness.

Strategy and focus are essential to this execution. There must be an understanding to what drives both today's and tomorrow's economy and where each critical cross-over opportunity exists in order to bridge current economic investment opportunities with unique outcomes that build critical mass for future emerging business investments. This requires the knowledge of market conditions, both locally and globally, to understand the forces at play. This resolve can only be honed through networking and seeking information, through discussions and reviews of leading informational sources that build awareness and understanding. There is no substitution for experience; this can only be gained by taking action and learning from both errors and successes. Retreat or surrender is never an acceptable outcome, only redeployment, mitigation, and progress will suffice.

There must be an exploitation of intelligent opportunities, and this can only be achieved by the use of cash to purchase relevant information and advice from the subject matter experts who exist in chosen niche opportunities; thus creating a unique hybrid strategy to use this intelligence to its advantage. Other SMEs have a broader knowledge of the market forces and should be chosen because they possess experience in dealing with such matters successfully. From their sage advice, a decision can be made as to what is worth honing and modifying and what should be avoided and why. This knowledge helps calculate the risk before employing the use of precious Hybrid Capital funds. Most of today's economic developers let the winds of fate push them and their ships against the rocks instead of harnessing the winds of global forces in order to navigate such storms and exploit the port of opportunity just over the horizon. Economic developers must solve their own problem strategies, which, in reality, is the unwillingness of politicians and local leaders who cannot admit not knowing what to do and unwilling to tell the public the truth about such and/or the necessary expense required to change the realities of their local economy. Cheap intelligence causes more waste and money spent than is prudent or wise.

Understanding and mitigating barriers to economic growth is the art and science of well-founded economic development practice. If there is no comprehension for what is realistically wrong with an economy, there is most likely no knowledge of what is right and why. There is no excuse for not understanding the SWOT analysis of a local economy and then knowing what steps to take in order to address each element identified in this analysis. Again, getting an outside, professional perspective, both unbiased and un-jaded by local opinions, is critical to understanding a starting point, developing an understanding of what capital will be needed and why, creating positive change and exploiting the low hanging fruits of opportunities, in fact:

> *Economic developers need to use their political leaderships to bring financial institutions, corporate, and community foundations into a room, and then develop a business plan that will develop our business community to build "patient" capital.* (**Mark Barbash**, *Professional Economic Developer, Columbus, OH*)

However, a decisive and fearless leadership is the critical missing element in today's communities. There is simply far too much apathy and paralysis today, so there is no gain to the understanding of what needs to be done and why; therefore there is no forging the plan to take action and remedy the situation before our leaders. The lack of attention to reality is undermining the abilities to respond to global threats in local economies. There is no substitution for leaders who step forward and set the pace to conquer the hill. These conquerors will step out and ask others to follow them without fear of reprisal or embarrassment to their constituents. They know well and good that they cannot get everyone to follow or wait for consensus prior to taking action. They also understand that others will follow when they see the resolve that inspires them to be part of the winning strategy. But they have to be willing, at first, to be the heal that steps gallantly when others wont, knowing they will be the eventual hero once they have taken the initiative without the support of their constituents who are mired in lost and impractical practices and expectations that will never come to pass again.

Yet who's to say this can't be fun and rewarding to those involved? While there are both risks and rewards to these calculated investments and the development of catalyst projects supported by new Hybrid Pots of Capital, there are windfalls. This process can be both exhilarating and exhaustive, but its process can be enjoyable. Engage others and create networking and brainstorming experiences that allow others to become a part of this metamorphic paradigm shift. Create new social events that build both the awareness of this need and the charted course for this new success while simultaneously building local capacity. Engage creatively and build the necessary players in this game of changing the outcomes of the local economy. When reality sets in and there is actual attainment, there will be many local friends and heroes to share in the revelry of this new success, and this experience will be much more rich and enjoyable when it is designed in a fun environment from the start. This legacy will spawn future local pioneers that will reshape the next economic expansion, and this institutional knowledge will build good will for future generations that will rise and take the challenge when their time comes.

Chapter Seventeen

"Rural Economic Development Renaissance: *Leveling the Playing Field for Equilibrium in Rural Economic Development*"

The mere mention of the word "rural" sends a mental picture to mind. The transfer of populations between rural, primarily agrarian based, economies to the urban cities, once the bastion of capitalism, has been enormous in the US. Even China faces this same transfer of populations. Many people fail to understand that more than 70% of the world's populations live in urbanized areas.

However, in the last decade, many US companies have found a renewed interest in rural areas. Yet still the trend is to locate in rural areas that are not backward in their political leadership, infrastructure deployment, workforce initiative, and quality of life amenities, such as cultural and safety influences. Today, many rural locations offer exactly what businesses say they need to be competitive; a low cost operating business climate, an available, affordable workforce with good work ethics, and a high quality of life.

With the added pressure of terrorism, political unrest and cost of energy will all increase, so rural locations are meriting a second look from major corporations before they outsource or go abroad; their key components today. In fact, in the future, many multi-national companies are going to choose to build in or very near to their markets for just these same reasons. The rural renaissance will be largely driven by this coming trend in the new manufacturing model. This is already being demonstrated by the Japanese, soon to be followed by the Europeans, and then the Chinese and East Indian will follow.

Many city dwellers might ask how culture can be rural. This is a problem and an opportunity many small communities face. Rural does not have to mean backward and remote. In fact, many site location projects are targeting rural unincorporated areas that are within 60 or 90 minutes from a major metropolitan area. There is no doubt, rural areas present many unique challenges to both survival in the global era and a community's thrive to get ahead. Rural areas are perceived to have a lower quality of life, and many urban dwellers who make this transition find the local leadership and social networks to be narrow minded toward new comers. In addition, the cultural issues that create a sense of a well-rounded place are more difficult in small communities. The access to theater and performing arts can be limited, but it can also be exceptional in towns that recognize art as culture, bringing with it a real sense of community. This same close-knit society also builds a sense of safety amongst its residents, yet it breeds outsider feeling for those new to the community. Overcoming this barrier is paramount. Meeting these challenges to open rural economies for the best and brightest to flourish will create new havens for quality of life fiefdoms. Each social group, the old timers and new timers, will need to depend on one another if they are to be competitive in the global era.

In addition to facing these social and cultural civic issues, rural communities have to be fearless in their resolve to address the key components that build competitive, modern economies and the necessary infrastructure required to succeed. There are several key tenets present in a rural economy that, if left to market forces, are amplified in their exposure to risk. If these tenets are not attended to, investments won't be made in most rural environments. The expectations for outcomes in a rural area are scrutinized even more rigorously. The following are basic examples of how rural communities can wage a campaign to increase their own value in the face of intense global competition for business retention and new business development.

Inward investment in the redevelopment of the areas existing retail, service, recreational, and cultural amenities is an absolute requirement. Rural communities cannot afford to leave such decisions and capital investments to chance. There has to be a specific game plan to address key investments to retool and improve existing businesses and the quality of life amenities, and part of this is this includes educational systems.

Creating a capital plan to attract funds to redevelop the downtown areas and improve the quality of life, including culture, function, expectations for shopping, and recreational environments. Historic heritage is important. Not every town has to have a unique place-based attraction, but they need to care about their local history enough to want to allow others to view key elements and periods of their history; this will build a sense of awareness, pride, and belonging. Every community needs what I refer to as a basic game plan of fundamental core concepts as starting points.

Develop streetscape designs, façades, signage, and landscaping requirements that denote a sense of pride and stylistic values important to residents. In most cases, the windfall to this is higher property values. Cutting-edge communities are constantly developing inward investment opportunities to funnel grants and loans toward this agenda, like small city community development block grants, affordable mixed retail lower floor and residential upper floor tax credit projects, historic redevelopment tax credit projects, and low interest revolving loan funds aimed at such projects from the country and/or its municipality.

Innovation and Entrepreneurial—Though many small communities always think small means not being able to do all the same things urban centers do, just the opposite is true. One cannot afford to have one's oars of the water in all aspects of economic development. To not have a stake in the new emerging knowledge economy is to set communities up for ultimate decline and eventual mothballs. Finding and creating a unique business incubation center to allow young or budding entrepreneurs to grow and flourish is a good starting point. Tying such centers, if possible, to a university, colleges and community colleges is a great foundation, even if it is done remotely. These centers need high-tech infrastructure, tools, and shared services to allow them to compete. Funding knowledge-based new research and development is a great secondary investment. This can entail funding competitive grants for SBIOR applications and specialized consultants in the preparation of such grants and linking these entrepreneurs to others in the field can greatly enhance the grown of at home markets for new ideas. In some states, competitions are held, such as in Arizona and in others, like Kentucky, states match their SBIOR award funds. States with large rural components should heavily consider this model approach to innovation. However, communities shouldn't wait for their states because this can be implemented and done on a community basis as well.

Workforce and Education Alliance—In a rural environment, resources are precious and usually sufficient if there is focus on accomplishing the task of addressing the needs for a modern workforce. Get back to the basics. Just as Germany and other European countries have done, our nation needs to approach education as the initial building block to a life-long process. There is a need to prepare pre-workforce members for employment in economic reality and the preparation of life-skills for each individual. There must be focus on the awareness of local economy and its existing industries and how they interconnect to the world economy. Then there will be the need to create alliances within the industries for apprenticeships and school-to-work program placements. Encouraging even college-bound students to get some work experience to better prepare them for the eventual reality of work is also important. Incorporating a joint education and employment work skills certification and assessment system, such as ACT Work-Keys, is also a good approach. This allows young students with current skills to interact with those necessary for certain occupations so they understand their areas of improvement, reach their goals, and know where they should seek current employment for jobs. This better matches our youth to meaningful employment rather than quantity-based employment that keep them flipping burgers their only choice. Using a skills assessment and employment certification system is not expensive, and it pays huge dividends once the infrastructure is in place. The ability to match youth to meaningful employment is critical to expanding and increasing experiences. The local reluctance to this is kids are tested enough and there is no authority or resources to test them further, but this type of program can be paid for through an economic development initiative, with the school board's approval. This testing will provide yet another means of holding the school board accountable for educational outcomes. But educators are also going to have to be part of this solution if we are to win.

Once a program like this is developed, it can easily be incorporated into an incumbent and dislocated workforce initiative at the community college level. The same holds true for those currently under-employed or unemployed. The faster these folks can be matched to dignified and meaningful employment the better off they and their families will be. There are many people out there who know they are underemployed, but they have no means of demonstrating this. The skills certifications give them a quantifiable manner in which to do so. The importance of getting employers to do occupational profiles is the underlying strength of this approach. If employers are not willing to be part of the solution, they need to quit complaining about educational results.

High-tech infrastructure—Building a high tech infrastructure is necessary. In some ways, small towns and cities have some advantages because they have less area to deploy and they have fewer competitors to negotiate with in their market, to achieve their provisioning. An essential roll-out includes high speed WI-FI spread spectrum networks that cover their downtown and even its outlying areas, so the entire community can not only plug in but also look and feel high-tech to visitors. Negotiating for high bandwidth digital fiber networks as part of an agreed upon utility improvements is also a possibility. As a community, a franchise can be passed for the requirement that all improvements must be underground by a certain date, and as such, must be modernized to the newest state of the art systems. These stacked wet and dry conduits not only allow for easier future modernization, but they also protect the grid against environmental damage. This means the community must partner with utility providers to find and fund new deployments in partnership with entrepreneurial attitude. These investments will allow the community and the utility to upgrade their appeal to new customers, adding new users.

Arts and Culture—Small towns' people don't have to act like "Red Neck Hicks," even though culture is an important element for place and pride in a community. Creating performing arts venues, visual arts displays and shows, craftsmanship artist fairs, and art studios can be a real upbeat element to any community. These allow for outlets other than merely commerce to occur. Some communities go as far as to create artist colonies and incubators to demonstrate this resolve. The building of a community theater or a visual arts center speaks bundles to the potential best and brightest new residents. The lack thereof will also cause many to overlook a community. If given a choice, potential residents will flock to communities with these amenities. Coupling these amenities with the redevelopment of a historic facility can achieve a double reward for a community.

Small Business Assistance—The biggest factor to growing a small business community is making sure it has access to capital. In addition, plugging this community into outside opportunities for assistance, like manufacturing extension partnerships, retail networks, educational technology transfer-based knowledge tools, innovation capitalization for new ideas, seed capital for new budding companies, and angels for start-ups, is essential. Even more important, developing skills in dealing with globalized markets, such as export assistance, is also essential. Distance to a metro is no excuse in the internet-enabled era for accessing the resources available. Often, the single biggest issue is access to affordable capital. Most communities approach the establishment of their revolving loan funds either as a corporate welfare system or an all in loan fund. In fact, in many cases, leveraging these funds with other national markets for capitalization, such as the Community Reinvestment Fund and the New Markets Tax Credit Program can create a leverage factor of 10 to 1. Even with limited resources, if utilized correctly, a small community can have an enormous affect on its local economy.

Furthermore, another big initiative many fail to pursue is simply creating and maintaining their SCORE and the Small Business Development Centers in their area. While their resources are limited, their knowledge and experience can really level the playing field for new or existing businesses to grasp how to best proceed.

Shovel-Ready Sites in a Cutting-Edge Industry Park—Instead of trying to be all things to all people, the most important factor for rural environments is to create a place where they can raise their flag to competition. Once this project is chosen, it must be fully improved for rapid development. All high-tech infrastructure must be at the curb (telecom, electric, gas, water, sewer) and, if necessary, all environmental evaluations must be completed and mitigated. Transportation and logistics (access to interstate, rail, air, and water routes) are paramount assets that must be provided, and this should partially drive the decision for where to plant this competitive flag. Fast-track permitting is essential to corporate decision makers and site location consultants. Availability is not enough, so if there is the possibility, having these sites pre-permitted for certain uses, such as light industrial, is essential. Get third-party endorsements for these shovel-ready sites, using site location experts. Even if a project isn't ready today, chances are it will be in the future and, if nothing else, these third-party endorsements mean something to other site location consultants. One of the major attractions to industry parks, especially those designed from a Greenfield is a campus-like amenity, such as fitness and recreational trails, picnic armadas, and sport's features such as basketball and tennis courts, and even softball, baseball and soccer field complexes can be incorporated into this design. These all can be used by the community, after hours, so again, multi-tasking pays-off. Green space is a great soft sell amenity. Let the parks and recreational staff members maintain them, and this will give an even greater benefit to a new industry park. Remember, this park is a commerce showcase, so don't go cheap or it will speak volumes about community pride and civic mind set. One of the most decisive assets can often be the designation of a site or the development of a childcare and daycare facility that can only be used by the tenants of the industry park's employees. This is a great resource for attracting a superior workforce.

Educational Outreach to Higher Education—Being rural and possibly remote does not allow for excuses. Universities and higher educational programs are a must for all residents. If a community doesn't have a community college campus, it should create a specific high-tech facility that will provide these services and negotiate for the delivery of services to its residents. If a community has a community college, make the necessary improvements and partnerships to make sure the most possible is delivered to its local residents. The two most common complaints for the best and brightest crowd are youth exportation and the lack of available higher educational resources. Providing these services sets a community apart from those that lag behind. Education is a strategic, intangible investment that will pay off while attracting high-wage earners to an economy.

Historic Preservation and Historical Education—Many communities, both urban and rural, make the mistake of getting attached to dinosaur facilities that are well beyond their usefulness but cannot be reasonably placed back into service. If a facility lacks significant historic value in a community, it has passed the test of "Raze it or Save it." If a facility has significant historic value, then finding a new and alternative use may be possible. This may require thinking out of the box, but maybe it is time to consider an affordable workforce housing project with "Low Income Housing Tax Credits." This facility may be the perfect place to create an artist colony or incubator, or a traditional business incubator. Perhaps another cultural, historic, or civic center may be needed. There are also other tax credit programs (historic tax credits, new market tax credits, brown-field tax credits) that should be considered, and these can be combined with other resources to maximize capital for redevelopment of such projects. If its original use is not marketable, a needed new niche that can serve multiple needs in the community and maximize community's resources and pride must be found. Once these have all been considered and they still won't work, then the facility can be razed. As Bob Ady once said, "It is the land underneath the facility that is important and the most valuable resource, so don't get caught falling in love with buildings."

Speculative Niche Opportunities—Markets are slow to recognize the value of unproven investment areas, especially those far from their normal routes of consideration. In order to level the playing field, many rural communities pick a niche and create a compelling set of incentives that are valuable to that niche, and then they cast their hook to land these deals. This can include the development of a below market cost speculative building for immediate use and, if chosen, a rapid roll out. Examples can include back-office call centers, light manufacturing buildings, office space with high-tech infrastructure, and distribution buildings for logistics. Making such facilities tenant ready with the most robust capabilities is essential.

Business Retention and Expansion—Since resources are tight in rural environments, the monies and time spent in this area are critical. At a minimum, there are three key components that should be done. First, use a technology platform to address surveying and tracking this business community's responses to best analyze its current economic situations. Use Red Flags for hot situations that need immediate mitigation and solutions to problems; Green Flags for identified opportunities that can create new economic investment business growth and new or retained employment; and Yellow Flags for areas that need further outside investigation and merit watching to see if the situation worsens. Finally, use strategic response team members (SRTs). These volunteers are very important, and training these volunteers to be efficient and proficient in their duties is essential. Reward these volunteers with praise, don't caudle them, and hold them accountable. The last and most important thing that can be done for a business community is keeping everyone educated on core strengths when compared to other markets, communities, and trends to be aware of and how to engage them collectively as a successful community. One of the most effective ways to make sure businesses feel important is to utilize the VIP tour approach; this makes members, both the community's elected and appointed, aware of local business issues and perceptions, keeping things real when making strategic economic development decisions.

Cutting-edge web—Because rural environments are many times overlooked, the most critical element they should possess is an aggressive and proactive marketing campaign that promotes their communities and areas to business decision makers and the site location industry experts. With the new internet-enabled technologies, this is much more available to many communities. The internet has done more to level the playing field for rural economic development than any other single asset. The focus now becomes building a robust, user friendly, and meaningful web site that provides the information users will desire and expect. Then, networking and marketing a community in the places where such decision makers will gather and discuss such investment decisions will more than likely have a better chance of taking place. Trade shows and industry niche gatherings are not the realm of just big city economic developers, and the old adage "Don't Ask Don't Get," should come to mind. If money isn't spent for good marketing, then there is less chance of competing.

Capital Formation—Establishing sustainable funding for initiatives coupled with a business plan approach that outlines the budget necessary to carry out this mission is essential. Once costs are estimated there must be the building of a revenue stream. This can be simple or difficult in its approach. The cost of business or sunk cost is a bad approach whereas the business investment approach is best. Then there must be the recognizing of those whom are giving an extraordinary amount of resources for doing so. Lastly, if the approach is fun and fulfilling to those involved, it will be even more successful. So, celebrate successes and praise volunteers and staff members for their efforts. Provide recognition, not only within the community but externally, in the state and industry. Do the little things to recognize those who help carry the water for this aggressive and proactive approach to economic development.

Some of our biggest successes come from capital campaigns in smaller communities that many underestimate their resolve to get ahead and therefore pay too little attention to them in the scheme of things. (**Terry Cusack**, *National Fundraising Consultant, Jacksonville, FL)*

Being rural does not mean being small-minded. Rural areas do not have to relegate being less of a global player in the economy and opportunities presented to others in urban environments. Being rural means having to strive even harder to not be stereotyped by others and overlooked by the investment world for potential opportunities. In fact, today, these qualities that are often cited as truly necessary to build and operate a new or expanding business opportunity may lie in the rural hinterlands of this country, but it is up to those areas to make their case for consideration. Taking care of their own business is only their concern. No one else owes them an equal opportunity or fair consideration, life is just not played by those rules, and as good as it may sound, it simply is not reality.

Many of these elements, if not all of them, can and should be interconnected to be effective. Those that multi-task and connect the proverbial dots to such opportunities get the greatest bang for the buck. In the end, as I have always said, communities that are winners help themselves, and they don't wait for others to come to their rescue. The rest just decline, become diminished, and eventually board up and blow away.

Chapter Eighteen

"World-Class Communities do World-Class Economic Development: Getting the Job done is Their Playbook for Success."

There is no substitute for solid, diverse and widespread economic development policies and practices for building and sustaining a local economy. When communities look at the best of the best and wonder how they got so lucky in their opportunities and successes in these tough and competitive times, they will find, if they dug deeper, a community that has a "can do" attitude. When this type of attitude is coupled with a leadership that challenges others to step up and be a part of the future, there is a winning combination. Today's world-class communities, no matter what size, have this similar trait. They do not wait for others to ride in and save them. They invent solutions and create opportunities that blaze a path to the future they envision for their communities. They understand calculated risks, catalyst investments, and the value of creating enough local capital to control and design their own destiny. They do not sit on their past successes, and they do not allow set backs to derail their journey.

But this process has to start somewhere; a community commitment to world-class economic development leadership and budgetary assignment of enough meaningful capital to energize the process and sustain it from start to perpetuity. From the professional's perspective, economic development is both rewarding and agonizing. Just as a local economy starts humming, the economy of the day throws new angles and evolutions that cause constant adjustments and reassessments in the playing field. This causes the need to create new plays in the playbook, so the game has to be played all over again. World-class economic development is holistic and diverse in its use of assets and its addressing a large number of simultaneous needs within a community. In addition, world-class economic development is collaborative, and it understands the need to collaborate with other players in order to move the ball forward and address the needs of a community, in the broadest sense. It has to have a wide base to be effective, and it has to be regionally aligned with other local economies in close proximity because they have a linked destiny for helping each other.

Diversity makes a world-class city. Diversity is of course the people, modes of transportation, air, water, land, and excellent educational opportunities from pre-K to graduate programs. Overall, a good quality of life is what matters most to both our best and brightest and our dull and less witty. Everyone wants a better life, and everyone feels they deserve it. (**Greg Owens**, *Professional Economic Developer, Miami, FL*)

Creating knowledge for reality and understanding the realm of possibilities is the starting point for world-class economic development. Understanding the drivers of the local economy and how current situations compare to regional, state, national, and world-level economic output, growth, and trend is essential. Knowing this starting point will build an effective game plan and gauge its progress during the process. This includes understanding what there isn't enough of and what trends will show if current situations continue (the plot line of what could be if this course is continued, or the cost of denial). There must be an understanding of the community's current and future needs, the impact its current economic situation has on its population, and what can be done to create a better quality of life, not just economically but socially, as a community that cares about its residents. World-class communities are places where people want to live, and these people are proud of their communities, and it shows. There is a sense of a symbiotic relationship that runs throughout the social fabric, and visitors can feel this relationship.

A 2005 Report to the US Economic Development Administration from the Council on Competitiveness suggested that over 50% of the U.S. annual GDP is derived from innovation in the economy. This became the thrust of their recommendations to the U.S. administration to empower American community economic development progress at harnessing new opportunities in the global economy. This report pointed out that innovation is occurring much more rapidly than in the past. It is becoming multi-disciplinary in nature because it can now combine industry innovations with bio-tech genetics, nanotech genetics, and nanotech robotics. This new innovative economy is more collaborative because it uses resources from many backgrounds and national origins. It engages customers and employees in finding new opportunities, solutions, and quality control measures to meet the expectations of the market. Most important is the fact that the US is not alone in this high growth competitive game of economic bounty to the winners and huge economic trauma to the losers, it is global in nature. The scary facts, according to the report, are that foreign born inventors and companies account for nearly 50% of all today's patents in the US. Sweden,

> *Finland, Japan, Israel, and South Korea all spend more on research and development as a portion of their GDP than does the US, and in 2004, China overtook the US's lead in the export of information communication technologies (ICT). Only six of the worlds 25 most competitive information communication technology companies are based in the US. And 14 are in Asia. This message carries a warning that America must heed. There is an immediate need to reinvigorate the economic development process and regain and sustain world-class economic prowess in the US. (Economic Development America Summer; 2006. Published by the International Economic Development Council on behalf of the US Economic Development Administration)*

Collaborating and creating linkages with key allies are world-class policies. Communities create a regional strategy to unite their peers in working together to change their future in a positive manner. They share resources and information and create a support system for fueling investments into key innovative projects within the region because they know what helps one partner will build strength for all the partners, and this benefits the whole region. However, the benefits must be equal to all members.

> *The global economic environment that we work in now has all kinds of opportunities and at all different levels. Every city does not operate at the same level in the global environment; therefore, each city has to truly evaluate and understand what its assets are and what market it chooses to target. It's not prudent for a small rural community to have the same targets of interests that an urban city may have. Based on some level of asset evaluation, a community must develop a list of targets that matches its assets and creates an environment, so companies can be successful.* (**Ronnie Bryant**, *Professional Economic Developer, Charlotte, NC*)

It must be mentioned that education is the key to success for economic development. For years, economic development has given business retention and the retention of its workforce and youth talent acknowledgement little more than lip service. In today's economy, human capital is the crucial supreme capital asset to success. A community cannot afford to lose its population (especially its youth) and business operations and continue to focus on filling the pot with merely new business opportunities alone. The remedy for this starts with solid educational experiences, rewarding business opportunities, and cultural amenities that will make the community's youth want to stay rather than seek greener pastures elsewhere. A world-class community focuses on the best educational system money can buy, and it creates the cash to build, grow, and maintain this system. Then there must be the accountability to this educational system to make sure it is performing and producing the results that meet the expectations of the community. These systems need smaller classroom sizes, more computer access, and a more diverse curriculum. They must work to produce better ACT/SAT scores and graduation rates. There must be programs for the at-risk population that will encourage good grades and staying out of trouble. Most importantly, students must be prepared for the workforce through the rewards of advanced opportunities for further education and employment connections.

There must also be the same level of care given to retaining and expanding existing companies in a community. Business retention is powerful because these folks are already invested in the community, and they are bright and innovative, just like those outside of the community that are typically being focused upon for business attraction opportunities. Engaging the existing businesses (retail, manufacturing, services, knowledge-based), especially focusing upon the core industries (those that export things made in the community to other places) is essential. Innovation has to be channeled and challenged at home, and working with the current manufacturing businesses to transition to the realm of advanced manufacturing will help them remain competitive. This will mean community leaders and other agencies involved must understand the business retention strategy; therefore, empowering them with the advanced tools they need will allow them to engage the business audience in their daily interactions.

Train call-teams and outreach personnel from the local community colleges, workforce providers and agencies, universities, chamber of commerce, and other service organizations to be on the look out for strategic information. Create web-based information portals that will collect information with each log in and will debrief each meeting with a business manager or owner. Send teams out with PDA-based email enabled information templates that can be used to gather information, instantaneously, for each visitation call. Create a responsive and aggressive customer care follow-up to these missions and intelligence assets.

Link each business with a possible solution and resource providers that will power the desire to create and expand. Business retention and expansion can be sexy, as well. Many entrepreneurial new markets can be uncovered and created from these existing businesses, if they are given the support to grow such ideas. In addition, the potential to create new entrepreneurial ownership for smaller businesses that may have owners with succession or retirement issues can be a huge boon to the local economy. These can all be cultivated and expanded upon in non-traditional approaches to out of the box business retention and expansion strategies.

World-class communities also have a depth of focus for creating multiple pots of capital leveraged with traditional capital in order to invest in the businesses that reside in their economy. They invest in bringing new infrastructure to their community, improving old infrastructure, and creating funds for improving the cultural and social amenities of their community. Business retention efforts have to be structured and methodical in their systemic approach to gathering and reviewing the information gathered and the data that flows from this aggregate compilation. Utilizing available Manufacturing Extension Partnerships (MEP), implementing technology-enabled business retention mobile communication intelligence tools, creating financial capital for growth and retention funding (gap funds, revolving loan funds, mezzanine funds, business improvement funds, infrastructure improvement investments), building cultural infrastructure through Future Funds and Opportunity Funds, and visiting corporate headquarters, at least annually, to build relationships both internal and external to their community business executives all intertwine well with energizing the innovative entrepreneurial economy. These all create grown-at-home efforts that bolster venues into today's emerging and high-growth economy. All world-class communities focus on building these knowledge-driven assets from within, and not just attracting them from abroad.

World-class communities then recognize the importance of the redevelopment of other non-sexy elements of the community, such as brown-fields. Brown-fields find more productive uses for old dinosaur facilities that are converted or razed and help them meet the community's need. It balances the need for these facilities and the land underneath them, which is more necessary for a productive and contributory role in the economy. World-class communities focus on their core, their downtowns, to make them clean, safe, attractive, and vibrant through new brown-field industry parks with focused incentives. They reuse only the dinosaur facilities that can be transformed into innovated projects, like affordable housing or art incubators, and they target funding to rebuild these areas and create new much needed and appreciated amenities where none exist today or too little are available to fill the expectations of the community, especially the innovative elements such as youth, heritage, and cultural forces.

Above all else, world-class communities focus on their workforce (human capital). This is their trump card in the poker hand of the global economy. Without an aggressive world-class workforce, a community cannot prevail against the forces of evolutionary progress in the economy. Traditional economic developers attend workforce investment boards, support state based employment centers, and take part in other natural workforce efforts. World-class economic development efforts challenge these agencies and partner with them to invent new venues, engage their existing workforce, and grow their new workforce entrants more efficiently. This involves calling ineffective programs just that, and redirecting funds into world-class initiatives that work, examining the best practices from around the globe, and then implementing these to fit the mold. Piracy, in this instance, is absolutely an expectation of a solid workforce development effort because this creates dislocated workforce mentors, skills testing, skills curriculum delivery and employment needs, and tracking and matching to skills participants (including those underemployed in this process). A healthy workforce is funded while it suffers the hardships of dislocated families through insurance access and day care facilities. Workforce services are brought to the employers, both to fund and expand the skills of those already employed. This workforce will customize its training to meet the future needs of these employees while promoting diversity and equal access of all its programs to all members of the community; therefore, provide a dignified skills improvement process for those seeking advancement and additional educational needs in a non-threatening environment.

World-class communities create a niche for attracting the core business opportunities that can be leveraged as part of their over-all economic growth strategy through a SWAT Team approach. They focus such investments on catalyst projects and business opportunities and situations that create ancillary positive economic outcomes spawned from the initial investment, and this is done by removing or reducing market entry risks and barriers. This is determined by the current situation, what drives today's economy, and what needs to be done to expand this economy and better new growth opportunities. World-class communities play from their strengths while improving their weaknesses. Some of the proven strategies to grow additional world-class economic opportunities are less about incentives and more about capabilities and availabilities of much needed resources. The creation and the operation of fast track permit systems, highly useful and relevant web sites, Greenfield industry parks, and specific incentives are a few of these strategies. Creating a local ombudsman, designing niche opportunities, enhancing economic zones, and funding financial tools are a few more strategies.

The growth of world-class communities is also determined by their ability to open their communities to more advanced infrastructures, such broad band and WiFi grids that allow not only residents but visitors better access to mobile communication. These cutting-edge communities design infrastructure and transportation grids that deliver the best quality of utilities and transport experiences for their population. They combine and expand utility provisioning that improve congestion, with fewer road cuts for trenching and burying the most robust infrastructure capabilities (fiber, gas, electricity, water, and sewer), using wet and dry vaults that allow the most cost-efficient deployment. These communities often engage in breaking down barriers for new cutting edge systems, such as area wide WiFi systems in their downtowns and alternative energy systems geared toward conservation efforts.

We have undergone a major transition over the past 10 years. The writings of Richard Florida and Tom Friedman have shown that real estate is no longer the primary issue in business development. It used to be that the primary drivers of business development in the 1960s were industrial parks and physical space for specific types of businesses. These are less critical now. Most of the companies that require a large real estate base have gone overseas, and this trend will continue, so property is not nearly as critical. In fact, the physical infrastructure that has been developed is going to be excessive as our industrial base continues to leave. The major needed physical infrastructure will be the focus on telecommunication infrastructure. There will be a movement away from heavy industries toward knowledge-based industries, which will require a robust telecommunication industry. A focus on educational efforts at a level above the economic development industry will be essential. Local leaders and economic developers are very real estate-based and transaction-oriented, and this is now outdated. Community leaders, businesses leaders, civic leaders, mayors, and those involved in public purpose decisions must be better educated, and they will need to understand the importance for the telecommunication industry and the technology it requires. In situations where communities want to be more competitive, good technology allows them to attract and retain high-quality employees. (Gary Fields, National Economic Development Consultant, St. Paul, MN)

World-class communities that benchmark themselves against the best and set their aim at getting to or surpassing these levels as part of their strategy develop the knowledge and the systems to provide a leadership that nurtures and grows the most robust action plans in order to attain the success they desire. This constant focus on their situation allows and affords them the vision to plan for today's successes and tomorrow's desires. These communities are out of the box thinkers and forward-minded, and their reality-based goals and objectives are tied to timelines, benchmarks, and milestones that produce progress and educate their citizens through accountability and transparency to their oversight and stewardship of their public resources and investments. The key to this scenario is the constant analysis of their local situation, which includes asking themselves to take perspective of their own outcomes, realities and responsibilities for their own future. I call this process my Seven Step Community Assessment Process: Step 1) Communities ask themselves where they are compared to other world-class communities in comparison to producing results and quality of life. They understand what drives their economy today and what is needed for tomorrow in order to remain competitive and continue their high quality of life. Step 2) Communities then address their strengths and opportunities for the greatest investment returns for their citizens. Step 3) these communities then discover their barriers and improve these areas. Step 4) Communities then need to discover what success looks like, how it is defined, how long it will take to address their opportunities and their weaknesses, and their realistic benchmarks and milestones for this transformation and growth. Step 5) Communities need to know their executable strategic investments for infrastructure, catalyst projects, and capital investments in order to level the playing field and create a competitive economic advantage that will enhance the quality of life for their residents, visitors, and business environments. Step 6) Communities then need to create funds that will pay for these investments. Can other funds be leveraged? How do they create a return investment capable of filling capital needs into perpetuity? Who can they get to participate in these investments? Step 7) Finally, communities need to educate and inform their citizens and partners. What is the best method to keeping their audience informed? Accountability and transparency is essential to gaining support and consensus in order to build future initiatives and provide a responsible leadership that will carry out the mission.

In the end, world-class communities are visionary and capable investment-oriented economies that are well led, well managed, and extremely positive in their analysis of what it takes to remain competitive and build a healthy future. These are communities that depend on themselves, not others, for solutions and resources that will improve their local situations. These communities are proud, and they are open to new ideas, new members, and new opportunities. These communities leave an impression because the leadership and its residents have done their job and left their mark on society.

However, the single most difficult hurdle a community faces is the commitment to address the capitalization and cost of community and economic development efforts. Local initiatives experience the same difficulties that the states and the nation face in today's scenario. In many cases, the fiscal systems are too burdensome on individuals and corporations alike. Taxation, user fees, and other governmental revenues need a complete and strategic overhauling; however, this does not mean there should be a lower over-all tax burden, merely a shift to a more reasonable policy for payment. For example, in the last two decades, the burden has been shifted from corporations to individuals, and from within the individual segment, wealthy to the middle and lower-class income wage earners. This shift has not created a more equitable quality of life for the working-class; in fact, it has deteriorated their over-all quality of life. Those who have reaped the rewards have also reaped huge economic wealth accumulation, so the equation has not served its purpose; there was no trickle down of economic growth equitably through all sectors of society.

World-class communities don't wait for the eventual changes in their fiscal systems to occur; they address the areas within their power to transform their financial systems and make them more equitable and effective and they meet their financial needs in this transformation. These communities realize it takes cash to run this transformation, and there is no poor or suffering in a community that raises its own cash, but quite the opposite happens, a robust economy with significant, vibrant activities. World-class Communities create what I refer to as Hybridized Capital Pools to solve their problems and fund the opportunities within their local area. There are many financial tools that can create funding for progress within a community, and these economic developments won't burden its citizens:

- Impact Fees for new residential and commercial development that will offset government services and extensions for new utilities and growth of infrastructure and educational facilities and services
- Fast Track Permit Fees.
- Parking Systems such as garages and meters.
- Fast Lane Transportation Passes.
- Toll Roads and Bridges.
- Hotel Bed Taxes.
- Recreational Ticket Taxes.
- Airport Taxes and Rental Car Taxes.
- Restaurant and Beverage Taxes.
- Sales Taxes dedicated to special purposes like stadiums, economic development, and performing art centers.
- Business Improvement Special Assessments.
- Tax Increment Financing Taxes.
- Parks and Recreational Assessments on Households.
- Utility Franchise Fee Taxes to improve advanced infrastructure.
- Community wide fundraising for Catalyst Projects (bricks, clicks, mobility, infrastructure, and shovel-ready customized sites for niche opportunities).

The biggest contributor to world-class success is the leadership of the community. This is hard to measure, but it is easy to spot; it is proactive, reactive, and inactive. The visionary community leaders understand that their business decisions need to be made on an informed basis, so they can make the best decisions possible. They seek out best practices from others, and then they seek to understand how to use this knowledge in order to create hybrid strategies for their own use. They do not undertake actions that are not related to driving them closer to their stated goals and objectives, and they do not allow situations and other pressures to divert them from these goals. First and foremost, they stay on task, creating continuity through leadership changes that assure the expectations of their public. These leaders do not allow the media to direct their opinions, and they govern with the full knowledge that they are accountable to public, not the press, enabling their world-class communities to establish metrics that keep their objectives and goals on target, comparing the opportunities to the possibility of furthering their cause for a positive impact, and these metric variables are continually tracked and measured. These leaders also make decisions that add value to their communities' goals and understand the importance for creating a valuable place for their residents, visitors, and businesses. They understand that each segment must pay their fair share in order to sustain and build the value of their locale. Most importantly, these leaders don't wait on consensus because they don't want to be held hostage by the weakest link, those who are afraid of change and progress.

World-class communities understand all places consider themselves unique and this value is intrinsic and intangible because it is always in the eyes of the beholder; thus their focus on business retention, expansion, and attraction is unique, addressing each business opportunity uniquely, as a custom situation. Their incentives policy is flexible and it can be applied to fixing the impediments that reduce growth and attraction. Incentives are not corporate welfare payments, they are funds used to level the playing field so businesses can thrive in their economy. Incentives matter in this perspective because they eliminate unusual risks and mitigate upfront hardships for forward-moving projects. These incentives are not grants; in fact, in most cases, they are investments, and they should be viewed as such. Incentives are used to create competitive advantages for local businesses so they can compete and prosper in the global economy, and there are many creative incentive types and uses:

- Mitigate costs for hiring, screening, skills assessments, and training a new or expanded workforce
- Relocate and attract key employees and talent critical to the success of businesses new to the locale
- Purchase the facility and/or site and prepare a due diligence analysis for new businesses
- Improve and develop the facility and/or site to the business' specific needs (unusual barriers)
- Remediate any site or facility's environmental issues
- Relocate and/or ship new specialized equipment, machinery, and fixtures to the facility and have them installed
- Improve the capacity of physical infrastructure for business uptime guarantees (wiring, roads, telecommunications, electricity, water, sewer, and gas)
- Avoid state sales taxes and special location-based taxes that create hardships in the early years of a business' development
- Reward the company for hiring its dislocated workers and train these workers for its business skills requirements

- Reduce costs of architectural, engineering, and landscape designs
- Mitigate, if applicable, the reuse and disposal of older facilities that are being abandoned in favor of a new location
- Provide new businesses with an initial bridge loan for the first 3 months of operation (a smooth transition from old to new operations)
- Provide funding for the cutting edge businesses that create cost-effective inspection and shipping of their products worldwide (support the intellectual capital to create the new system design)
- Create for these businesses the most favorable business climate for the sustainable development and presence in the global economy (trade zones, enterprise zones, specialized districts such as TIF, Historic, Technology, and Brownfield)
- Allow low-Interest, favorable, and patient capital loans for these facilities and/or sites and their, equipment, machinery, fixtures, process design, relocation, and start-up transitional working capital

Furthermore, world-class communities do not give the proverbial farm away; in fact, this is quite the opposite they are smart investors. They understand that every catalyst investment project must have measurable metrics for investment returns, both directly and indirectly, generating job retention for those who live and work in the region and attracting those outside the region. This will also generate substantial new economic impact on the local economy and tax bases for the various levels of government jurisdictions. There must be a means to repay the actual out of pocket expenses associated with this opportunity, so this is, in fact, an investment rather than a gift. The indirect benefit associated with this project is the diversification of the local economy that is less dependent on fewer industries for vitality. This could include the removal of a blighted parcel or a dinosaur facility that is no longer viable for reuse, one that is draining the tax base and no longer an asset to the community, economically. This could include cleaning up a site or parcel that is harmful to the local environment or it could address the specific needs within the community, such as daycare, at-risk workers, the under-employed, dislocated workers, and infrastructure modernization and upgrades. However:

> *This is not done in a vacuum. Economic developers have a multi-tiered process for addressing how much and when to make such investments. They look at the project's projected return on investment (ROI) scenario to see what the investors internal rate of return will be and how that compares to other markets and the national averages. When necessary, funds can be used to boost the return in investment. Secondary to this, economic developers ask an unbiased third party professional firm to do this assessment from a financial analyst view (in KC, they used Integra Analysis, from Chicago).*

They look at whether the project is correcting or removing blight and the diversification it provides to their market. The last step is the "If Not But For Clause." Are these funds essential to the success of the project? Today, KC Economic Development is beginning to develop a set of formal procedures to use in doing these analyses that assure the continuity of the process each time. (Jeff Kaczmarek, Professional Economic Developer, KC, MO)

It is important to realize there is no size requirement for the world-class communities; only a mindset. World-class communities come in big, medium, large, and super sized examples. They exist in all areas of the world. Anyone who visits these places is aware of their uniqueness. Every community should address this evaluation and start this journey because this will create the best possible future for its residents and visitors. Though world-class is not inexpensive, it is the most desired and valued scenario. Its investment return is not necessarily measured, tangible variables, but its pride and well-being are measured greatly. These investments are perpetual, and they can run far beyond today's capabilities. These world-class measurements can be reached, or they may already be reached, in a community, but in order to measure these measurements, allow me to give you a quiz:

Place a 1 if the following statements are apparent or true and place a 0 if they are not evident or if they are false for the community in question. Veritas Vos (The Truth will set you free)

1. Does this community have specific and quantitative (not intangible) goals and objectives that indicate it is currently or soon to become a world-class city? The key point here is in setting actual targets for the genuine catalyst projects that indicate world-class mindsets, such as master planning a community's growth and vision for where it wants to be in a decade and what it will take to get there. Does the community actively review and utilize best practices from other locales to understand how to address its own issues?

Score: ☐

2. Has this city identified a unique selling proposition (USP) that establishes a sense of place and purpose that resonates both internally to its residents and externally to others? With more than 12,000 economic development groups across the US, has this community's leadership clearly documented what makes its community or region truly different and special to others, and has this been validated from the perspective of unbiased third party experts?

Score: ☐

3. Does the local leadership (elected and appointed) fully understand what it takes to be competitive, both today and tomorrow? Does this local leadership play an active role in helping the city organize and fund the efforts for success?

Score: ☐

4. Has this community completed a SWOT analysis that will target its "best bet" (what I refer to as the low-hanging fruit on the tree of opportunity) for new development opportunities? If so, has this city's leadership identified and prioritized target core industries and economic investment activities where current or future developments demonstrate a competitive advantage?

Score: ☐

5. Has the economic development organization in this community developed a visually attractive, up-to-date, and easily navigable website that is useful to those who seek answers to the pertinent questions most prospective businesses need to know when researching a new location for business decision purposes? Does this organization understand how to gain competitive intelligence from the deployment of such useful information or is this website merely one way traffic?

Score: ☐

6. Does the local elected and appointed leadership go to great effort to educate and inform the electorate and business community about the economic and social issues at work within the city? Do they outline the need for visionary investments and solutions for addressing such issues?

Score: ☐

7. Does this city have a cutting edge vision and investment strategy for empowering and improving the educational attainment and outcomes for its students and youth? If so, does this strategy include work skills assessments and curriculum tied to the skills not only required today but tomorrow? Do they reward youth educational attainment and the programs that join together youth and businesses in order to fulfill both educational and workforce needs and desires?

Score: ☐

8. Does this community have a vibrant and robust method for empowering and investing in new entrepreneurs and innovation-based intellectual capital development such as patents, new business ideas, and products? Is this tied to the university and community college infrastructure for additional support? Is there business incubation space available for new entrepreneurial businesses that do not create an economic hardship for the new entrepreneur in this city?

Score:

9. Does this city have unique workforce development programs that truly assist in the transition of its under-employed or dislocated workers? Does the economic development effort specifically target workforce members, making them aware of expanding business opportunities and reducing stressful economic conditions for their families?

Score:

10. Has this city or region created hybrid investment capital for new business opportunities and innovative business expansion projects from local resources that can make such investment decisions locally? Does this include customized incentives to lower business investment risks for making significant investments into the community? (For example, can this community provide as much as 20% of a project expense to support key catalyst projects?) Are these funds available for easy access when necessary or is there a large amount of discussion and cultivation that must go on to raise such resources? Experience suggests that "crash" programs, or programs created rapidly to address unforeseen situations, tend to lack a true capacity of accuracy when it comes to private investment decisions.

Score:

11. Has this city invested in performing and visual arts as well as natural and historical museums for its residents? Is this community aggressively creating a renewed aesthetic quality and thematic appeal to its core city center, making it attractive to residents and visitors alike? (This also includes after hour activities that draw people into the city while providing a safe and clean environment for their enjoyment.) Does this city have ample and expansive green space for its residents and is it requiring such green spaces for new development and general community growth?

Score:

12. Has this city or region enjoyed a continued population growth since 2000? Does this growth include the 18-30 year old age group at the same or greater rate than the general population growth?

Score: ☐

Tally up these scores, and then it will be apparent whether or not the city being quizzed is a world-class city or if it is in need of help:

- 0= This community has a long journey ahead, so get started now!
- 1-4 = This community may have some basic knowledge for what it means to be world-class, but it needs a greater focus and resolve toward achieving its expectations.
- 5-7 = This community is well poised to expand its horizons and seek greater results.
- 8-10 = This community's leaders are wise and resourceful, and the journey to world-class is easily within its reach.
- 11= This community is very close, but it must press on to its final reward of prosperity with a purpose, for both its city and its residents.
- 12= The person who scored this has either lied or his or her city is one of the few in the world that is uniquely positioned to exponentially benefit from tomorrow's progressive economy.

Chapter Nineteen

"Been There Done That and Bought the T-Shirt: Lessons learned!"

There are a few simple areas many economic developers should heed to if they want to survive in this tumultuous industry. Each member of this professional economic development organization must demand great resolve, good business acumen, a rigorous continuation to his or her education, and a honed improvement of his or her craft, and all these can be attained through practical experience. As some often tout, "Hindsight is always 20/20." As Bob Seger once vocalized, "I wish I didn't know now what I didn't know then."

There are several issues that beg attention when attempting to survive as a professional economic developer. The following are a few simple reflections of the perceptions I have gained throughout my years as a professional economic development practitioner. These are all directed to the others whom practice the art of economic development.

Contracts and Interviews:

Always remember the interview is the most critical process in determining whether this community or organization is right for you and your family. Don't dodge your known weaknesses in this interview; be candid, and let the interviewees know about your weaknesses. Ask how you will be supported or how those in light of these expectations will be dealt with. In addition, you don't want to win the offer if it isn't the best place for you, professionally, or your family's quality of life. You need to respectfully stress that the interview is a two way street; you are looking at them as much as they are looking at you. Remind them that their realistic, candid conversations about the real problems of the organization are critical to your own considerations as much as your responses to their own questions.

Do not take a position without a proper severance package less than 3 months, and I always recommend 6 months; this should include your paid benefits, accrued time off, and sick leave. This is not a question of if this will be needed; it is a question of when you will need it. This is a very political business and leadership changes many times lead to an inexperienced and naïve public and private leaders who simply do not understand the need for proactive economic development practices and the changing demands of growing an economy.

Media Coverage:

Yes, for the most part, media coverage is a double-edged sword. It can be powerful and sexy when times are good and your actions seem to generate positive sentiment, but some reporters can be the most yellow-tainted, uneducated writers you will ever meet, especially when a reporter builds or creates a fictional opinion that is directly opposed to economic development practices. A reporter can portray you as a vile proponent of corporate welfare against the public spender of hard earned tax dollars, calling you a wasteful steward of public funds and trust. This type of reporter is constantly seeking sensationalism and the chance to become the next (imagined) Pulitzer Prize winner, and you are his or her ticket to the ceremony. Furthermore, because this is the age of "Google," these stories will follow you throughout your career, creating a place where bloggers will write all kinds of useless and meaningless crap about you and your profession. Do everything you can that is right, and do this with integrity. Answer the media's questions with the answers to questions you wish them to have asked and emphasize your own points. Support your own points with facts. If the situation spirals out of control, call upon your board for a series of actions and opinions on the topic, taking the pressure off you and placing it on the organization. Then hold an editorial board meeting that will openly discuss the topic and address these issues in a controlled environment. Let your board members step up and, with their proper preparation, address key issues because people will better respect their local organization more than the outsider; you.

Public Speaking and Presentations:

Always be ready to speak of your profession and trade, whether the issues are ad hoc or requested. Be accessible to the public and make sure they feel you are their champion, not some stranger who is merely earning a pay check. Be both empathetic and sincere in your conviction of what needs to be done and why. Give clear examples for how positive outcomes will take place. Use every opportunity to address the public like each is an educational, internal marketing opportunity, not a task or chore you regretfully perform as a mundane necessity.

Know your industry and its every detailed fact. You should never be afraid to debate or discuss your industry practices because you are the expert, even though once you arrive they may make you feel like the newly dubbed "Village Idiot." You are, in fact, the local economist in charge of creating outcomes that will improve the quality of your constituents' lives, and this is a huge responsibility; one you take very seriously.

Best Practices:
To quote Sir Francis Bacon, "Knowledge is truly power." In economic development, you have to approach each opportunity and problem from the aspect of institutional knowledge. Who in your industry has faced this before and how did they handle it? What other experts have experienced this, and what would they bring to the table if they were hired to give you an impartial and unbiased opinion? What was redone differently and how might this be utilized and applicable to your own situation? You must create hybrid solutions built upon several best practices and institute these practices in order to avoid the mistakes they disclosed to you during your interviews with these folks. You must do your own primary research by talking to those who have gone down the path you are about to follow because very few problems exist that have not been addressed by other communities; learn from their successes and failures.

Catalyst Projects:
Every great community has its constant funnel of projects. These projects, once completed, will change the dynamics of its economy through mitigating its barriers to economic growth and spawning its additional leveraged and ancillary investments. Those communities that do not have at least one of these projects are not engaged in the art of economic development or the building of their local economy, and these communities are not yet ready for your talent.

The First 100 Days:
There is nothing more critical to a newly hired economic developer than his or her first 100 days. You must get out and meet the community's key decisions makers and influencers in these decisions. Doing this will help you gain their perspective of the current state in their local economy, so you can develop an acumen for the situation. Once you have compiled and reviewed this assembly of information, you must be diplomatic. Never give away your own perceptions just observe others'. Ask tough questions during your interviews and seek others who should be interviewed, and do not allow bias opinions to sway you away from these future interviews. Ask the type of questions that will give you an early SWOT assessment. At this point, it is absolutely necessary that you do not gather this collective, newly-gained wisdom and hold a meeting to tell your opinion because this is when you will need to decide who and how this message should be delivered, and this must be done through a third-party's expert emissary. You must lead these decision makers into believing they directed your opinions through a third party's assessment and enlightenment exercise.

Annual Reviews:

If you don't get the metrics for how successes and compensations will be measured up front, your aim will be an ever elusive target after the first year, and this target will continue to become more elusive. Major League Economic Development Players nail these details out of the park before they join an organization. Once the entire team can discuss their criteria with you, you are not yet ready to take home plate because they hold all the bases. Once you believe home plate is within your grasp, you could most likely be tagged by the ball; therefore, a move to a new location where future negotiations can be better thought out.

Performance Accountability:

If you don't know what a win looks like to your leadership, how are you supposed to meet their objectives? Within your first 100 days, interviews are your best plan to picturing what your leadership considers as win for the economic development game, but all parties must agree, so these wins must be written agreements. These written agreements are living documents, evolving as time passes, and a major part of your annual review conversation. Once these metrics are known, build them into your monthly executive dashboard report, so you can demonstrate to your board and its community leadership the progress being made by you and your team.

Dealing with Site Location Consultants:

In general, site location consultants are not a difficult lot. Your best bet is to respond to their questions both quickly and with exact and accurate information specific to their request. Make sure you can cite your sources and offer their dates of executions. Recent data is the currency of validity for these information sleuths. The number one thing to remember is these consultants are not there to pick you as a winner, but to eliminate you from their list. They are looking for faults and deficiencies. The last and best community or site left at the end wins the deal. In this game, surviving each cut matters. Your web site is your number one portal to gaining site location relevant information, so you need to make sure this web site is easy to navigate and filled with useful information, not merely sales speeches. Quality information trumps electronic blather every time.

Using Incentives & Calculated Risks in Deals:

If you do not have a local incentive analysis and incentive policy, you will need to develop one, quickly. When opportunities present themselves, you have to know what you have to offer, how to make it relevant to the industry's need, and how much of it to offer, responsibly, given their commitment to invest in your community. Without guidelines, metrics, and protocols, you will not be capable of responding rapidly or prudently, and then you will likely be eliminated from consideration, or you may risk exploitation. Your lack of thought about the actual value of the deal to the community in economic impact is relative to local investments that will give an unreasonable ROI. If you cannot calculate the risks and rewards, Major League Economic Developers will trump your deals and win every hand, like expert poker players.

Using Consultants:

Most consultants want to convince you they can do it all; they are the turnkey solution to all your problems and worries, but this is simply bull! Most consultants have their niche expertise, so you need to hire those consultants that fit your niche needs, on a case by case basis. Then, by making sure each reviews the other's work, duplicitous outcomes won't be created; rather, each will build upon the other's observations, providing you with a hybrid superior product.

Facing Economic Realities in Your Communities:

No community likes to hear the hard facts about its weaknesses and its threats, but there is a real need to give your most accurate opinion of these. Your job is to be the local expert that addresses the hard issues; thus leading the community to better outcomes. Education and leadership is the key to getting this done. Rome was not built in year, and with this knowledge, you must lay out a charted course that the community can both comprehend and support. However, you must take small steps until you build enough momentum to increase your speed.

Networking with your Peers:

There is no way you can become or remain a world-class economic developer unless you are actively engaged in the intelligence and thought discussions amongst your peers. These discussions should not only be mandatory to your schedule, but they should be enjoyable, too. While each economic developer is a competitor on a daily basis, each is still brothers and sisters in arms, each sharing a kindred spirit for helping one another receive a healthier quality of life. As these discussions proceed, each economic developer will reap a greater professional and personal satisfaction.

Leadership:

Those who step out and lead their peers are those who will feel the just rewards for giving freely of themselves to their trade. Knowledge shared is exponentially returned to those who give it freely. The combined wisdom of so many is at your disposal once you show the courage to lead and offer your resources for making the industry a better place to work and garner better results for your greater constituency.

I hope you have enjoyed this journey through my experiences, reflections, and optimisms about how the economic development industry can and will continue to make positive outcomes for our nation's residents. Our struggle is not easy, but it is a task worth the effort. There is simply too much at stake, and if we do not raise the bar and spur others to march forward into the economic chaos that confronts us today, we will lose the battle. Good Luck.

THE FINAL CHAPTER

"The Pillars of the Next Frontier, for Economic Development, for the Future"

Economic developers are equivalent to the modern-day Knight's Templar. How so? Because we are a small but passionate group set out against the odds to fend off the roving bands of bandits and threats that attempt to harm our citizens in their journey to economic prosperity. We hold our training and our passion for the cause as the decisive factor that creates our advantage on the battlefield, when we engage our opponents. Our presence in the foray creates a sense of confidence in those who venture into the fray from our side, and this tips the scale to our side because of our enormous ability to take on greater odds, with less resource, yet we still carry the day. We are also misunderstood, maligned, and mysterious to those who are not familiar or experienced with our tactics and solutions to do good for our citizens and communities. We are often criticized by those we seek to protect, yet for all these stresses and under-appreciations, economic developers find great personal reward in their work. What we do is patriotic and beneficial to society, and we find great solace in these benefits to others.

> *Today's economic developers are deal doers. They accomplish things by using the tools available to them, and they make projects happen. As they work each transaction or deal, they simultaneously work toward the next deal or transaction. They are deal makers and transaction specialists, but I refer to them as transactional economic developers. Some are more administrative or strategic, but all who work real estate development, financing, business recruiting, or any sort of transaction can be called transactional economic developers.* **(Jeff Finkle**, *Professional Leader of Economic Developers, Washington, DC)*

Our order, the economic development organization, cannot afford to lose sight of the enormous tasks that lie ahead if we are to create a vibrant and fair 21st century. We must stand in the face of change and beckon others to follow us forward, into the unknown of new opportunities without freezing in their steps and hoping change will pass, and the past will resurface. This means we must lead when no one else will, even when our actions are not always understood or feared. We must have the courage, resolve, vision, and leadership stamina to step out when others cower in their seats or remain anchored to unrealistic views. To do this, we must become experts at the forces that will drive the new frontiers of this century. From my perspective, we must promote the following without fear:

- Education that is accountable and performance-based
- Workforce transition strategies, programs, and policies that replace lost jobs with equal or better jobs and preserve their economic security
- Energy is the next big thing, and those who solve the replacement of fossil fuels will reduce terrorism tensions, improve our climate and planet issues and generate the greatest wealth on the planet
- Business Climate Reform, not how much tax is paid but how it is paid. There has to be more equilibrium between the book ends of wealth and poverty. This would also include fiscal responsibility for retirement, trade gaps, national debt reduction, and monetary strength of the dollar.
- Political Reform and how we are governed, what is tolerated, and what undermines our republic and the individual rights of our citizens by making politics too elitist for the common folk to participate in and share their adequate influence
- Innovation is the key, and we must empower and support accelerated and advanced research and development of the best products and ideas in the world. The increase of our innovation index will spur the exponential growth of the knowledge economy
- Immigration is not a bad thing; it fuels the best and brightest from the around the world to come to America with hopes of starting and developing their own version of the "American dream"
- Infrastructure must be dealt with. We have neglected to keep pace in all manners of our nation's community and interstate infrastructures, from rail to roads, utilities to telecom, and across the board, we are woefully falling short of our other competitors around the globe.
- Manufacturing matters. We have to make things, not just create ideas, if we are to be successful. We have to create a level playing field for America's manufacturers, so they can thrive, rejuvenate, and rebuild our prowess in a holistic and diversified base that is sustainable to our own national economy needs

To be yourself in a world that is constantly trying to make you something else is the greatest accomplishment. **(Ralph Waldo Emerson)**

My hope is that each of you will be fearless in your passion as an economic developer, community leader, or concerned citizen and embracing the concepts I have both shared and explored may help. If you do join me in this cause, this century will indeed be even more wondrous than the last. While these pages may seem to be filled with fanciful predictions and premises, they are grounded in what is known to be factually-occurring situations that, for the most part, are daily addressed in denial. To be counted and stand for something matters as a citizen of our nation, state, community, and planet, there is no more noble cause than to make a difference in the lives of others. This effort will not be without its self-sacrifice, and its journey in this first part of the century is going to be more difficult than many of us can imagine. If we can just remember this; the Dark Ages were a tough and difficult time, yet from that experience, the development and the notion of democracy, basic human rights, and the concept of equality evolved from the chivalrous codes that held true through this era. Living through the Dark Age would not have been pleasant, but the end result changed the world as we know it today. Through our fearlessness and our passions, we can also hold true to our chivalrous codes and change the world's tomorrows.

Author's Notes

As you can imagine, I have spent quite a bit of time surfing the web for information I felt relevant to consider, both pro and con, along with my own perspectives, in an attempt to be well rounded. The following web sites played a major role in my analysis:

U.S. Supreme Court upholds Smoke Stack Chasing Incentives:
http://www.stateline.org/live/ViewPage.action?siteNodeId=136&languageId=1&contentId=112763

Georgia Offers Korean Car Manufacturer $400M in Incentives—ABC News
http://abcnews.go.com/Business/WNT/story?id=172946O&page=1

Chasing the Smokestack a Strategic Policymaking
http://papers.ssrn.com/sol3/papers.cfm?abstract_id=317930

Political Opposition to Gubernatorial Smoke Stack Chasing
http://sppq.press.uiuc.edu/3/3/abstracts3.html

Globalization's impact on state and local economies, policy research
http://www.blackwell-synergy.com/doi/abs/10.1111/j.1541-1338.2001.tb00191.x?cookieSet=1&journalCode=ropr

Toyota Incentive Deal Debate
http://www.news-record.com/apps/pbcs.dll/article?AID=/20060423/NEWSREC0101/604230305

Toyota Technical R&D Deal
http://www.siteselection.com/ssinsider/incentive/ti0504.htm

Toyota Indiana Business Growth & Reuse of closed Facility
http://www.glpi.org/newsfiles/SIADeal.pdf

GM Deal for Business Retention in NY
http://www.siteselection.com/ssinsider/incentive/ti0009.htm

http://www.findarticles.com/p/articles/mi_m3165/is_n4_v26/ai_8952399/pg_2

Foreign Direct Investment perspective on incentives race
http://www.fdimagazine.com/news/fullstory.php/aid/937/US_in_overdrive.html

Incentives comments from media perspective
http://www.statesman.com/business/content/business/stories/archive/112904_dell.htm

Ernest & Young Cash Cow Incentives (Boeing Example included)
http://www.effwa.org/main/article.php?article_id=69

Developing a Place for World Class Destination Attraction Kansas City, MO
http://www.schlitterbahn.com/corp/media/vacation-village-factsheet.asp

http://www.schlitterbahn.com/corp/media/vacation-village.asp

http://www.bizjournals.com/kansascity/stories/2006/01/23/focus11.html

http://kansascity.bizjournals.com/kansascity/stories/2007/01/01/daily25.html

Mike Mullis Harley Deal in Kansas City
http://www.glscs.com/archives/4.97.HarleyDavidson.htm?adcode=90

The Sample of Numerous Incentives Deals and Policy Positions recently including Cabela's $127M retail deal in West Virginia
http://www.sb-d.com/issues/winter2004/aroundthesouth/index.asp

The ability grow manufacturing and quality jobs locally (making things) is essential to renewing American competitiveness. There is no wealth in servicing visitors and recreational amenities alone, you have to innovate, design, manufacture and sell products to be a healthy well rounded economy.
http://orsted.nap.edu/openbook.php?record_id=11024&page=1

Developing new cutting edge strategies to renew manufacturing competitiveness is essential. The use of Manufacturing Extension Partnerships (MEPs) can be a critical first step. Many times this can lead to better and more efficient operations

and when coupled with proper modernization and energy efficiency incentives it can give U.S. manufacturers a new edge in competing.
http://www.apolloalliance.org/strategy_center/strategies_for_clean_energy/mfgeff.cfm

Retooling manufacturing is critical and it is essential to sustaining our global economic posture and repairing the damage to our middle class quality of life.
http://www.mma-net.org/newsinfo/news.asp?NEWSID=176

The Rat Race to compete with ultra low cost labor in Mexico which might run about $2.40 per hour versus $.30 cents per hour in China versus $20 per hour in the U.S. is a real paradox for not only multinational firms but small and medium companies. NAM and other groups feel that only through equipment modernization and research & development expenditures coupled with workforce development tax credits can U.S. companies hope to compete. Some would rather offshore and outsource than take the long-term capital risk. Incentives, business climate involvement in business cost burden and national trade policies are the key to survival.
http://www.businessfacilities.com/bf_06_09_cover.php

Corporation for Enterprise Development, Special Report "Smoke Stack Chasing, 2000" Larry Buchholtz & William Schweke
http://sadrc.cfed.org/publications/accountability/Accountability%20Jan%2000.pdf

National Conference of State Legislators—(Immigration) http://www.ncsl.org/programs/press/2007/pr070419immigration.htm

U.S. Conference of Mayors—(Climate Change)
http://www.mayors.org/climateprotection/

National League of Cities—(immigration)
http://www.nlc.org/ASSETS/53FC69B744CC4884AD40B6C2503A8C37/07_ImmigrationReform.pdf

National Association of State Development Agencies—(Incentives)
http://www.nasda.com/

C2ER (The Council for Community and Economic Research) formerly known as **ACCRA** (American Chamber of Commerce Research Associates)
http://www.c2er.org/incentives

Institute of Electrical and Electronics Engineers (IEEE) (Innovation & Tax Credits)
http://www.ieeeusa.org/policy/positions/basicresearch.pdf

European Association of Development Agencies—(Creating jobs that matter)
http://www.eurada.org/doc/cohesionpolicyE.pdf

Progressive Policy Institute-*Federal Economic & Public Policy* (*http://www.ppionline.org/ppi_ci.cfm?knlgAreaID=125&subsecid=162&contentid=254284*

Council on Competitiveness—Road Map to Innovation
http://innovateamerica.org/pdf/NAS-NII-A_Roadmap_for_American_Innovation.pdf

Corporation for Enterprise Development—(Incentives)
http://www.cfed.org/focus.m?parentid=34&siteid=2346&id=2346

Urban Land Institute-Global Competitiveness
http://www.uli.org/Content/NavigationMenu/News/LeadsTipsandIdeas/Leads_Tips_and_Ideas.htm

Citizens for Fair Taxation-Freedom Works (Steve Forbes and Dick Armey Board members)
http://www.freedomworks.org/informed/key_template.php?issue_it=17

National Association of Workforce Professionals-Emerging Issues
http://www.nawdp.org/SummitDiscussionDraft.pdf

World Economic Forum—The Global Competitiveness Report
http://www.weforum.org/en/initiatives/index.htm

Rand Institute-Forces shaping the US workforce
http://www.rand.org/pubs/testimonies/2007/RAND_CT273.pdf

Brookings Institute-Transitioning the US Workforce in the global economy
http://www.brook.edu/comm/infocus/wageinsurance.htm

CATO Institute-Subsidies and entitlements and trade imbalances
http://www.cato.org/pub_display.php?pub_id=8195

Hudson Institute—Foreign Policy
http://cffss.hudson.org/files/publications/TrumanEventSummary_july172006.pdf

American Enterprise Institute-Capitalism and Democracy are they interlinked?
http://www.american.com/archive/2007/may-june-magazine-contents/does-economic-success-require-democracy

Research Institute for Sustainable Energy (RISE)—Energy Solutions for this century
http://www.rise.org.au/

Industrial Asset Management Council, IAMC—Business Development transactions
www.iamc.org

There were also a fair amount of special reports I reviewed while creating both this book and my other book, *Who Moved My Smoke Stack?* The following reports played a major role in my considerations, and each is available via the web, as PDFs:

- Alternative Energy for Economic Development by Louise Anderson, IEDC Staff
- Why Any Town needs a Young Professional's Organization, Rebecca Ryan
- Cool Communities presentation by Rebecca Ryan
- The Creative Class a Key to Rural Growth, David Mcgranahan
- How to Cut Green House Emissions Now—Brookings Institute, Mary Graham
- Tackling Trade & Climate Change-Brookings Institute
- Striking the Right Notes on Entrepreneurship—Richard Florida Speech
- Legislative and Guiding Principles—IEDC
- The Past and Future of America's Economy—unknown author
- Framing Paper Weak Market Cities-Brookings Institute
- Workforce 2020 Overview by Dick Judy

Index of Key words

Workforce development—17, 29, 32, 78, 127, 135, 174, 183, 197
Innovation—25, 29, 32, 33, 36, 49, 57, 69, 88, 101, 109, 110, 120, 121, 129, 134, 135, 141 147-149, 151, 152, 158, 164, 166, 171, 173, 183, 192, 198
Brownfield—174, 175, 179-181
Site Selection—78, 80, 81, 104, 107, 136
World Class Communities—23, 66, 68-73, 75, 76, 115, 137, 149, 152, 157, 170, 171, 173-181
SWOT Analysis—15-17, 88, 143, 144, 160, 182
Seven Step Strategy—71, 87, 88, 96, 176
Community Cycles—39, 77
Placed Based Strategies—55, 65, 69, 71, 80, 85, 163
Business Retention & Expansion—128
Business Attraction—15, 17, 70, 78, 80, 94, 128-130, 145, 146, 173
Infrastructure Development—78, 127, 172
Pillars of the Next Frontier for Economic Development—191
Knights Code—46, 47
Fearless Leadership—14, 45, 160
Education—27-32, 35, 36, 41, 44, 50, 60, 62-68, 72, 77, 88, 93, 104-116, 118, 124, 125, 134, 150-153, 157, 163-167, 170-178, 182, 185, 186, 189, 192
Best Practices—21, 22, 33, 34, 72-74, 85, 91, 144, 152, 154, 174, 178, 181, 187
Globalization—9, 13, 25-26, 29-30, 33, 38, 42-43, 77, 80, 94, 103, 113, 128, 135, 141 195
Global Economy—7, 17-19, 22, 25, 27-29, 42-44, 57, 61-62, 78, 81, 109-110, 118, 121, 132, 135, 137, 146, 148, 150, 157, 171, 174, 179, 180, 198
Knowledge Economy—164, 192
Technology Based Economic Development—36, 52
Internet Strategies—35, 38, 42-44, 63-64, 110, 124, 128, 166, 168, 173
Community Profiling—54-60, 77
Dinosaur Facilities—155, 167, 174
Business Incubation—127, 164, 183
Shovel Ready Sites—17, 134, 155, 166, 168
Speculative Buildings—168

Incentives & Inducements—*16, 18, 67, 69-70, 93-95, 100-107, 118, 121, 123, 125, 131, 134, 146-147, 155-157, 167, 174-175, 179, 183, 188, 195-198*
Hybrid Capitalization—*146, 154*
Revolving Loan Funds—*127, 157, 163, 166, 174*
Venture, Angel and Seed Capital—*121, 127, 144, 152, 166*
City Rankings—*62-65, 80-83*
IEDC Data Standards—*16, 136-140, 144*

I would also like to credit my fellow authors who have blazed a trail that inspired my two books. For the last two years, I have spent much of my available free time consuming the written chronicles of others and what has been stated, believed, and perceived as far as the state and conditions of our socio-economic and environmental predicaments are concerned. I now acknowledge these books I have reviewed while preparing my own.

Rural Communities, "Legacy + Change" 2nd edition
Cornelia Butler Flora, Jan L. Flora

Bowling Alone, "The Collapse and Revival of American Community"
Robert D. Putnam

Building Communities From The Inside Out, "A path toward finding and mobilizing a community's assets"
John P. Kretzmann, John L. McKnight

Lost Landscapes and Failed Economies, "The search for a value of place"
Thomas Michael Power

Boom Town USA, "The 7.5 keys to big success in small towns"
Jack Schultz

Smart Communities, "How citizens and local leaders can use strategic thinking to build a brighter future."
Suzanne W. Morse

Life 2.0, "How people across America are transforming their lives by find the Where of their Happiness."
Rich Karlgaard

Asset Building & Community Development
Gary Paul Green, Anna Haines

Community Building: What Makes It Work, "A review of factors influencing successful community building"
Paul Mattessich, Barbara Monsey, Corinna Roy

Cities Ranked & Rated, "Cities Compared & Contrasted in 10 Categories"
Bert Sperling & Peter Sander

The Samurai Leader, "Winning Business Battles with Wisdom Honor and Courage of the Samurai Code"
Bill Diffenderffer

Managing The Whirlwind
Michael Annison

Flat Tax Revolution, "Using a postcard to abolish the IRS"
Steve Forbes

The Great American Jobs Scam, "Corporate tax dodging and the myth of job creation"
Greg Leroi

The Undercover Economist, "Exposing why the rich are rich, the poor are poor-and why you can never buy a decent used car"
Tim Harford

Marketing in the Public Sector, "A Roadmap for improved performance"
Phillip Kotler, Nancy Lee

Collapse, "How societies choose to fail or succeed"
Jared Diamond

World out of Balance, "Navigating global risks to seize competitive advantage"
Paul A. Laudicina

People and the Competitive Advantage of Place, "Building a Workforce for the 21st Century"
Shari Garmise

Lockout, "Why America keeps getting immigration wrong when our prosperity depends on getting it right"
Michele Wucker

Fortune Favors the Bold, "What we must do to build a new and lasting global prosperity."
Lester Thurow

Winning the Global Game, "A strategy for linking people and profits."
Jeffrey Rosensweig

I Want That, "How we all became shoppers."
Thomas Hine

The Marketing of Nations, "A strategic approach to building national wealth."
Phillip Kotler, Somkid Jatusripitak, Suvit Maessincee

The Global Me, "New Cosmopolitans and the competitive edge: Picking Globalism's winners and losers."
G. Pascal Zachary

The New Normal, "Great Opportunities in a time of Great Risk."
Roger McNamee, David Diamond

On Becoming Fearless, "Love, Work and Life."
Arianna Huffington

The World is Flat, "A brief history of the twenty-first century"
Thomas L. Friedman

Fostering Sustainable Behavior, "an introduction to community based social marketing."
Doug McKenzie-Mohr, William Smith

Sun Tzu Was a Sissy, "Conquer your enemies, promote your friends, and wage the real art of war."
Stanley Bing

The 2 Percent Solution, "Fixing Americas Problems in ways liberals and conservatives can love."
Matt Miller

Where We Stand, "Can America make it in the global race for wealth, health and happiness?"
Michael Wolff, Peter Rutten, Albert F. Bayers III

Marketing Places, "Attracting Investment, Industry, and Tourism to Cities, States and Nations."
Philip Kotler, Donald Haider, Irving Rein

Social Marketing, "Improving the Quality of Life."
Philip Kotler, Ned Roberto, Nancy Lee

Marketing Asian Places, "Attracting Investment, Industry, and Tourism to Cities, States and Nations."
Philip Kotler, Michael Hamlin, Irving Rein, Donald Haider

The Extreme Future, "The Top Trends That Will Reshape the World for the Next 5, 10, and 20 Years."
James Canton

Making Globalization Work
Joseph Stiglitz

Place Creation, "A Groundbreaking Manifesto for Real Estate Professionals." Version 1.1
Bradley A. Smith, Kevin W. McCarthy

The Rise of the Creative Class, Richard Florida

War On The Middle Class" How the Government, Big Business, and Special Interest Groups Are Waging War on the American Dream and How To Fight Back.
Lou Dobbs

Revolutionary Wealth, "How it will be created and how it will change our lives."
Alvin and Heidi Toffler

Field Guide To The Global Economy, Revised & Updated
Sarah Anderson, John Cavanaugh, Thea Lee

Printed in the United States
98135LV00002B/154-222/A